Controlling Vegetable Pests

Created and designed by
the editorial staff of
ORTHO BOOKS

Project Editor
Cynthia Putnam

Manuscript Editor
Susan Lang

Writer
Pamela K. Peirce

Designer
Gary Hespenheide

Ortho Books

Publisher
Edward A. Evans

Editorial Director
Christine Jordan

Production Director
Ernie S. Tasaki

Managing Editors
Robert J. Beckstrom
Michael D. Smith
Sally W. Smith

System Manager
Linda M. Bouchard

Product Manager
Richard E. Pile, Jr.

Marketing Administrative Assistant
Daniel Stage

Distribution Specialist
Barbara F. Steadham

Operations Assistant
Georgiann Wright

Technical Consultant
J. A. Crozier, Jr., Ph.D.

Address all inquiries to:
Ortho Books
Chevron Chemical Company
Consumer Products Division
Box 5047
San Ramon, CA 94583

2	3	4	5	6	7	8	9
92		93		94	95		96

ISBN 0-89721-230-4
Library of Congress Catalog Card Number 90-86161

Chevron Chemical Company
6001 Bollinger Canyon Road, San Ramon, CA 94583

Acknowledgments

Photo Editor
Pamela Peirce

Copy Chief
Melinda E. Levine

Editorial Coordinator
Cass Dempsey

Copyeditor
Barbara Feller-Roth

Proofreader
Deborah N. Bruner

Indexer
Elinor Lindheimer

Composition by
Nancy Patton Wilson-McCune

Editorial Assistant
Laurie A. Steele

Associate Editor
Sara Shopkow

Photo Assistant
Mary Sullivan

Production by
Studio 165

Separations by
Color Tech Corp.

Lithographed in the USA by
Webcrafters, Inc.

Consultants
Dr. George Bird, Michigan State University, East Lansing, Mich.
Kate Burroughs, Harmony Farm Supply, Sebastopol, Calif.
William Cheney, USDA Farm Advisor, Salinas, Calif.
Ramon Georgis, Biosys, Palo Alto, Calif.

Permissions
Thanks to Mary Louise Flint for permission to adapt the nematode control chart from her book, *Pests of the Garden and Small Farm: A Growers Guide to Using Less Pesticide.* (Mary Louise Flint, Statewide Integrated Pest Management Project, University of California, Division of Agriculture and Natural Resources, Publication 3332, Davis, Calif.)

Special Thanks to
Jo Brownold; David Dixon; Fetzer Valley Oaks Garden, Hopland, Calif.; Evelyn Holt; Mary Holt; Sandy Jones; Garry King; Robert Kourik; Richard Molinar; Pat Morgan; Mudd's Restaurant, San Ramon, Calif.; Dannette Peltier; Michael Peltier; George Edward Welles

Front Cover
Inspecting plants regularly allows early detection and easier control of pest infestations.

Title Page
Pale yellow corn earworm eggs will be clearly visible against purple corn silks.

Back Cover
Top left: The insecticide pyrethrum is derived from the colorful pyrethrum daisy.
Top right: Yellow sticky traps are used to control adult whiteflies in this tomato planting.
Bottom left: Handpicking is an effective way to get rid of many pests.
Bottom right: Lady beetles help vegetable gardeners by feeding on aphids.

Photographers
Names of photographers are followed by the page numbers on which their work appears. R=right, C=center, L=left, T=top, B=bottom.

William D. Adams: 66R, 86R, 87BL, 92C, 104L, 129TL, 133R, 134R
Max Badgley: 16TL, 17BL, 34T, 59TR, 63R, 64R, 67BR, 76TR, 84L, 84R, 115R, 118L, 120TL, 120BL, 130BR, 131R, 132R
Allen Boger: 50L, 130L
Ralph Byther: 72L, 83R, 85BL, 92TR, 99R, 102L, 105TL, 106TR, 109R, 111TR, 112L, 113L, 113R, 114L, 123L, 135R, 138R, 139L
Clemson University: 83TL, 93L
Rosalind Creasy: 4, 9, 19, 52L
Samuel Cotner: 92L, 121L, 127R
J. A. Crozier: 114R
James F. Dill: 41B, 61BL, 67TR, 73TL, 75TL, 77TL, 86TL, 87TL, 89C, 90R, 96R, 100L, 123R, 131L, back cover BR
Robert A. Dunn: 73R
Charles Marden Fitch: 20, 33B, 82BR, 98L, 99BL, back cover TL
David Goldberg: 146L, 146R
Dennis H. Hall: 62R, 110L, 127L
Lionel Handel: 58R, 59L
Duane L. Hatch: 57R, 107R, 126R
Saxon Holt: 6, 8, 11, 12L, 13, 14, 21, 22, 23, 24, 29BL, 29R, 30, 31, 32, 35, 36, 37, 40, 43, 44, 47, 48, 149T, 151, back cover BL, TR
R. K. Horst: 58TL
Stephen A. Johnston: 70C
Steven T. Koike: 62L, 71BL, 85TL, 85R, 103L, 106BR
Thomas J. Koske: 93R
Ray R. Kriner: 64L, 79TR, 88TR, 90L, 95R, 97BL, 108L, 126L
Wojciech Lucka: 38, 41T
W. J. Martin: 128R
Charles A. McClurg: 52R, 61R, 77BL, 88BL, 129BL, 129R, 140R, 149B
Eugene Memmler: 83BL
Paul Meyers: 39T, 39B, 54L, 65L, 76TL, 91L, 97TR, 134L
Arthur A. Muka: 73BL
Joe Ogrodnick: 26R, 108TR, 108BR, 122R
Oregon State University, Dept. of Entomology: 111BR
Ortho Photo Library: Front cover, 29TL
A. O. Paulis: 83C
Pamela Peirce: 1, 16CL, 50R, 51R, 56, 57L, 60L, 74C, 99TL, 100R, 117L, 132L, 137L, 137R
Thomas Perring: 16TR
R. P. Puck: 59BR
Purdue University: 58BL, 82TR, 128TL, 128BL
R. C. Rowe: 122L
Avin D. Rutledge: 72R
Anita Sabarese: 152
C. T. Schiller: 27B
Arden F. Sherf: 70L, 76BL, 79BR, 80L, 91R, 105R, 116TR, 116BR, 119TL, 124L, 135L
Michael Smith: 53R
Kenneth A. Sorensen: 68L, 95L, 98R, 107L, 115TL
Donald Specker: 55TR, 55BR, 89R, 119BL
Norm Thomas: 7T, 7B, 133L
University of Illinois: 74L, 79L, 82L, 86BL, 88BR, 97TL, 109TL, 111TL, 111BL, 112R, 116BL, 130TR, 138L, 139R, 148
Paul C. Vincelli: 69L, 69TR, 70R, 109BL, 110R
Ron West: 16CR, 16BL, 16BR, 17T, 17C, 17BR, 26L, 33T, 34B, 42, 51L, 53L, 54L, 55L, 60TL, 60R, 63L, 65TR, 65BR, 66L, 67L, 71L, 71TR, 74R, 75TR, 75B, 76BR, 77R, 78, 87R, 88TL, 94, 96L, 97BR, 101TL, 103R, 105BL, 115BL, 118R, 119R, 120TR, 120BR, 125L
Thomas Zitter: 27T, 68R, 69BR, 80R, 81, 89L, 92BR, 101BL, 101R, 102R, 104R, 106L, 116TL, 117R, 121R, 124R, 125R, 136, 140L

PRINCIPLES OF PEST CONTROL

There are many ways to deal with pests in the vegetable garden. This chapter outlines the basics of pest control and explains how to make informed choices.

Controlling Vegetable Pests

TECHNIQUES FOR SUCCESS AGAINST PESTS

The methods described here will help you carry out environmentally friendly pest control confidently and effectively.

ENCYCLOPEDIA OF PESTS

Before taking any action against the pest you are fighting, you should find out as much as possible about it. The descriptions and photographs in this chapter will help you do that.

Principles of Pest Control

There are many ways to deal with pests in the vegetable garden. This chapter outlines the basics of pest control and explains how to make informed choices.

G rowing a vegetable garden inevitably brings home gardeners into conflict with harmful insects, plant diseases, and other pests. Luckily, there are many options for dealing with these destructive agents. There is no one right or wrong way to control most of them, but rather a choice of methods ranging from altering the way you grow plants, to using biological helpers, to applying pesticides.

Within each broad technique are additional choices. For example, altering the way you grow plants encompasses methods such as planting resistant varieties, rotating crops, and solarizing the soil. The biological helpers available to home gardeners include many naturally occurring creatures as well as an increasing number of beneficial insects, mites, and nematodes that you can buy.

Depending on the pest and the plant, the pesticide you choose may consist of insecticidal soap, a copper compound, or one of several plant extracts. The pesticides cited in this book are generally of the lowest order of toxicity. There are other chemical methods of control that have passed rigorous testing and the approval of the Environmental Protection Agency (EPA), but they are beyond the scope of this book.

In many cases, fighting a pest may call for a combination of methods. Here again, you will probably be presented with choices. The tactics you choose may depend on the size of your planting, the climate in your area, your available time, and other factors. As you become more experienced in pest control, you may find that you prefer certain tactics over others. But, with the help of this book, you will find that you nearly always have a choice.

A well-thought-out pest control plan, which may include a combination of techniques, will keep your vegetable garden beautiful and productive.

THE BASICS OF PEST CONTROL

The first principle of effective pest control in the vegetable garden is to avoid problems by giving plants the best possible growing conditions. Read about the needs of each crop in Ortho's book *All About Vegetables* or another basic vegetable gardening book. Plant at optimum times, following seed packet directions for spacing and planting depth. If you start seeds indoors, be sure that the seedlings are at the proper stage for transplanting and are adequately hardened off (gradually acclimated to outdoor conditions) before you put them into the ground. Provide plants with a suitably sunny location, well-drained soil with an appropriate pH level, adequate fertilizer, sufficient moisture, and protection from strong winds.

Watch carefully for problems as they develop. Reviewing descriptions and photographs of insects and diseases (see the third chapter) will help train you to notice the signs of trouble. It's also a good idea to talk to neighbors and find out what problems have developed in their gardens. Experienced gardeners can tell you which problems are serious in your area and when to look for them. You may find, to your relief, that many of the problems you read about are unlikely to appear. Although the number of potential pests may be overwhelming, only a few usually appear in any one garden. Your neighbors may also provide good advice about vegetable varieties that not only produce well locally but resist attack.

From the time you sow seeds or plant seedlings, your garden will benefit from frequent observation. Make it a point to inspect the garden often, at least three times a week. At first you may notice a problem only after it has become obvious, but as you become more aware of what to look for, you will learn to recognize early signs of trouble. A problem caught within the first few days is easier to solve than one discovered a week or two later.

After noticing that a plant may be in trouble, your next step is to identify the problem accurately and decide how to handle it. Sometimes, it is very easy to recognize the problem—for example, an insect devouring a leaf. In this case, you need only identify the insect and find out how to keep it within bounds. In other cases, you may see similar damage but no insect or other pest. Then you need to use special observation skills to try to catch the pest in the act. (See page 26 for information on how to develop your skills of observation in the garden.)

A disease may also be obvious, as when a typical leaf spot appears or when you see the mottled, malformed leaves characteristic of a mosaic virus. But sometimes you may notice only that a plant is not performing well; it may be small or discolored, or it may produce a poor harvest. If so, find out about the needs of that crop and try to provide better growing conditions for the remainder of the season; if it is too late this year, improve conditions next year. Laboratory analysis is needed to identify some problems, such as most nematode pests (see page 148). Before consulting a laboratory make sure that the problem isn't due simply to poor growing conditions.

A problem may turn out to be physiological; instead of being caused by an outside agent, this type of problem is due to a combination of genetics and growing conditions. For example, blossom-end rot on tomato is caused by a mineral imbalance brought about by uneven watering. Some tomato varieties are more susceptible to the problem than others.

Not all insects in the garden are harmful. Don't jump to the hasty conclusion that an insect is a pest unless you have positively identified it or have seen it not just on a plant but actually eating the plant. Many insects are neutral: They do not harm crops. Some insect are beneficial: They prey on the harmful insects that eat crops. In addition, lizards, snakes, many kinds of birds, and numerous

If you grow your own seedlings indoors, harden them off gradually until they are ready for the more severe climate of a garden.

other wild animals are either neutral or beneficial. Only when you have clearly identified a pest should you be ready to consider control measures. The descriptions of pests in the third chapter will help you identify harmful agents in the garden. If you still can't determine which pest is at fault, a good nursery or garden supply store may be able to offer assistance, or you can consult the local cooperative extension office.

When you know which pest you have, read about it and decide how to handle it. In some cases, control may not be necessary or even possible. In many other cases, control will be warranted and control measures will be available. Applying the right control measure at the right time may help break the pest's life cycle. Select the appropriate control methods (see page 22 for advice on how to choose among different solutions) and carry them out correctly (see the second chapter). Take note of how your control efforts turned out. The results may be apparent immediately, as when an insect stops eating a crop, or you may have to wait until the following season to see the outcome. If the control measures failed, try other tactics.

You will find that you can conquer most, although probably not all, of the problems that appear in your garden. A home gardener can grow a much wider variety of vegetables than the average farmer, because the small scale of a garden allows for much greater attention to the special needs of different crops and to time-consuming pest control methods. Even so, certain insects or diseases may be so prevalent in some locations that it may not be worthwhile to plant some crops. You may choose to cope with such pests by avoiding the plants they attack and replacing them with immune or less susceptible crops.

ENVIRONMENTALLY FRIENDLY METHODS

A method of pest control is considered to be environmentally friendly if it poses minimum hazard to people, domestic and wild animals, and the environment inside and outside the garden. The method must meet the following criteria.
• Minimum toxicity, both immediately and in the long term, to humans and other mammals
• Minimum toxicity to beneficial creatures in the garden, including birds, reptiles, spiders,

The Six Steps of Pest Control

These steps will allow you to manage garden pests, including diseases, effectively and in a manner that is friendly to the environment. The emphasis is on maintaining good plant health and recognizing and dealing responsibly with problems before they get out of hand.
• Provide plants with good growing conditions.
• Watch for symptoms on plants and for signs of pests.
• Identify any pests, and decide if and when to control them.
• Choose one or more methods of control.
• Use the method or methods correctly.
• Decide what to do next year.

Positive identification is important before you act to control an insect. The convergent lady beetle (top) should be encouraged and the Colorado potato beetle (bottom) should be controlled.

Applying regular doses of a liquid fertilizer, such as fish emulsion, will help crops hold their own against certain diseases.

attack by a particular insect or disease; this lets you know which conditions to avoid. Unfortunately, not all pests are attracted only to plants growing under poor conditions. Slugs, snails, and many kinds of insects feed heartily on the healthiest crops.

Plant Resistant Varieties

When they are available, resistant varieties are an easy and inexpensive solution to problems. Disease resistance is more common than resistance to insect and other animal pests. Some plant varieties withstand attack by several different destructive organisms. For example, the highly popular 'Better Boy' tomato is resistant to fusarium wilt, verticillium wilt, and certain nematodes. In cases where there are many strains of a disease or many species of an insect pest, you may have to consult a local nursery or the cooperative extension office to find out which resistant plant variety will work in your area. Many resistant varieties are referred to in the pest descriptions in the third chapter. Also see the lists and charts of resistant varieties on pages 141 to 147.

Even if resistant varieties are not listed for particular pests, that does not mean they are not available. Look for them in mail-order catalogs and other plant sources. Plant breeders are constantly at work developing superior garden plants, so watch for new resistant varieties in the marketplace.

Diversify and Rotate Crops

Growing many kinds of crops offers advantages to the vegetable gardener. The odors and sights of diversified plantings may confuse some insect pests and encourage beneficial insects. At the very least, diversity will leave you with some crops if one or two are decimated by insects or diseases.

Rotation means not growing the same crop in the same place year after year. Crop rotation is a particularly useful control for many soil-borne diseases, and it may help you avoid some other soil-dwelling pests as well. By alternating susceptible crops with immune crops, you can interrupt the life cycle of a pest and cause it to die out. Once the population has subsided, you can grow the susceptible crop again. Continuing a rotation is important to prevent the pest from building up to large numbers again. Even when you don't have evidence of a harmful

amphibians, and beneficial insects above the ground and in the soil
• Minimum disruption of the environment outside the garden by toxic materials washing into sewers or waterways, flowing downhill, entering the biological food chain, or dispersing into the atmosphere
• Minimum use of nonrenewable resources and maximum use of recycling

Every gardener must make personal decisions about gardening methods, weighing the importance of a particular crop against the means of preserving it. Knowing the choices will help you make those decisions. Here are some of the most important environmentally friendly tactics.

Grow Healthy Plants

Although good gardening practices are a general preventive technique, in some cases they are critically important in combating a problem. Extra attention to plant nutrition and watering may get a crop through the season when it is exposed to certain disease organisms or to a moderate nematode infestation. Sometimes, you will read that specified conditions, such as excessively wet soil or too much nitrogen fertilizer, make a plant vulnerable to

agent, rotation is a good idea, because it will nip incipient problems.

Sometimes, a fallow period—one in which soil is left bare in a part of the garden—is included in a rotation. This is especially useful in combating pests, such as root-knot nematodes, that attack most crops but die out fairly quickly when crops are absent. Solarization, a method of increasing the temperature of the soil by covering it with a clear plastic tarp, may be used during a fallow period to increase the death rate of disease spores, nematodes, weed seeds, and other harmful agents. (See page 30 for directions on solarizing the soil.)

Obtain Pest-Free Seeds, Starts, and Other Materials

Infected seeds spread some diseases. Potato tubers, sweet potato roots, and garlic and onion sets may also carry diseases. If you live in an area where a particular seed-borne disease is prevalent, saving your own seeds, tubers, roots, and bulbs is chancy. You also take a risk when you plant tubers, roots, and bulbs sold as food by a grocery store, since grocery produce is not legally required to be free of plant diseases.

Seeds purchased from a reputable source are likely to be healthy. Since fewer diseases occur in arid regions of the West, seeds grown there are more apt to be free of certain diseases. In some cases, there are certification programs in which seeds, tubers, roots, and bulbs are sampled for evidence of disease; if any shows up the entire batch of stock is destroyed.

If you have any doubt about the quality of the seeds you have obtained, you may be able to kill the disease organism by soaking the seeds in warm water for a specified number of minutes. (See page 32; also refer to the third chapter to find out which disease organisms may be killed this way.)

Seedlings and perennial rootstocks can also bear disease; look for those that are certified to be disease free. Even the soil around plant roots can carry unpleasant surprises in the form of disease spores or pest nematodes. Commercial seedlings should have been grown in a clean, sterilized medium, but beware of gift plants dug from other gardens. It is wise to observe gift plants in a quarantine area of the garden before locating them near other plants.

Purchase soil, compost, mulch, and other amendments from reputable dealers. In many cases, packaged materials are certified pest free; however, the quality of bulk materials

Plant a diversity of crops and locate each in a different area of the garden every year.

often depends on the sanitation and other practices of individual dealers. Materials obtained from questionable sources may be infested.

Break the Pest's Life Cycle

Often, the life cycles of pests have weak points—periods in which your actions may cause a pest to die. For example, many insects pupate, or go through a resting stage encased in a cocoon or hard shell, in the soil. They are vulnerable during this inactive period between the larval and adult stages. If you plow the soil one or more times after the insects pupate, you will kill many and expose others to predators.

You may be able to schedule a planting to avoid a pest's active period. Often, insects emerge when the air or soil reaches a certain temperature in spring. You may escape serious damage if you plant a crop early enough so that it is already past its most vulnerable stage when the pest emerges. In the case of a pest like the asparagus aphid, you may be able to delay the susceptible stage of the crop until many of the aphids have starved for lack of their preferred food (see page 60).

Some pests have alternate hosts. This means that when the pests are not injuring your crop, their primary host, they are living on some other plant. For example, in many areas the green peach aphid spends the winter on peach and other dormant fruit trees before moving to spinach, potato, and other vegetable crops. You may prevent infestations on the vegetables by spraying the fruit trees with a dormant oil. Many pests live on weeds when they are not on domestic plants. Although it is always a good idea to keep weeds from competing with crops, it is especially important to eliminate weeds that harbor pests. Knowing which weeds pests prefer allows you to do that.

Most kinds of disease spores require a moist environment for a certain number of hours before they can germinate. Thus, a common means of preventing diseases that attack aboveground plant parts is watering at ground level—by furrow irrigation, soaker hose, or drip irrigation—rather than by overhead sprinklers. Spreading a mulch under the plants may reduce the splashing of disease spores onto leaves during rainy weather.

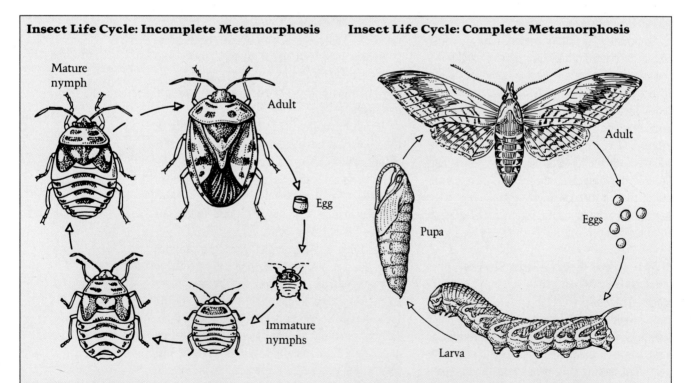

Insect Life Cycle: Incomplete Metamorphosis

Mature nymph

Adult

Egg

Immature nymphs

Insect Life Cycle: Complete Metamorphosis

Adult

Eggs

Pupa

Larva

The life cycle of the harlequin bug follows a pattern known as incomplete metamorphosis. An egg hatches into a wingless nymph that feeds, grows, and sheds its skin several times. After each molt it looks increasingly like an adult. A winged adult emerges after the last molt. Stinkbugs, squash bugs, thrips, and earwigs also follow this pattern.

The hornworm illustrates complete metamorphosis, a kind of insect life cycle marked by drastic changes in appearance. Eggs hatch into wingless larvae that molt and grow, then enter a resting stage called a pupa from which the adult emerges. Caterpillars are the larvae of moths or butterflies, maggots the larvae of flies, and grubs the larvae of beetles.

Top: Children can freely explore a garden in which pests are controlled by such methods as handpicking or breaking a pest's life cycle.
Bottom: Weeds and crops in the same plant family are likely to share pests. This gardener is pulling lamb's-quarters, a relative of Swiss chard, to keep pests from spreading to the adjacent chard planting.

Finally, keeping the garden clear of debris will help control many problems. Some pests hide in stacks of flowerpots or piles of brush. Decaying plant debris may provide a place for insects to hide during the daytime or to spend the winter; disease organisms may survive for years in plant debris. Good garden hygiene means digging under or composting spent crops. Remove them from the garden if the debris carries, or is suspected of carrying, a harmful organism that can survive burial or composting.

Remove Pests and Infected Plant Material by Hand

Handpicking can be a very effective way to control insects in small plantings. It is most effective when the pest you are hunting is clearly visible and slow moving; handpicking is the foundation of most successful efforts by home gardeners to control the brown garden snail. Pests that feed during the day are the easiest to handpick, although you can hunt night feeders in the daytime if you know where they hide. Picking off damaged leaves will slow the spread of leafminers and some diseases,

including certain kinds of leaf spots and powdery mildew on cucurbits.

Handpicking is not a perfect control. Even when you pick regularly, you may still miss some pests. However, most crops will tolerate a low rate of pest damage without loss of yield. Also, not all damage is serious. For instance, several pests, including the imported cabbageworm and cutworms, eat holes in the outer leaves of cabbage, but the holes are usually not deep enough to seriously damage the head.

Sometimes, a whole plant or an entire planting should be removed. This is often the case when a plant has a virus, since there is no cure for plant viruses. They are often spread by insects or by contact, so an infected plant may serve as a source of infection for other plants. For example, aphids spread viruses among squash plants by feeding on a virus-infected plant and then on healthy ones; likewise, gardeners may spread tobacco mosaic virus by brushing against an infected tomato plant and then against a healthy one. Many other kinds of diseases are also best controlled by removing the affected plants as soon as you notice the symptoms.

Even if you are able to control diseases well enough to harvest a crop, you should always remove infected plants as soon as the harvest is over. This is also a good idea if your plants are infested with insects that reproduce continually, such as whiteflies or mites. Plants seriously damaged by nematodes should also be removed; allowing the plants to remain in the soil only encourages the nematode population to increase.

Use Visual and Olfactory Repellents

Some methods of controlling pests depend on unpleasant scents or frightening images. These tend to be less effective than methods that exclude, remove, or kill the pests, because they are less final. A repelled pest is still there; it still has physical access to your plants and, under pressure of hunger, it may ignore the repellent. However, some repellents are useful, especially in combination with other control methods.

Birds may be frightened by an inflatable owl or snake or by a bull's-eye pattern on a balloon, but they may also become accustomed to the object and ignore it. Deer and rabbits may be deterred by the scent of a commercial repellent or by materials such as blood meal, but they too may overcome their fear as the repellent becomes familiar.

The idea that certain plants can be interplanted in ways that repel insects has been a popular one for many years. Often, the suggested companion plants are strong-scented herbs. Although only some of these relationships have been tested, they have consistently shown poor results. Some repellent plants reduce the number of pest eggs on adjacent crops, but only when the repellent plant is seeded so

A frame of polyvinyl chloride tubing covered with plastic netting forms an enclosure that will protect crops from bird damage.

Removing crop plants as soon as they are finished bearing is a good garden practice, and it is important in controlling certain pests. Here, a gardener is pulling spent bean plants.

densely that it substantially reduces the yield of the crop plants.

More promising is the use of plant extracts to spray on crop plants as repellents. In a laboratory test Colorado potato beetles preferred starvation to eating eggplant leaves sprayed with an extract of the herb tansy. Some gardeners swear by a spray containing garlic, onion, and hot pepper extracts as a repellent for various beetles, weevils, and leafminers. Although there is no guarantee that the spray will be effective, you may want to try it; see the directions on page 34. One commercial formulation combines extracts of kelp, English ivy, Dalmatian sage, garlic, and eucalyptus oil. Gardeners have reported success using it against aphids, whiteflies, mites, slugs, and snails. Insect repellents may prove to work best in combination with trap crops or baited traps (see pages 14 and 36); the idea is to make the main crop less attractive and to drive the pest into the trap.

Since repellents are only a mild deterrent, local conditions may override their effectiveness. Your local pest birds may ignore inflatable owls in your garden because a gardener in the next block has been using them for years. Local insects may be genetically different from those repelled by a plant extract in other areas, or they may have fewer alternative food sources in your neighborhood, causing hunger to overcome revulsion.

Create Barriers to Pests

Physical barriers can be a practical way to keep pests away from plants, particularly seedlings. For example, collars made from tin cans will stop cutworms, and plastic netting will prevent birds from pecking the plants.

Older plants may also be protected by barriers. For example, developing potato tubers kept well covered with soil are less likely to be damaged by blight or by the potato tuberworm. A strip of copper foil fastened to the frame of a raised bed will serve as a barrier to slugs and snails (see page 56).

A new family of materials known collectively as floating row covers can provide protection for individual plants or entire plantings. The covers are made of lightweight, translucent synthetic materials. Unlike clear plastic they are porous. You can water right through them. Since they let in air, they needn't be removed unless temperatures are very high or the crop requires pollination by insects. A floating row cover offers protection against many otherwise hard-to-control insect pests. For example, even if your garden has a severe cabbage maggot infestation, you can still produce undamaged radishes and turnips under a floating row cover; just be sure that the edges are tucked firmly into the soil all around the planting. Most floating row covers can be used for at least two seasons.

Set Traps to Catch Pests

If you know what attracts a pest, you can set traps for it. Traps may be unbaited or baited. Often, unbaited traps depend on the pest's need for daytime cover. For example, rolled-up newspapers will attract earwigs, and wide boards propped 1 inch above the soil surface will draw snails. This type of trap must be emptied daily or it will become a protected site from which the pest can feed every night.

Baited traps use an attractant substance to lure pests. Beer traps are a common method of catching slugs, and they can also be used to catch earwigs. The yeasty odor of beer attracts the pests, which then drown. Commercially available traps use a malt-based bait to achieve the same result. A cut potato buried just beneath the soil serves as a baited trap for some kinds of wireworms.

Traps containing insect sex attractants, known as pheromones, attract male insects. Such traps are often used by farmers to monitor the number of moths in their fields so that they know whether to spray or apply other control measures. Pheromone traps may be used in the same way in home gardens. For example, by knowing when corn earworms become active,

you know when egg laying is about to begin; that allows you to begin spraying the bacterial insecticide *Bacillus thuringiensis* (Bt, see page 41) to control the newly hatched worms at their most vulnerable stage.

Sticky traps are flat surfaces painted a color, usually yellow, that attracts pests; the surface is then coated with a sticky substance. Like pheromone traps, sticky traps are useful for monitoring pests, but they can also help control the pests if enough traps are used. (See the directions for making and using sticky traps on page 37.)

A trap crop is one that is grown to attract a pest away from a crop that you intend to harvest. You can use the same crop, started a bit earlier, or another crop that the pest likes even more. For this method to work, you must either kill the pest on the trap crop or remove the trap crop along with the pest before the crop you are protecting is at a vulnerable stage. Try starting a few trap crop plants indoors in containers before it is warm enough outside to plant the desirable crop. Then, at the normal planting time, set the container plants in the garden to attract the pests.

Encourage Beneficial Creatures in Your Garden

By constantly destroying pests, naturally occurring predators and other beneficial creatures provide considerable help in the battle to save crops. Usually, gardeners don't realize how much help they are getting until these

Left: A collar made from a tin can with the ends removed is a good protection against cutworms. Right: Commercially available slug traps come with a malt-based bait.

natural enemies fail for some reason. In the Northeast, farmers and gardeners often get such a demonstration when a cold, wet spring kills the natural enemies of the fall armyworm. Free to multiply unharmed by its enemies, the pest marches northward in alarming numbers, consuming a wide variety of crops in its path.

Naturally occurring beneficial creatures are ideal pest control agents. Not only are they free and environmentally harmless, but they hunt the pests for you. You can encourage these helpful creatures by providing a welcoming habitat and by avoiding pesticides that are toxic to them (see page 38). The following are some of the many predators, parasites, and other creatures that may dwell in your garden.

Aphid midge Several kinds of aphids fall prey to the larvae of this tiny black fly with long legs. Active at dusk and during the night, the adult flies feed on the honeydew, or partially digested plant sap, excreted by aphids. On plants infested by aphids, they lay eggs in proportion to the density of the aphids. The legless light orange to red larvae eat the aphids, leaving dried blackened aphid bodies as evidence of their feeding.

Lady beetles Both the larvae and adults eat insect eggs and soft-bodied insects, particularly aphids. In addition to the common convergent lady beetle, with its 12 black spots, there are types of lady beetles with 2, 7, 9, and 15 black spots on red wing covers. Some lady beetles have 2 red spots on black wing covers; other lady beetles are completely black. Smaller blackish or gray lady beetles feed on spider mites and whiteflies. Learn to recognize lady beetle larvae, which eat more pests than the adults. They are shaped like tiny alligators; the most common types are black with orange or yellow spots.

Lacewings Green lacewing larvae and brown lacewing larvae and adults feed on insect eggs and soft-bodied insects. (The adult green lacewing eats pollen rather than insects.) Lacewing larvae resemble the alligator-shaped larvae of lady beetles, except that they are gray-green or gray-brown. The adults are small, with large transparent wings.

Predatory wasps Many native wasps hunt pest insects. They are often seen patrolling the garden rows or flying off carrying a caterpillar. Even yellow jackets, which are considered annoying at times, hunt caterpillars when they are feeding their young early in summer.

Parasitic wasps A number of tiny wasps are parasites of many kinds of pest insects. (Technically, the wasps are parasitoid, since they kill their hosts.) Each type of wasp usually parasitizes one kind of insect, often a single species. The wasps lay eggs in the host insects—in the eggs, larvae, or adults. One common parasitic wasp lays eggs in adult aphids, creating aphid mummies (see pages 16 and 63). Another lays eggs in hornworms, eventually killing them; look for parasitized hornworms with small white wasp cocoons on their backs.

Syrphid flies The larvae of these beneficial creatures, also known as hover flies, eat aphids, mealybugs, and scales. The adults, which pollinate plants, are often seen hovering like tiny helicopters over flowers. With their black and yellow or black and white markings, they resemble wasps but do not sting.

Tachinid flies The legless white larvae, or maggots, of these flies parasitize armyworms, beetle larvae, corn borers, cutworms, and stinkbugs. The bristly black, gray, or striped adults resemble houseflies but are usually larger.

Ground beetles Usually shiny and often black but sometimes iridescent, ground beetles live in burrows in the ground, although they may climb to hunt. Some eat caterpillars and others eat small snails or snail and slug eggs. Some feed on both insects and plant material, although they don't damage plants significantly.

Rove beetles These slender, usually black beetles have short wings that leave much of the body exposed. Some types raise their rear ends as if to frighten potential predators, but they do not sting. They range from minute to 1 inch long. The diets of various rove beetles include mites, root maggots, slugs, and snails. They can be found on the soil surface and in surface debris.

True bugs Several members of this insect group prey on other insects. Damsel bugs eat

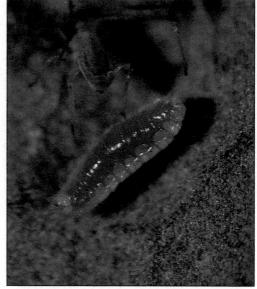

Top left: The ⅓-inch-long brown lacewing (shown here) and the slightly larger green lacewing eat aphids and other soft-bodied pests and many kinds of insect eggs.

Top right: The orange to red larva of the aphid midge is only ⁵/₃₂ inch long, but each eats up to 30 aphids.

Center left: Aphids killed by parasitic wasps become distended and brittle. A round hole shows where young wasps exited from these aphid mummies.

Center right: For their size, lady beetle larvae eat more aphids than adult lady beetles. The ⅓-inch-long larvae look like orange and black alligators.

Bottom left: The braconid wasps that parasitize aphids are tiny and do not sting humans.

Bottom right: Predatory paper wasps hunt caterpillars and other pests daily while they are feeding their young. Tolerate wasp nests in areas that you don't enter often.

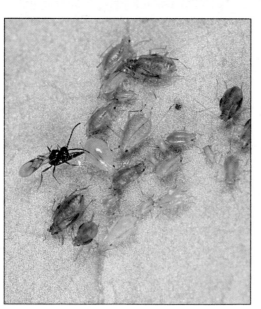

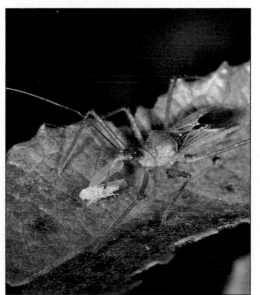

Top left: Plant shallow-necked flowers to provide the pollen that syrphid fly adults need for reproduction. Syrphid fly larvae eat aphids, leafhoppers, and other pests.
Top right: Ground beetles, which feed mainly on insects, are usually shiny black, although some are iridescent.
Center left: Two predatory mites of the species Phytoseiulus persimilis *are seen attacking a pest mite.*
Center right: Rove beetles typically lift their rear ends into a defensive position when disturbed, but they do not sting.
Bottom left: When fully grown, minute pirate bugs are less than ⅛ inch long. This minute pirate bug nymph is about to feed on corn earworm eggs.
Bottom right: Assassin bugs, which eat almost any insect, will render a powerful sting if you touch them. Although these predators vary in appearance, all species have elongated heads.

aphids, leafhoppers, and small caterpillars; they also feed on plant-eating true bugs, such as the tarnished plant bug and the harlequin bug. Assassin bugs attack almost any kind of insect. Bigeyed bugs live on small insects, insect eggs, and mites. Although tiny, minute pirate bugs eat many kinds of mites and insects, particularly thrips.

Predatory mites   Several kinds of beneficial mites feed on pest mites. Some predatory mites can be purchased, although many occur naturally in gardens.

Honeybees and other pollinators   Although they do not destroy pests, honeybees are considered beneficial insects because they pollinate plants. The larger bumblebees, syrphid flies, and many other insects are also pollinators.

Vertebrate predators   In every area some native amphibians, including salamanders and toads, and some native reptiles, including snakes and lizards, prey on garden pests. Birds such as the robin, flicker, and mockingbird also devour many insect pests.

Soil-dwelling organisms   The soil contains many living creatures, most of which are microscopic. Some attack living plants, but the majority are either harmless or beneficial. Among the helpful organisms are many fungi, bacteria, and tiny animals. They break down organic matter, transform soil chemicals into forms that plants can use as nutrients, and release antibiotic substances into the soil. Research has shown that mycorrhizal fungi, which live in symbiosis with plant roots, help plants combat soil diseases. Beneficial nematodes attack soil pests, and actinomycete bacteria kill harmful nematodes. By aerating the soil, earthworms help reduce the incidence of disease due to poor drainage.

Disease organisms   Many fungi, bacteria, and other naturally occurring disease organisms attack pests, often providing significant control. You may see dead fuzzy brown or reddish aphids that were killed by a predatory fungus. Polyhedrous granulosis viruses kill many caterpillar pests in vegetable gardens. These helpful organisms are being identified gradually, and a few have been developed for commercial release.

Release Purchased Helpers

At one time the main predatory insects available for sale were the praying mantis and the convergent lady beetle. Now, more predatory and parasitic creatures appear on the market every year. The old standbys are no longer the only, or necessarily the best, choice. Although the praying mantis eats pests, it is not very specific. It will eat just about any insect, including many harmless and beneficial insects.

The convergent lady beetle eats aphids and other pests, but it often flies away from the garden in which it was released. The aphid midge and the green lacewing are more likely to remain and feed in your garden. The larvae of the aphid midge are aphid predators, and green lacewing larvae eat aphids and many other pests consumed by lady beetles.

Some tiny beneficial wasps can be purchased to control insects in vegetable gardens. For example, trichogramma wasps control many kinds of caterpillars by parasitizing their eggs, and a whitefly parasite (*Encarsia formosa*) lays eggs in and feeds on the greenhouse whitefly.

A relatively new helper on the market is the spined soldier bug. This insect, which has proved quite capable of stopping the Mexican bean beetle, also preys on the cabbage looper, the imported cabbageworm, and other pests.

Predatory mites, which are available for purchase, may help to control pest mites. Before buying mites, check with the supplier to make sure that you are getting the most useful species for your environment and for the pests you are fighting.

Two microscopic organisms are among the most effective biological controls you can buy. These are predatory nematodes and the bacterial insecticide Bt, which is sold under various trade names, including Dipel® and Thuricide®. Bt is a bacterium that infects and kills various pest insects without harming beneficial insects or any other animals. There are several formulations of the bacterium, three of which are useful in the vegetable garden. *Bt berliner-kurstake* kills many kinds of pest caterpillars, such as the cabbage looper, the imported cabbageworm, the diamondback moth larva, the corn earworm, and hornworms.

Javelin® is the trade name of a strain of *Bt berliner-kurstake* that is especially effective in controlling armyworms and loopers. *Bt san diego*, sold under the trade name M-One®, kills the Colorado potato beetle.

Predatory nematodes are relatives of the nematodes that eat plant roots, but these useful creatures seek out and destroy insect pests in the soil and in protected places on plants. They destroy carrot weevil larvae, cutworms, Japanese beetle larvae, root maggots, seedcorn maggots, wireworms, and other pests. The most commonly available species, *Neoaplectana carpocapsae* (Nc for short), works well for most purposes. Another species, *Heterorhabditis heliothidis* (Hh for short), is more effective against Japanese beetle larvae and root weevils because it moves faster and travels deeper in the soil.

Choose Pesticides With the Least Environmental Impact

Some products for controlling garden pests are relatively nontoxic to humans and other creatures. Certain others, although moderately toxic, do not remain active in the environment for very long and thus are minimally disruptive.

Insecticidal soap This pesticide acts by damaging the insect's protective covering, causing it to dehydrate. It is no more toxic to humans and other mammals than any soapy water. Commercially available insecticidal soaps have been formulated to kill targeted pests—aphids, whiteflies, caterpillars, stinkbugs, some beetles, and certain other insect pests—without damaging the plants they are intended to treat. The insecticidal soap must be sprayed directly on the insect in order to kill it. One commercial formulation combines soap with citrus oil; the soap acts as a surfactant and the citrus oil actually suffocates the insect. See page 44 for instructions on using insecticidal soap.

Diatomaceous earth A dust made from the fossilized shells of tiny aquatic algae, diatomaceous earth kills some kinds of soft-bodied insects by piercing their protective covering and causing them to desiccate. Since it is not selective, it will kill beneficial as well as pest insects. Some gardeners swear by it; others find it a nuisance to keep reapplying. Dusted on

moist plants, diatomaceous earth is most effective during hot, dry weather; you needn't reapply it as often, and pests are less likely to recover as during cool, moist weather.

Elemental sulfur In dust or spray form, this mineral element is used to control some mites and many plant diseases. Some people have an allergic reaction to sulfur. Do not use it just before harvesting food that you intend to can, since traces of sulfur will form sulfur dioxide and may cause the containers to explode.

Copper compounds Various copper compounds—including liquid copper fungicide, fixed copper fungicide, and bordeaux mixture—are used to control certain diseases. They are relatively low in toxicity to humans and other mammals, although they will harm fish. In theory, heavy use could cause a buildup

There is no waiting period when you use biological helpers, such as Bt or predatory nematodes. You can enter the garden, harvest, and eat the crops anytime.

in the soil, but some organic farmers have tested the soil after extensive use of copper and have not found a problem. Copper materials can damage plants, especially during hot weather and when used at high rates on young plants. Wearing protective gear is particularly important when applying these materials, since some people are very sensitive to them.

Pyrethrum products   Derived from a kind of chrysanthemum that has insecticidal properties, pyrethrum products consist of the ground-up flower pyrethrum, and pyrethrins, the toxins extracted from that flower. Although pyrethroids take their name from the same flower, they are synthetic chemicals that last longer in the environment than natural pyrethrum products.

Pyrethrum, a dust made from the whole flowers, is relatively low in toxicity to humans and other mammals, although it causes allergic reactions in some people. Pyrethrins, which consist of six active chemicals extracted from the flower, is somewhat more toxic since it is more concentrated, but it is much less likely to cause allergic reactions. Pyrethrins are usually applied as a spray.

Pyrethrum products are toxic to honeybees, fish, and aquatic invertebrates that fish eat; however, they have only a brief effect in the environment, since the toxins break down in a few hours when exposed to sunlight.

Pyrethrum and pyrethrins work in direct contact and are noted for their quick knockdown effect. Pests hit by a pyrethrum toxin are stimulated and often move from their hiding places before becoming paralyzed. They will die if the dosage was sufficient; if not, they may recover. That is why instructions for using pyrethrum products sometimes advise you to apply the product once to flush out the pests and a second time to kill them. It is also the reason that pyrethrum is sometimes combined with rotenone or other chemicals that will finish off the pests. Pyrethrins may be sold in combination with synergists, such as piperonyl butoxide, that block an insect's ability to recover from the knockdown.

Ryania   Extracted from a tropical shrub, ryania works both on contact and through the stomach. It has a low toxicity to humans and other mammals, and will not harm beneficial mites, parasitic wasps, lacewings, or lady beetles. It remains active in the environment up to 14 days, but its low toxicity to beneficial organisms mitigates the fact that it persists so long. Ryania works best in hot, dry weather, since rain and dew wash it off plants. It is usually applied as a dust. Ryania is currently available; however, manufacturing sources continue to dwindle, and the product may not be obtainable in the future.

Sabadilla   An extract of the seed of a tropical lily, sabadilla is applied as a dust and works both on contact and through the stomach. It has a relatively low toxicity to humans and other mammals and little effect on common beneficials. Sabadilla is especially effective against leafhoppers and many true bugs, including the tarnished plant bug and the adult squash bug. It breaks down rapidly in sunlight and air, remaining effective for up to a day. Sabadilla can be used in cool, rainy, or damp weather, since the active ingredient is not water soluble.

Pyrethrum is derived from a very pretty daisy that is also sold as an ornamental plant.

Rotenone   A substance extracted from the roots of a tropical legume, rotenone is effective on contact and through the stomach. It kills beetles, caterpillars, thrips, weevils, and other pests. It is available as a dust or spray. Since rotenone is very toxic to fish, it should not be used in a manner that may allow it to get into waterways. It will kill some beneficial insects, although it is not toxic to honeybees. In strong sunlight rotenone breaks down, becoming non-toxic in one to five days.

Rotenone may be the least toxic insecticide available for certain hard-to-kill beetles. If rotenone is the only pesticide listed for an insect, look for it in formulations that also contain pyrethrum or pyrethrins, or these chemicals plus ryania. These combinations reduce the amount of rotenone required to kill the pest.

OVER THE HORIZON

New pest control methods that are friendly to the environment will continue to become available in the coming years. Plant breeders are constantly developing new resistant vegetable varieties. More and more beneficial creatures will be sold to control garden pests, and an increasing number of them will be beneficial soil organisms that are able to control soil pests. Insect pheromones will be used to make insects too confused to mate. Plant extracts will be developed to discourage insects from feeding or to attract them to traps. The following are a few of the promising techniques just over the horizon.

Parasitic wasps are being trained to select and find corn earworms. United States Department of Agriculture scientists have found that behavioral conditioning can make the wasps much more effective hunters, a feat previously thought impossible. The scientists hope to have trained wasps ready for large-scale release soon.

Chemical extracts of onion plants show promise in controlling white rot fungus, a serious soil pest of onion, garlic, and shallot. Researchers have isolated the chemicals that trigger growth of the soilborne fungus. When they apply these chemicals to the soil before the crop is planted, the fungus starts to grow

New environmentally friendly methods of keeping vegetable crops healthy and productive are continually being developed.

but then dies from lack of food. These chemicals are not yet commercially available.

Neem, an extract from a tree native to India, holds promise as one of the most useful pesticides. It acts as an insect growth regulator, causing the insects to die before they mature. It also reduces egg laying and causes insects to stop feeding. In addition, it has proven effective against some kinds of harmful nematodes and soil fungi. Neem is biodegradable, and it has a very low toxicity to mammals, birds, honeybees, predatory mites, and predatory wasps. The product has been approved in the United States, under the trade name Margosan-O®, for use against some pests of ornamentals; it is currently being studied for possible registration for use against pests of food crops.

CHOOSING AMONG SOLUTIONS

Before you can make an informed choice about control methods, you should find out as much as you can about the pest you are fighting (see the third chapter). It is important to consider several factors when deciding among control methods.

First, ask yourself whether now is the right time for each tactic suggested. For example, planting a resistant variety is an excellent idea, but only early in the season. If an insect is already feeding on a crop, another tactic is clearly in order.

When you have narrowed the choices to those applicable now, you must consider the time and money involved in each. You can figure out the total time by estimating or recording the amount of time to implement the method in one unit, then multiplying that by the total planting. The unit can be one plant, a fraction of a row, or a certain number of square feet. Suppose you are debating whether to handpick insects or spray Bt in a small planting of young broccoli. You find that it takes 1 minute to handpick insects on one plant; since you have four plants, the whole job will take 4 minutes. You estimate that spraying Bt will take 11 minutes: 5 minutes to mix, 15 seconds to spray each plant, and another 5 minutes to clean the sprayer. For four plants handpicking is faster. However, if you had 40 broccoli plants, handpicking would take 40 minutes and spraying would take 20 minutes. Spraying continues to gain a time advantage as the planting gets larger.

Some of the best pest control methods are free, or nearly so—for example, wrapping a seedling stem in paper to exclude root maggots, or keeping down weeds to avoid the pests they

Knowing the size of the area requiring treatment will help you compare the time and expense involved in various pest control methods.

carry. Other methods require an expenditure. To calculate the cost, note the price of a product and the number of plants or square feet it will treat, then calculate how much you will need for your garden. For example, suppose 1 unit of predatory nematodes costs $15 and treats 225 square feet. If your garden is 15 by 25 feet, or 375 square feet, you will need 1⅔ units of predatory nematodes; since you must purchase whole units, you will have to buy 2 units at a total cost of $30. Suppose you decide to apply the nematodes twice, at the two periods of maximum root maggot damage. Since each unit must be used up all at once, you will need to purchase 2 additional units for the second application. The total cost for the season will be $60.

You must consider the degree to which various methods affect the environment. For example, if two pesticides will handle the same problem, choose the one that is less toxic to humans, birds, and honeybees, and lasts for a shorter time in the environment.

In some cases, the recommendations in this book will conflict—for example, when advice to clean up debris conflicts with advice to provide cover for predators. Then you will need to weigh the advantages and disadvantages of each course of action.

Often, you will want to use more than one tactic at a time—for example, planting a resistant variety, rotating crops, and avoiding overhead watering. If you want to test a specific tactic, you must try it alone. For instance, if you want to know how well diatomaceous earth works, apply it alone and not when you are releasing beneficial insects or applying another pesticide. Ideally, leave some plants untreated. If the untreated plants show more pest damage than the treated ones, you know the treatment made a difference.

Another consideration is the severity of the situation. If you are seeing only an occasional cabbage looper, handpicking is a logical tactic. But if your cabbage or other plants are covered with young loopers, Bt could save the day. If the loopers are nearly full-grown and thus less susceptible to Bt, you may choose to apply pyrethrins or sabadilla.

Sometimes, when a pest has built up to large numbers, you may gain control by spraying or dusting the plants once and then releasing a predator. For example, use pyrethrum or rotenone to reduce the Mexican bean beetle population, wait a few days while the insecticide breaks down, and then release spined soldier bugs. The pest population will then be at a level that the predator can control.

Sometimes the presence of a pet will influence the choice of methods for protecting a vegetable garden from pests.

Techniques for Success Against Pests

The methods described here will help you carry out environmentally friendly pest control confidently and effectively.

Some pest control techniques seem straightforward enough at first. For example, looking at a plant seems easy, especially if the plant is about to produce something delicious for your dinner. But the way you ordinarily look at garden plants may allow problems to spread unnoticed. Once you know exactly when, where, and how to look, you are more likely to catch a problem before serious damage occurs. The same concept applies to handpicking. Knowing how to catch a wily pest dramatically increases your chance of eliminating it.

On the other hand, planning a crop rotation may seem complex and mysterious at first. But once you understand the theory, you will find that you are able to create elegant rotations that either prevent many soilborne problems or let you continue to garden while you starve the invading soil pests.

One of the most sophisticated pest control methods is biological control. In this chapter you will learn how to attract beneficial creatures to your garden, schedule releases of purchased helpers, including predatory nematodes, and apply the bacterial insecticide *Bacillus thuringiensis* (Bt).

Also included is the information you need to use chemical pesticides wisely. Choosing an appropriate applicator will make your job easier and more accurate, and a few precautions will allow you to use pesticides in ways that protect people and the environment.

After you harvest a crop, amend the soil and plant a different crop than was growing there before. Crop rotation is an effective way to escape many soil pests.

OBSERVATION

Plants may or may not respond if you talk to them or expose them to classical music, but it's a fact that the time you spend observing your plants pays off in healthier crops. When you look at plants often, you begin to understand how they should look at each stage of their growth, and you learn to recognize any changes that signal trouble. Careful observation is the foundation of any prevention program as well as the first step in any treatment plan.

How to Search Plants

Look over an entire planting on a regular basis, starting when the plants are young. If one or a few plants are small and weak compared to the others, it is wise to remove them. Such plants may have been grown from infected seeds, or they may have a disease spread by insects.

As plants develop, check them regularly for evidence of disease or insect damage. A 10-power hand lens will provide a closer look. Be sure to examine the undersides of the leaves, where many insects and diseases appear. Also check the growing points at the top of the plant and the leaves nearest the ground; these are areas in which insects and diseases often begin their damage. If you see chewed leaves but no pest, try observing early in the morning when pests move more slowly. To find night feeders, either hunt after dark with a flashlight or search hiding places during the daytime.

What to Look For

First look for obvious damage, such as leaves and fruit that have been eaten by pests with chewing mouthparts. Then look for damage caused by sucking pests: leaves that are pale, stippled, bleached, or twisted. Next, you must hunt for the damaging pest and identify it. If you can't find any pests, try laying a white cloth under the plant and tapping the plant until pests fall onto the cloth. (Start with a light tap, although it may take a sharp rap to dislodge some kinds of pests.) Use your hand lens to identify the catch.

Sometimes, eggs reveal the presence of insects. Typically small, insect eggs are often laid singly or in groups on the undersides of leaves. Once you have learned to recognize the insect eggs, you will have an early warning of the pest. Exercise some caution in destroying any eggs, since some beneficial insects also lay eggs on plants. Watch long enough to be sure that you are seeing the guilty creature before you begin to combat it.

Another common way to detect an insect is to look for its frass, or excrement. Caterpillars often leave a greenish or brownish material that may be easier to see than the pest itself. Aphids and whiteflies excrete honeydew, a clear, sticky substance consisting of partially digested plant sap, which coats infested leaves.

Look for spots, blotches, and growths on the leaves, stems, and fruit. These may be caused by leafmining insects or by any number of diseases, including leaf spots, blights, rusts, and viruses. Observe the shape and color of the spots; also note whether they consist of more than one color, contain an ooze or powder, and develop first on the lower or upper surface of the leaves. Whether they appear at the bottom or the top of the plant may be another important clue. Be sure to check the stem at the soil line for discoloration and for obvious disease organisms, such as fungal strands.

Left: Striking in appearance, stinkbug eggs resemble little barrels.
Right: When European corn borer eggs reach the black head stage, they will hatch within 36 hours. Knowing this lets you plan control treatments to coincide with the hatching.

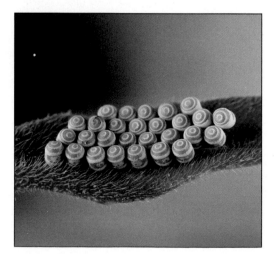

Watch for plants that wilt or even fall over even though they are adequately watered. These plants may also be smaller than others planted at the same time. The problem may be a boring insect in the plant stem (this is especially likely in cucurbits and corn), an insect or other creature damaging the roots, or a wilt disease clogging the water transport system in the plant. Check the stem for entry holes made by a boring insect. Then dig soil away from the base of the plant and examine the upper roots; if there is no evidence of a pest, dig up the plant and examine the roots for decay and for galls that indicate root-knot nematode damage. Cut through the lower stem, both lengthwise and crosswise, and look for orange, reddish, brown, or black discoloration typical of a wilt disease.

Check the pest listings under the crop in question in the third chapter; look for a description of symptoms that approximates what you see. Although this book covers the most common problems gardeners across the United States are likely to encounter, all possible symptoms and causes are too numerous to list. Remember, too, that a pest is not always responsible for a problem. For example, leaf discoloration may result from physiological conditions, such as underwatering, poor fertilization, or air pollution. If you can't identify a problem, you may want to try to improve growing conditions before you check further. However, if the symptoms strongly suggest a pest and you can't identify it with the help of this book, seek advice from the local cooperative extension office.

CULTURAL TECHNIQUES
You can prevent or control pest problems in the vegetable garden by altering the way you grow plants, by choosing varieties that are less likely to be attacked, and even by not planting susceptible crops for a period. All of these are cultural techniques.

Plant Resistant Varieties
If you know which pests are likely to turn up in your garden, you can seek plant varieties that offer genetic resistance to them. There are many varieties that resist certain diseases and a smaller number that resist certain insects. Nematode-resistant varieties can be grown successfully in soil infested with nematodes.

Seed packet labels often include letters following the name of the plant variety; the letters indicate the pests that it resists. At present, this labeling is largely confined to resistant tomato varieties. For example, *VFFNT* after the name of a tomato variety indicates that the variety resists verticillium wilt, two races of fusarium wilt, certain nematodes, and tobacco mosaic virus.

More and more resistant varieties appear on the market yearly, thanks to aggressive plant breeding programs. Some are breakthroughs, offering resistance where none existed; others replace current resistant varieties. Sometimes, a replacement variety is unchanged in resistance but offers improved qualities, such as larger and sweeter fruit. At other times, a new variety is bred because an older one is no longer resistant. A disease may suddenly be

Top: Two-tone mottled leaves are a typical symptom of virus diseases. This squash plant has papaya ring spot virus.
Bottom: Many fungus and bacterial diseases cause leaf spots. The fungus disease early blight of celery, also known as cercospora blight, has infected this celery plant.

able to penetrate the resistance, or more commonly a new race of disease may appear in some areas.

Plants with the strongest resistance adversely affect the growth of a pest, repel it, or fail to attract it. Tolerance is a weaker form of resistance. A tolerant variety will be attacked by a pest but will still bear a satisfactory crop. Resistance does not mean immunity. Even resistant plants may succumb if conditions are particularly favorable for a pest or if there is a very high concentration of the pest. Using resistant varieties does not allow you to neglect other methods of prevention and control.

Many resistant varieties are mentioned in the pest descriptions in the third chapter and others are listed on pages 141 to 147. Just because resistant varieties are not listed for a particular pest does not mean that they do not exist, although in many cases that may be true. Occasionally, cooperative extension offices are aware of vegetable varieties that perform well locally and resist local strains of insects and diseases. Always be on the lookout for resistant varieties offered by mail-order catalogs and nurseries. If you can't find varieties that resist certain pests, request them; widespread demand for resistance to a particular pest will encourage breeders to develop suitable varieties.

Rotate Crops

Crop rotation can prevent outbreaks of many soilborne diseases and certain other soil pests. It can also be used to control these problems if they appear.

The first step in planning a rotation is to group plants that are susceptible to the same problems. Usually, these are members of the same plant family—for example, the cabbage family, the cucurbits, and the tomato family. If you don't know which pests you have, or you aren't aware of any in your garden, grouping plants by family is a good place to start. Rotate these crops together. A three- to five-year

---

Plant Families

The most commonly grown vegetable crops belong to the following plant families. Usually, the families are rotated together, since the members are susceptible to many of the same pests. Perennial crops, such as asparagus, artichoke, and rhubarb, cannot be rotated with annual crops. If perennial crops are affected by soil pests, remove the crops and plant new pest-free rootstocks in a different area of the garden.

Beet Family

Beet
Spinach
Swiss chard

Buckwheat Family

Rhubarb

Cabbage Family

Broccoli
Brussels sprouts
Cabbage
Cauliflower
Chinese cabbage
Collards
Cress
Horseradish
Kale
Kohlrabi
Mustard
Radish
Rutabaga
Turnip

Carrot Family

Carrot
Celeriac
Celery
Parsley
Parsnip

Cucurbit Family

Cucumber
Gourd
Melons
Pumpkin
Squash
Watermelon

Grass Family

Corn

Legume Family

Bean
Cowpea
Pea
Peanut

Lettuce Family

Artichoke
Chicory
Endive
Jerusalem artichoke
Lettuce

Lily Family

Asparagus
Garlic
Leek
Onion
Shallot

Morning Glory Family

Sweet potato

Tomato Family

Eggplant
Pepper
Potato
Tomato

rotation is ideal—that is, grow each plant family in a certain part of the garden only once in three to five years. Plant crops from a different plant family in that spot the next time. Try to keep at least a one-year interval even if you are certain that no pests are present, because yields commonly decline when the same crop is grown repeatedly in the same soil.

If you know that a certain pest is in your garden or that it is a problem in your area, you can design a rotation to combat it. Find out how long the pest can survive in the soil, and note which crops it affects. If the pest can be eliminated within the time allowed by your present rotation and if it affects members of only one plant family, no changes are needed. But if the pest lives longer than the interval you have scheduled, you must lengthen the amount of time that you plant nonsusceptible crops. Some pests affect crops across plant

family lines. For example, the sugar beet cyst nematode injures the roots of beet and spinach as well as cabbage-family crops, so you must include all these crops in a rotation group designed to fight the pest. If you are combating the spotted cucumber beetle, you must rotate cucurbits and corn together, since the pest feeds on both at different stages of its life.

When you are rotating, you must be aware of any fruit crops, ornamental plants, weeds, and cover crops that are alternate hosts for the pests that attack your vegetable crops. Be sure

Top left: A tomato flower has both male and female parts: Five stamens (male) press closely around a central pistil (female). Since the parts almost touch, tomato flowers are self-pollinated by light breezes.
Top right: On squash plants bees deliver the pollen from male flowers, such as this one, to female blossoms. The female flowers develop into zucchini fruit.
Bottom left: A tomato relative, eggplant also has five-petaled flowers and a similar arrangement of male and female parts.
Bottom right: In the cucurbit family there are separate male and female flowers. The beginning of a fruit behind the lemon-cucumber flower on the right indicates that it is female. The flower on the left is male.

Sample Rotation Plan

In this typical rotation plan, members of the tomato, cabbage, and legume family are grouped together. Because of their similar soil needs, root crops can be rotated together, unless a disease appears. Radish is often rotated with the root crops, since it is in the soil so briefly that it usually escapes cabbage-family pests; if such a pest appears, plant radish with other crucifers. The miscellaneous group consists of vegetables that don't fall into other categories.

Group 1 Tomato Family	Group 2 Cabbage Family	Group 3 Legume Family	Group 4 Root Crops	Group 5 Miscellaneous
Eggplant	Brussels sprouts	Lima bean	Beet	Corn
Pepper	Cabbage	Pea	Carrot	Cucumber
Potato	Cauliflower	Snap bean	Garlic	Lettuce
Tomato			Onion	Zucchini
			Parsnip	
			Radish	

If a soil disease has made it impossible to raise a favorite crop in your garden, you may choose to grow the crop in a sterile potting mix in containers for a while.

that the alternate hosts are not in the planting area while you are keeping the soil free of susceptible crops. In most cases, you must avoid only a few kinds of plants. However, if you are combating the fungus disease verticillium wilt, you must avoid many commonly grown vegetables, fruit crops, and ornamentals (see the list on page 147).

At its most formal, rotation requires dividing the garden into sections and keeping records, so that you don't repeat a susceptible crop in less than the specified time. See page 28 for a list of the most commonly cultivated vegetable crops in each plant family. A sample rotation plan is shown above.

Rotation is more difficult and less effective in a small garden. A small yard may not offer three or four different locations where, for example, tomatoes may be grown. Also, the different planting locations in the garden may not be far enough apart to effectively stop the spread of diseases. Still, it is a good idea to rotate as well as you can. If a pest is particularly serious, consider not growing the host crops at all for a few years. As an alternative, grow the susceptible crops in a sterile potting mix in containers until the pest dies out.

Solarize the Soil

Also known as soil tarping and soil pasteurization, soil solarization consists of trapping the heat of the sun under a clear plastic tarp to kill many soil pests. The tarp is placed over the soil surface for from four to six weeks during the warmest part of the year. How hot your soil gets depends on the weather conditions and where you live. Under the intense sun of the Sacramento and San Joaquin Valleys of California in early summer, the soil 2 inches deep usually reaches 140° F and the soil 18 inches deep is generally elevated to 102° F at the end of solarization.

The process has proved capable of controlling verticillium wilt, some fusarium wilts, clubroot, southern blight, lettuce drop, root rots, and other diseases. Although it won't control nematodes completely, it does reduce infestations. In combination with other methods, soil solariza-

Plants seem to grow better in soil that has been solarized even when there were no known pests in it. For best results, solarize an area at least 6 by 9 feet.

tion allows shallow-rooted crops to be grown in nematode-infested soil (see page 151). It also kills many kinds of weeds and weed seeds, especially those of weedy grasses.

Although researchers aren't quite sure why, plants often grow better in solarized soil, even when no pests were known to be present. Solarization seems to make nutrients temporarily more available, and it may also allow greater proliferation of some helpful soil organisms. The positive effects of solarization last for two to three years.

Soil solarization is most effective during hot, sunny weather. Cloud cover, fog, and wind are detrimental to the heat-capturing process. Heavy rains are also a handicap, because standing water cools the tarp and must be swept off. Begin solarization when you expect four to six weeks of clear, warm weather. Mid-July is probably the best time to start, although local conditions may allow success at other times between May and September.

The area to be solarized should be at least 6 by 9 feet, since smaller areas will lose some heat, especially at the edges. The soil will heat more uniformly if you weed the area, till it well, and break up any large clods. Fertilize as if you were about to plant. If you intend to water with a buried soaker hose or a drip irrigation system, install it now. Avoid air

pockets between the soil and the plastic by raking the surface of the ground so that it is level and smooth.

Water the area to be solarized, using your irrigation system or a sprinkler. Water for an hour or two, or until you are sure that the moisture extends at least 2 feet deep; then water again two days later. This double watering encourages some of the disease spores to germinate. It also ensures that the soil will be moist before you put on the tarp. Moist heat is more lethal to soil pests than dry heat.

Although 1-mil polyethylene tarp is the most effective in building up heat, it is easily punctured by handling and strong winds. For a more durable tarp, use 1½- to 2-mil plastic. Ultraviolet-stabilized polyethylene will last the longest; unstabilized types will begin to break down and crumble in six to eight weeks.

Spread the plastic over the prepared area and tuck all the edges firmly into the soil. To cover a large area, join tarps together with transparent tape or duct tape, or glue them with a long-lasting, heat-resistant glue. (The tape is also handy for mending the tarp if it tears during solarization.)

If it rains while you are solarizing, sweep any standing water off the tarp, since it will reduce the heating of the soil. Remove the tarp when you are ready to plant. If the soil is too moist for planting when you uncover it, let it dry for a few days. Be very careful not to undo what you have accomplished. Don't bring soil from untreated areas into the solarized area. Mulch the paths to the treated area with wood chips or sawdust, so that you won't track contaminated soil into the clean area. Don't transplant seedlings from untreated seedbeds into the treated area. Also, avoid disturbing the solarized soil as much as possible; try to plant within the top 2 inches.

Treat Seeds in Warm Water

Often, you will encounter instructions to soak seeds in warm water for a certain amount of time to eliminate seed-borne diseases. This method is contingent on the seeds being able to withstand a higher temperature than the disease organisms. To carry out this method properly, you must follow directions exactly, because hotter water or a longer period than recommended may kill the seeds.

To treat only a few seeds, place the seeds on a small square of thin cloth; gather up the edges of the cloth and tie them with string. Prepare two pitchers of water, one with cool water and one with hot water. In a small, deep bowl, mix the water until it is at the recommended temperature; use a meat thermometer

to check the temperature. Submerge the pouch of seeds, leaving the ends of the string out of the water so that you can lift out the pouch. Stir the water a little to make sure that the seeds are thoroughly wet. Leave the thermometer in the bowl, and add hot water if the temperature starts to dip. As you add the water, stir constantly so that the heat is evenly distributed. At the end of the specified time, lift the pouch by the string and submerge it immediately in cool water. After the seeds have cooled for a few minutes, remove them from the pouch and let them dry.

MECHANICAL AND PHYSICAL TECHNIQUES

Sometimes, the most direct approach to pest control is the best one—for example, handpicking pests off plants. Other mechanical and physical techniques that are effective in the vegetable garden include removing diseased and infested material, applying a floating row cover, and setting traps.

Handpick Effectively

Successful handpicking begins with observation—and observation is more effective when you know as much as possible about the habits of the creature you are hunting. Read about a

Before you handpick a pest, familiarize yourself with its habits. Be sure to check the undersides of the leaves, where pests often feed.

pest to learn when and where you may find it; make note of any tricks it may have for evading capture, such as falling to the ground, running quickly, or visually blending into the plant it is attacking. Try to find out the earliest it may appear in your garden, so that you can hunt it before it has a chance to multiply.

Try to learn how long it takes for a pest to complete its life cycle and the length of the various stages. Timing may be crucial; for example, when you are handpicking eggs that hatch in four to seven days, handpicking twice a week will prevent the eggs from hatching whereas once a week will not.

Search one plant at a time, looking it over methodically and removing all pests. Some gardeners are willing to crush pests by hand, but there are several alternatives if that doesn't appeal to you. Slow-moving pests can be dropped into an empty jar. Faster-moving insects can be prevented from escaping by dropping them into a container partially filled with soapy water. If that doesn't kill them, try floating a few drops of horticultural oil on the surface of the water. As another alternative, fill the container with beer instead of soapy water. Dispose of dead insects in the trash, or bury them in the garden.

Special techniques may be useful in hunting certain kinds of pests. If the insects typically drop to the ground when disturbed, you may be able to use that habit to catch them. Place a cloth on the ground under the plant and tap the plant sharply so that the insects fall onto the cloth; dispose of the pests by shaking the cloth into a bucket of soapy water.

A borer can be extracted from a plant after it has bored into the stem. With a razor or sharp knife, make a lengthwise slit in the stem and remove the insect. The plant can survive a lengthwise cut because the water- and food-conducting cells run longitudinally in the stem. The cut may heal on its own, or you can bind it with a plant tie. On cucurbit vines, mound up soil around the slit part of the stem to encourage new roots to grow there.

Very small pests, such as whiteflies, can be swept up with a vacuum cleaner. Although vacuuming will not capture all the pests, used in combination with other controls it will help reduce their numbers. Place the vacuum bag in a sealed plastic bag and freeze it overnight before discarding it.

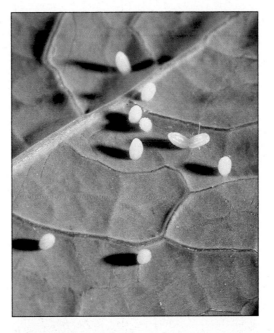

Top: The imported cabbageworm lays eggs on the undersides of the leaves of cabbage-family crops. If you destroy all the eggs you can find every three days, you will drastically cut the population of caterpillars.
Bottom: Many insect pests are camouflaged. Can you see the seven imported cabbage-worms feeding on this Chinese cabbage plant?

Top: When a plant is heavily infested with aphids, mites, or other rapidly reproducing pests, you may choose to remove the entire plant. This tomato shoot is coated with potato aphids.
Bottom: If only an occasional leaf is affected by an insect or a disease, you may be able to nip the problem by picking the damaged leaves. There are serpentine leafminers in this fava bean leaf.

Remove Diseased and Infested Material

Good sanitation is an excellent method of pest prevention, since many kinds of insects and diseases overwinter in or under garden debris, including rotting fruit. The best way to dispose of healthy plant debris at the end of the season is in a compost pile. Diseased plant parts or entire plants should be removed from the garden, because the diseases can easily survive the temperatures generated by the average compost pile. Although you may think that gardening will result in higher trash bills, an active program of prevention should keep uncompostable waste to a minimum.

Consult the third chapter to find out whether you should remove individual leaves or whole plants. If whole plants are to be removed, note whether they should be removed as soon as you see the problem or immediately after harvest. Also, note whether removing the top of the plant is adequate or whether you must dig up the entire plant, including the roots. In some cases, you may have to remove surrounding soil as well.

Leafminer damage, cercospora leaf spot of beet, and powdery mildew in its early stages on squash and other cucurbits are examples of localized problems that can be slowed by removing damaged leaves.

Viruses are a prime example of diseases that usually call for removal of the whole plant as soon as you see the symptoms. There is no cure for plant viruses, and infected plants may infect others, either by direct contact or by insects feeding on them and then on healthy plants. By removing the infected plants, you will reduce the chance of losing more plants during the season.

Southern blight, a fungus disease especially common on peanut, is an example of a problem requiring removal not only of the whole plant but also the surrounding soil. Since the fungus infests the soil quickly, fast action is needed. As soon as you recognize the problem, immediately

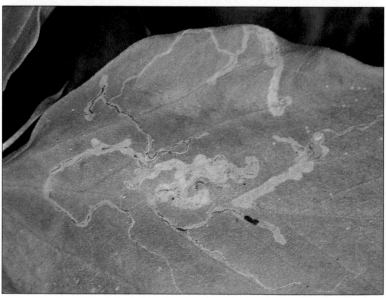

Making Repellent Sprays

Many gardeners experiment with homemade plant extract sprays as repellents for pest insects. One of the most commonly used is a spray containing garlic, onion, and hot pepper. Put the following ingredients in a blender: 1 clove garlic, 1 small onion (coarsely chopped), and ¼ teaspoon cayenne pepper (or several small chile pods). Add a little water, and blend. Wear rubber gloves to protect yourself from the chiles. Strain the slurry though cheesecloth, then dilute the liquid with 1 quart water; add 1 teaspoon liquid soap to help the spray stick to the plants. This spray may be effective in repelling the bean leaf beetle, the cowpea curculio, the Colorado potato beetle, flea beetles, the Japanese beetle, leafminers, and the Mexican bean beetle.

If you want to try other plant extracts, the process is the same. You will have to experiment with plant materials and concentrations.

remove the plant and surrounding soil for 6 inches in every direction. Be sure to scoop up all the fungal resting bodies, which resemble mustard seeds.

Some diseases, such as downy mildew and powdery mildew, cannot survive in the soil, but they can overwinter in plant debris. Therefore, infected plants should be removed as soon as the harvest is over. Plants that are severely infested with small pests, such as aphids, mites, and whiteflies, should be removed from the garden as soon as you see that you have lost the battle with the pests. If you choose to leave the plant in the ground because the crop is still harvestable, dispose of it immediately after harvest.

There are various ways to dispose of diseased or infested plants. They include burying them outside the garden area, depositing them in the trash, and burning them, if that is feasible and legal in your area. In theory, carefully controlled composting will kill many of these pests, but it usually involves greater care than most gardeners exercise. Compost diseased and infested debris only if you are confident that your compost pile heats to 160° F.

Apply a Floating Row Cover

Floating row covers are made of spun-bonded polypropylene and other synthetic fibers. These fabrics offer some protection from cold early in the growing season; if the edges are sealed, they also exclude many kinds of flying and crawling pests. They are superior to covers made of polyethylene plastic, because they let

Small bubbles of floating row cover will protect seedlings from insects and other seedling pests if you tuck the edges firmly into the soil. Remove the cover as soon as the plant begins to push against it.

A frame covered with a floating row cover will protect these radishes while they grow to maturity. Lift the cover only to thin and harvest the crop.

in water and air. You can water right through a floating row cover, and it isn't necessary to lift the cover unless temperatures are very high. The covers are called floating because they are so light that they rarely need supports to keep them above the plants. Only in very windy locations is there a danger that they may abrade plants; in these areas supports are recommended.

Floating row covers are typically sold in strips 5 to 8 feet wide and 20 feet or longer. One strip can be used to cover an entire bed, or the material can be cut into pieces to protect smaller plantings or individual plants. Make sure that the piece of material is larger than the area you wish to cover, so that there will be room for the plants to grow. Place the cover over the plants and tuck all the edges firmly into the soil. Gather the cover as you go, making a bubble in the center. Be very sure that no openings remain around the edges, or harmful insects may work their way inside. Lift the cover when the plants begin to push against it; if the crop requires pollination, uncover it when blooming starts.

Although a frame is not necessary to prevent damage to plants, it may be useful for providing easy access to blocks of seedlings or small plants. To tend plants you simply lift the frame and lower it again instead of having to

remove the cover and tuck it in when you're through. Make a rectangular frame of thin strips of wood, with a 2-inch-wide board at ground level. Use a staple gun to attach the row cover. For maximum security staple the cover to the inside of the bottom board. Place the frame over the seedbed, and press it 1 inch into the soil to form a seal.

Use Traps Wisely

Baited traps are used for a number of pests, such as earwigs, the Japanese beetle, slugs, and snails. It is important to consider the range of the pest and its probable path through your garden; set the trap away from your crops but where the pest is likely to encounter it. Flying insects, such as the Japanese beetle, have a fairly large range, so the trap needn't be placed adjacent to the crop you are protecting. In fact, it is better to set it farther away, since the beetles might damage the crop while congregating around the trap. Earwigs, slugs, and snails have a smaller range, but the principle is the same. Place traps where they will lure the pests away from your crops.

Most pheromone traps (see page 14) are effective for monitoring pests; they let you know when a pest has become active so that you can plan treatments. An exception are Japanese beetle traps baited with both a floral scent and

Top: Place traps, such as this homemade beer trap, where they will lure pests away from rather than toward the endangered crops. Bottom: If you intend to control a pest rather than monitor it, choose a sticky trap with a large enough surface area for the job.

Making Sticky Traps

The sticky trap is an effective device for monitoring pests. Many insects are attracted to yellow traps, although flea beetles and the tarnished plant bug are more attracted to white. Pests drawn to the trap are unable to escape the sticky surface. Small traps resembling tongue depressors that are stuck in the ground or hung from plants can be used to monitor whiteflies, winged aphids, and other pests. Larger traps, at least 1 foot by 1½ feet, can be used to help control pests. Space traps every 15 feet early in the season for prevention; once the pest is on the plants, space traps every 3 to 5 feet. Set the traps out of the direct sun and at the same height as the plants you wish to protect.

Some commercial sticky traps come already coated; you discard the traps when the surface is covered with insects. If you need many traps or if you are combating a heavy infestation, you may want to buy reusable plastic traps, which come with a can of sticky coating that you paint on the surface. When the coating is used up, make your own by mixing 1 part petroleum jelly and 1 part liquid dishwashing detergent. When the trap is full of insects, clean it with vegetable oil.

To make your own yellow sticky traps, paint plywood rectangles with Rust-Oleum® yellow (659) paint. Coat the surface with the mixture of petroleum jelly and detergent.

a pheromone; they can be used to catch the pest because they lure both sexes. Insect traps baited with pheromone alone attract only males; since the few males that fly free may fertilize most of the females, such a trap is effective only as a monitoring agent. A more promising use of pheromones, not yet widely available, is twist-on dispensers containing large doses of attractant that confuse the pests so badly that they are unable to mate successfully. These may reach the home gardener market soon.

If you intend to use a toxic bait, such as a snail bait containing metaldehyde, take precautions so that the product is out of the soil and inaccessible to children and pets. You can purchase plastic bait stations, or you can make your own by cutting a hole in the side of a small plastic container with a lid. Be sure to remove the label from a food container.

BIOLOGICAL TECHNIQUES

Once you realize how many helpful creatures are available to help control pests, the natural world seems a friendlier place in which to garden. Biological techniques include making your garden more inviting to native predators,

and other beneficial organisms, and releasing purchased helpers to supplement those found naturally in your garden.

Make Native Helpers Welcome

The naturally occurring predators, parasites, and other helpful creatures in your garden make up an unnoticed, sometimes unappreciated army that keeps pests from building up to destructive numbers. You may observe more pests following certain weather conditions, because the conditions happen to favor the pests over their natural enemies. Pests may also build up when a garden doesn't provide enough food or cover for the beneficial creatures. Native helpers can fail when an area has been subjected to the indiscriminate use of broad-spectrum pesticides—that is, pesticides that kill a wide range of organisms.

Keep to a minimum your use of pesticides that kill beneficial creatures. Spray only when you know that pests are present, and then treat only the plants that are under attack. Choose pesticides with a low toxicity to birds and other wild creatures. Pesticides that are not toxic to honeybees will also spare many predatory and parasitic insects. If you do use honeybee-toxic

A border planting of fennel will attract beneficial wasps, lady beetles, and other enemies of corn pests.

materials, use them in ways that spare the beneficial creatures in your garden (see page 45). To protect these creatures, choose pesticides that do not persist long in the environment.

One of the ways in which you can assist native helpers is to grow plants with small flowers. Many beneficial insects, including lacewings and syrphid flies, need to eat pollen and nectar in order to complete their life cycle; many other helpful insects can use pollen and nectar as a temporary food supply in the absence of pests. Dill, fennel, sage, thyme, Roman chamomile, yarrow, and a number of other herbs are good choices, as are clover and daisy. Allow a few carrot, onion, parsley, and cabbage-family plants to overwinter and bloom in spring. Make sure the plants you are growing to attract native helpers aren't plants that will harbor an insect or a disease with which you have had a problem. For example, if your peas fall victim to pea enation mosaic, don't plant clover, since it harbors the virus. Seed mixtures of attractant plants are sold commercially; before buying one find out what's in the mixture so you don't accidentally introduce a problem plant.

Beneficial insects, especially parasitic wasps and honeybees, appreciate a source of drinking water. Use a birdbath or a large terra cotta saucer filled with water. Place rocks or gravel in the container to break the surface of the water so that the insects can sip without drowning.

To attract helpful creatures that live in the soil or crawl on its surface, avoid the use of pesticides in and on the soil. Soil-dwelling creatures will be more plentiful if you leave an area untilled and covered with a permanent mulch. Mulched paths can serve this purpose. Rocks and pieces of wood will provide a cool, moist hiding place for ground beetles, salamanders, and other helpers.

Here again, you will have to balance creation of a habitat for soil-dwelling predators with practices such as turning the soil to kill pests and cleaning up pest hiding places. Experience will show you what attracts helpful creatures and what draws pests. Design any rocky niches or other hiding places for native helpers so that you can quickly check for slugs without disturbing the beneficial creatures.

Organic soil amendments increase the helpful fungi and other soil microorganisms that assist in controlling pest nematodes and soil diseases. When adding organic matter it is better to add composted rather than fresh material, since the organisms that break down fresh material are more likely to attack living plants. Creatures that live on composted matter are more likely to be harmless.

Buy Beneficial Insects and Mites

Although encouraging native predators and parasites is more effective in the long run than releasing a few purchased beneficials, those that you buy may be very helpful in certain cases. Before purchasing beneficials find out

Top: Garter snakes, such as the one shown here, help control garden pests and do not harm humans. Bottom: When you come across a salamander like this red-backed type, be careful not to harm it so that it can continue devouring aphids, beetles, slugs, and sowbugs.

Release purchased beneficial insects only when the pests they eat are present. These green lacewing eggs, which arrived mixed with rice hulls, are being released near aphid-infested red okra.

the best time to release them, how many to apply, and how often to repeat the applications. Often, repeat releases should be timed to coincide with different phases of a pest's life cycle.

Aphid midge (*Aphidoletes aphidimyza*)
This beneficial insect, which is sold as a pupa, should be distributed around plants in early spring or at the first sign of aphids. Soon, the adult midges emerge, mate, and lay eggs among aphids on the plant leaves. As long as aphids are present, the midges multiply quickly, completing their life cycle in about three weeks. There are several generations a year. To ensure a thorough cleanup of aphids, you can release midges every week for two to four weeks.

Convergent lady beetle (*Hippodamia convergens*) Although this predator is readily available, there is considerable controversy about whether it will stay or fly away when released. The problem is that lady beetles are most often gathered in the wild at a time when their life cycle calls for them to take a long flight. They overwinter in higher elevations, then in spring they use stored fat to fly to lower elevations to feed.

Studies with marked lady beetles have shown that the individuals that appear in a garden after a release usually are not the ones that were released there. Although there is no guarantee that the lady beetles will stay in your garden, several factors may make them more likely to do so. Those released after June are more apt to remain, perhaps because they have worked off their fat by then. Lady beetles that have been shipped with a sugar feedant or released in a garden sprayed with a commercial insect feedant (usually sugar and yeast based) may stay around longer. Heavy concentrations of pests may tempt some lady beetles to remain. Wet down the area before releasing lady beetles, and set them free in the evening. If they still fly away, console yourself that they are helping other gardeners; remember, too, that lady beetles released by other gardeners may fly to your garden.

Green lacewing (*Chrysopa carnea*) Sold as eggs, green lacewings are often shipped with a few inactivated moth eggs that will serve as food if any lacewings hatch before you place them in your garden. Wait until the weather is warm before releasing this predator, since it doesn't thrive in cool temperatures. Distribute two green lacewing eggs per square foot. For extra protection you can set out more lacewing eggs every one to four weeks. Green lacewings may become established in your garden, although this is not likely in cool-summer areas.

Predatory mites These predators are most commonly used in greenhouses, although several species are also helpful in gardens. Consult a supplier about the best species for your garden and the pests you are fighting; also, ask about the timing of the first release and the intervals between subsequent releases. Predatory mites are usually shipped as adults mixed with corn grits and killed grain mites. In some areas they are delivered on the bean plants on which they were raised.

Spined soldier bug (*Podisus maculiventris*) A recent addition to the list of biological helpers available for purchase, the spined soldier bug has been sold primarily to control the Mexican bean beetle. Growers and gardeners are reporting that the predator also eats other pest insects, including the cabbage looper and the imported cabbageworm. It feeds by paralyzing its prey and sucking out the body fluids. A single release of young bugs can provide one to three months of control. Apply spined soldier bugs when bean plants are sprouting, before the Mexican bean beetle is numerous. If the beetle has already caused considerable damage, use rotenone every three days until the spined solider bugs arrive; then release them three days after the last pesticide application.

Trichogramma wasp (*Trichogramma pretiosum*) Helpful in controlling caterpillar pests of vegetables, trichogramma wasps are shipped while still in the moth eggs they have parasitized. When the adult wasps emerge, they seek new pest eggs to parasitize. The release should be timed to coincide with the egg-laying periods of the pest moths. Wait until you see the first pest moths, or find out when they usually appear in your area. Set out the wasps every week or two, repeating the application three times.

Whitefly parasite (*Encarsia formosa*) Sold as a control for whiteflies, this tiny wasp is shipped in the parasitized whitefly larvae or pupae. It is effective as a control only when the whitefly population is very small—less than one per plant. The wasp is most helpful in a greenhouse, from which it cannot escape or blow away, although it may provide some help in a partially enclosed garden protected from strong winds. Release two wasps per square

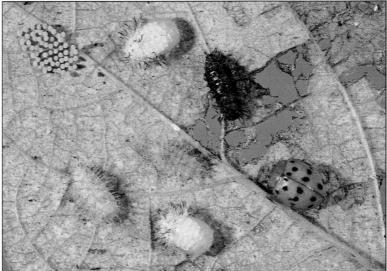

foot of garden, and repeat every two weeks for a total of four releases.

Put Bt to Work

The bacterial insecticide Bt causes an infection in certain insects, first paralyzing and then killing them. The insects may live for several days after they are infected, but they stop feeding almost immediately.

The insecticide must be placed where it will be eaten, since it must be ingested in order to kill. It is effective only when the insects are at a stage in which they are feeding vigorously. Caterpillars are most susceptible to Bt beginning a couple of days after they hatch until they are half grown. This is the period during which they feed most voraciously. If you wait until the larvae are larger, it may be too late for Bt to be effective.

Top: Spined soldier bugs create a drama on a small scale by impaling insects, such as this imported cabbageworm, and sucking out their body fluids. Bottom: This dark brown Mexican bean beetle larva has been parasitized by the wasp Pediobius foveolatus.

Bt put an end to the damage caused by this hornworm.

Use Predatory Nematodes

These beneficial nematodes seek out insect prey, enter them, and feed inside. As the nematode feeds it releases a bacterium that lives in its digestive tract; it is this bacterium that causes the pest to die. Cutworms may die in as little as 2 to 5 days, and Japanese beetle larvae and root weevils succumb 10 to 30 days after infection.

A typical package of predatory nematodes contains 10 million individuals, which will treat 225 square feet of garden. Although about 44,445 nematodes per square foot seems like overkill, that number is needed if all the pests are to come into contact with at least one nematode.

Nematodes require a moist environment. They can be mixed with water and sprinkled on the soil, or they can be sprayed on plants with ordinary sprayers. To avoid exposing the nematodes to sunlight, apply them right after sundown. When releasing them on the soil, make sure that the soil is moist, then water gently after the application. Keep the soil moist but not soggy. To kill insects that hide in plant crevices, spray nematodes on the plants; be sure to follow the instructions on the label.

Predatory nematodes can survive in the soil for up to 15 months, including one winter with temperatures below 0° F. However, they are active and plentiful enough to be effective against a serious pest infestation usually for only two to three weeks after they are released. To kill pests that feed for more than a month, reapply predatory nematodes every three weeks. If a pest has more than one generation a year, repeat the applications when the greatest number of larvae are present.

CHEMICAL TECHNIQUES

There may be times when hand control or pesticides with naturally occurring formulas do not work. In cases like this, you may wish to use chemical techniques. When you choose a chemical pesticide to control a pest, pay close attention to the correct method of using the chemical. A pesticide applied incorrectly may spare the pest you meant to kill, and it could even damage the plant you meant to save. Care is also needed to minimize hazards to yourself, those around you, and the environment.

When you use a pesticide, you are legally required to read and follow all the directions on the label. Reading the label is more than

The insecticide can be applied as a spray, a dust, or baited granules or pellets. If an insect typically ingests a large amount of exposed leaf, you can kill the insect by coating the leaves with Bt spray or dust. Be sure to cover the whole plant, including the undersides of leaves. If an insect typically ingests only a small amount of plant surface, you may need to add a bait to the Bt to make sure that the insect eats enough to kill it. One such product, Entice, can be added to a spray. Baited Bt granules dropped into corn leaf whorls will control the European corn borer, and baited pellets will attract and kill cutworms.

Although Bt does not infect humans, treat it as you would any pesticide. Since Bt is a living organism, it is especially important to follow the directions on the label for avoiding very hot or cold storage temperatures.

just a duty: The label provides you with valuable information that you need to be a responsible gardener.

First, check the label to learn the active ingredients. This information may appear in the name of the product, or it may appear only in small type under the heading *active ingredients*. This is where you will learn if the product contains pyrethrins or pyrethroids, or whether it contains rotenone alone or in combination with other ingredients.

Then check to find the list of pests the product is meant to control and the list of crops on which it can legally be used. Be sure that the pest you intend to control and the crop you wish to protect are both listed on the label. If food crops are not listed, it is illegal to use the pesticide on them. Whereas sources of information other than the label, such as suggestions in this book, are intended to guide you, the label is the final word on whether a particular pesticide is appropriate for your situation and the manner in which it should be applied.

Not only is it illegal to use a pesticide on pests and crops that are not listed on the label,

Release of predatory nematodes in garden soil requires only mixing the nematodes with water and applying them with a watering can.

Resources for Gardeners

H ere are some sources for beneficial insects and mites, floating row covers, tools, and other products related to environmentally friendly gardening. Some of the companies charge a nominal fee for their catalogs.

Common Sense Pest Control Quarterly
Bio-Integral Resource Center
Box 7414
Berkeley, CA 94707
A quarterly magazine with information on many aspects of environmentally friendly pest control, including some lists for products. Subscription includes membership in the Bio-Integral Resource Center, which offers advice and other benefits.

Gardeners Supply
128 Intervale Road
Burlington, VT 05401
Pest control products, including floating row covers and applicators. Also garden tools and low-risk seed starting setups.

Gardens Alive!
Natural Gardening Research Center
Highway 48, Box 149
Sunman, IN 47041
Pest control products, including biological agents, floating row covers, and applicators.

Harmony Farm Supply
Box 460
Graton, CA 95444
Pest control products, including biological agents, seeds for green manure, floating row covers, and applicators. Also tools and irrigation supplies.

Necessary Trading Company
New Castle, VA 24129
Biological pest control agents and other garden supplies.

Peaceful Valley Farm Supply
11173 Peaceful Valley Road
Nevada City, CA 95959
Pest control products, including biological agents, seeds for green manure, floating row covers, and applicators. Also tools and flower bulbs.

Rincon Vitova
Box 95
Oakview, CA 93022
Wide selection of beneficial insects and mites.

Using Insecticidal Soap

Although a solution of household liquid soap (not detergent) can be used as an insect spray, commercially available insecticidal soaps are more likely to kill pests without harming the plants they are intended to treat. The commercial products do a good job of controlling a number of pests, but only if the products are used correctly. To use them well you must understand how they work. Soap does not repel an insect; nor will it kill an insect that walks on or even eats a previously sprayed leaf. The soap works only when it is sprayed directly on the insect. It destroys the cell membranes of insects, causing them to desiccate and die. When you spray an insecticidal soap, try to reach every nook and cranny of the plant where pests might be lurking. Be sure to spray the undersides of the leaves and the growing tips. Let soap spray drip into the base of unfurling leaves and under artichoke scales, for example.

Usually, more than one application is required. This allows you to control insects that have arrived on the plant since the last spraying. Also, an insect may be susceptible to soap spray for only part of its life cycle. Eggs are usually immune. For example, even if you kill most of the larval and adult whiteflies on a plant, the infestation will recur as soon as the eggs begin to hatch. Rather than wait for all the eggs to hatch, spray every few days to kill newly hatched insects. The label may advise you to reapply the spray every two to three days as long as insects are present.

Insecticidal soap may harm some plants. Check the product label for warnings. If you have any doubt, test the spray on a small part of the plant and check for damage a day later. If none is apparent treat the entire plant.

Since the soap is effective only when it is wet, delay drying by adding ¼ teaspoon of any vegetable oil per 1 quart spray. (Test a small area of the plant, then wait 48 hours to make sure that the oil causes no harm.) Further slow the evaporation of the soap by applying it in the relative cool and calm of the early morning or evening.

You may want to add rubbing alcohol to the soapy spray to make it adhere better to waxy-leaved plants, such as many crucifers. Add ½ cup rubbing alcohol per 1 quart soap spray. Again, test a small portion of the plant before spraying the entire plant. Be aware that temperature is a factor when spraying alcohol on plants. The alcohol will evaporate quickly during warm weather, but it may burn plants during cool weather.

Insecticidal soap is effective only if it is used with soft water. Hard water, which has excessive calcium or magnesium, deactivates the soap. If you are using a ready-mixed soap spray, you won't have a problem; if you are diluting a concentrate, you will need to know if your tap water is soft enough. Test water for hardness by adding ½ teaspoon insecticidal soap to 1 cup water and shaking it. If a foam forms, the water is soft; if not, the water is hard. If your tap water is hard, you have two options: Either use distilled water or add a water-softening agent, such as Calgon®, according to label directions. Test a small portion of the plant to make sure that the water softener doesn't cause harm.

Soap spray will kill insects and mites only if it is sprayed directly on them. Be sure to spray it on the undersides of the leaves and into plant crevices where pests may hide.

but it could be hazardous or, at the very least, useless. If the crop is not listed, you may be harming the plants or yourself; if the pest is not listed, you may be wasting your effort.

Read the instructions carefully for mixing and using the pesticide. Be sure that you understand how to make the proper dilution, when and how often to apply the pesticide, and whether the product can be used at the same time you are using another chemical. If you have any questions about the use of a pesticide, call the National Pesticide Telecommunications Network at 800-858-7378. (Operated by Texas Tech University, the network is funded by a grant from the EPA.) For questions relating to a spill of or accidental contact with any Ortho product, call 800-457-2022.

Use Proper Precautions
When mixing and applying a pesticide, check the label for information about protecting yourself. The instructions are the legal requirements, although you may choose to take additional precautions. When you use any pesticide, wear a long-sleeved shirt, long pants, socks, and closed shoes made of leather or a relatively nonabsorbent man-made material. You may want to wear a pair of gloves, made of unlined rubber or neoprene. In addition, a dust mask is a sensible precaution when applying the sprays and dusts cited in this book. A dust mask is also recommended when applying materials that may irritate your respiratory system or activate allergies, such as copper products, diatomaceous earth, and sulfur.

Apply dusts and sprays only when the air is calm. Dusts are particularly likely to drift in a light breeze. Before applying the pesticide, clear the area of any items that may become contaminated, such as tools, toys, and pet items, especially pet food and water dishes. If there is a likelihood that outdoor furniture may be contaminated, remove or cover it. When you are finished applying the pesticide, clean the applicator according to the label directions. Store any unused pesticide in the original container in a cool, dry place out of the reach of children, preferably in a locked cupboard. Never store it near human or pet food. If you get any pesticide on your clothes, launder them by themselves in the washing machine.

Finally, protect yourself by meeting or exceeding the time guidelines required between the use of a pesticide and the harvest of the crop. Some pesticides, such as insecticidal soap and pyrethrum, require no waiting period. Others demand an interval of one or more days. Check the label for current information. Keep children and pets away from the treated crops during the waiting period.

Protect the Environment
Whenever there are several options for controlling a pest, always choose the one that presents the least hazard to the environment. If several pesticides are effective, choose the one that is least hazardous to humans and to other creatures you don't want to harm. In addition, choose a pesticide that does not persist in the environment but rather breaks down quickly to harmless substances.

Minimize the amount of pesticide that you release into the environment. Use pesticides only when the pest is clearly present on the crop or when experience has taught you that its appearance is inevitable. Apply the pesticide only to the affected plants, and only as often as the label recommends. Mix only the amount needed for one application. Purchase pesticides in quantities only as large as you need, so that you never have large amounts to discard if you don't use them up. If the pesticide will harm fish or the aquatic invertebrates that fish eat, be very careful that it doesn't seep into waterways. Although small-scale garden use is less likely to contaminate water than large-scale agricultural applications, contamination is still possible if your garden is near a pond, creek, or other body of water. Be very careful to avoid breezes in the direction of the water or surface runoff into it. If the soil is dry, decrease the chance of runoff by watering the garden before you spray.

Another serious concern is the toxicity of the pesticide to honeybees. This is important not only because honeybees are helpful and economically important, but because the pesticide will probably kill other beneficial creatures along with the honeybees. The only pesticides recommended in this book that will kill honeybees are pyrethrum products. However, because pyrethrum and pyrethrins break down so quickly, they can be used with minimum harm. If flowers are blooming apply these pesticides in the late evening, when bees are in their hives; the chemical will be largely inactive by the next day when the bees begin to fly and pollinate.

Dusts are more harmful to honeybees than sprays. If you are treating a crop that is pollinated by bees, avoid using dusts that are toxic to the insects if the plants are in bloom. Microencapsulated pesticide products—time-release materials that make a pesticide toxic over a longer period—are the most hazardous to honeybees. The bees pick up small beads of the pesticide on their bodies. None of these products are currently registered for use on food crops, but their use on nearby flowers may kill bees and other insects that are helpful in the vegetable garden.

Finally, dispose of unused pesticides and empty containers as responsibly as possible. (Now is the time you will be glad you bought small amounts.) If you must discard leftover pesticides, read the label for instructions. It is also a good idea to call the local health department to find out if there are any local ordinances on pesticide disposal and if there are collection sites that have been set up to receive such products. Never dispose of unused pesticide down a drain or add it to your household trash.

Using the Best Applicator for the Job

When you are choosing an applicator for a chemical pesticide, a microbial pesticide such as Bt, or a repellent spray, you should select one that is suited to the size of the job and the precision required to do it well.

Applying Sprays

Garden sprayers differ widely in size, price, and accuracy. Many pesticides come in ready-to-use, trigger-operated sprayers. Or you may choose to buy a concentrate and dilute it in a trigger sprayer. Inexpensive and accurate, these sprayers offer some variation between fine and coarse spray. The sprayers have two drawbacks: They do not operate well when aimed upward, making it difficult to spray the undersides of leaves, and they are tiring to operate. Use them for small jobs, where accuracy is important and you have time to make sure that the leaf undersides are well coated. If you need to treat more than 10 plants or more than a 10-foot row, you will find it more practical to use a sprayer that you don't have to squeeze to operate.

Pressurized sprayers come in several sizes. They are accurate; you can aim upward to reach under leaves, and you can adjust between a fine and a coarse spray. The smallest pressurized sprayers hold about a quart of liquid, which will cover roughly 50 square feet of plants. For small jobs these minisprayers are a very useful alternative to the hand-operated trigger sprayer. A few strokes of the pump give them enough pressure for a minute or more of spraying before you need to recharge.

For midsized jobs there are pressurized sprayers ranging from 1 to 2 gallons in capacity. (Generally, 1 gallon of spray will cover about 200 square feet of plants.) Some new models automatically repressurize either by rechargeable batteries or by a system in which the sprayer is charged while it is filled by a garden hose. Look for a sprayer with a built-in pressure release valve, so that you can let pressure out without having to spray extra pesticide.

For very large gardens 5- or 10-gallon backpack and wheeled sprayers allow you to spray without refilling. (Usually, 5 gallons of spray will cover about 1,000 square feet of plants.) Backpack styles have a pump that you operate as you spray; larger wheeled models generally work on battery-operated motors.

A hose-end sprayer can cover a large area quickly but without great precision. Because it is difficult to prevent the spray from landing on untargeted plants, a hose-end sprayer is best reserved for areas larger than 400 square feet and for spray materials, such as insecticidal soap, Bt, and liquid copper fungicides, that will not kill beneficial creatures. A siphon mechanism mixes a solution of the spray material with water from the hose to a preset dilution. However, great care must be taken to achieve the correct dilution ratio; otherwise, the spray may be either ineffective or damaging. Some hose-end sprayers have an adjustable nozzle, which can be aimed either down or up, making it easier to reach the undersides of leaves.

Applying Dusts

Two types of tools offer different benefits as dust applicators. One is a trombone slide-type pump, which delivers a fine stream of dust. It is the preferred applicator for small jobs and for those requiring precision. One commonly available brand shoots the dust at a 45-degree angle, making it easy to cover the undersides of leaves.

The other type of dust applicator is operated by turning a handle as you walk. Although not as precise as the trombone-type pump, it delivers an even cloud of dust that does a fairly good job of covering the undersides of the leaves. It is preferred for larger jobs, because it covers a big area quickly.

Injecting Drops

Sometimes, you may want to place droplets of a material in very specific places on plants. For example, injecting drops of mineral oil into the tips of ears of corn is a control for the corn earworm (see page 87). For a small planting of corn, an eye dropper is sufficient. For a large planting you will find an oil can more efficient.

Injecting predatory nematodes into the stems of squash plants is a control for the squash vine borer (see page 97). You can purchase garden syringes that hold either 2 or 4 teaspoons of liquid.

Top left: Trigger sprayers allow accurate coverage of small plantings, although you will have to lift leaves to spray under them.
Top right: Use a hose-end sprayer for larger plantings when precision is not a requirement.
Center left: An oil can is useful for applying mineral oil to a large number of plants.
Center right: Pressurized sprayers, such as this 1-gallon model, are convenient and accurate.
Bottom left: Rotary dusters handle big dusting jobs fast. A dust mask will prevent respiratory irritation from dust particles.
Bottom right: A trombone duster is better for small jobs and jobs requiring accuracy.

Encyclopedia of Pests

Before taking any action against the pest you are fighting, you should find out as much as possible about it. The descriptions and photographs in this chapter will help you do that.

In this encyclopedia you will find common problems affecting the most widely grown vegetables. You will be able to look up symptoms, find out the cause, and choose from several possible solutions. For each crop problems are arranged by category: physiological problems, insect and other animal pests, and diseases. Within each category is an alphabetical listing of ailments or pests. A special listing of seedlings starts on the following page.

Physiological problems are caused by poor growing conditions, not pests. Here is where you will learn the remedies for such problems as bitter cucumbers and blossom-end rot on tomato.

Next, you will find a list of common pests. Most of these are insects: aphids, beetles, caterpillars, maggots, plant bugs, thrips, and weevils. But insects are not the only animals that beset garden crops. Other animals, from snails to practically invisible pest nematodes, also bring disaster to plants.

A list of diseases completes each listing. Parasitic fungi show up as rusts, mildews, leaf spots, and other blemishes on plants, or they may appear as rots or wilts that cause plants to collapse. Parasitic bacteria cause a fewer number of diseases, including bacterial leaf spots, rots, and wilts. Plant viruses are often responsible for general stunting, plant deformities, and abnormal mottling of the leaves.

Use this chapter to find out the nature of your enemy and how to combat it. Armed with the information from the following pages, you will be able to choose the control methods that are most appropriate for you and your garden.

Regular inspection has brought this broccoli planting to maturity with relatively little damage. As the plants begin to bear, continuing inspection will keep the heads from being injured.

Crusted clay soil can damage seedlings, such as this bean. To loosen clay soil add organic matter before you plant.

A combination of bright sun and cold nights has damaged this poorly hardened-off tomato seedling.

SEEDLINGS

PHYSIOLOGICAL PROBLEMS

Cold Stunting

Although seedlings come up they grow slowly; they may look unhealthy, and the leaves may be yellow or purplish. Transplants may take a very long time to begin to grow and then may never reach full size. Although these symptoms can result from insect or disease damage to the roots, they are frequently caused by planting in soil that is too cold for the particular plant. Bean is especially prone to stunting and yellowing when the soil isn't warm enough. Check the needs of your crops and resow seeds when the soil is a more suitable temperature.

Transplants grown indoors or in a greenhouse will grow slowly and may become stunted if they are set out when the soil and air are too cold. However, they will tolerate cool conditions better if they have been properly hardened off. This means exposing them gradually to the outdoors. Of course, even harden-

ing off won't acclimate seedlings to extreme conditions.

Poor Germination

You may find that none, or only some, of the seeds that you planted come up. Sometimes, the problem is not an insect, an animal pest, or a disease, but rather improper growing conditions. Here are some possible reasons for poor germination.

• The seedlings may not have been able to penetrate the soil. Before planting, loosen the top 6 to 8 inches of soil and break up large clods. Remove pebbles and other debris from the top 3 inches of soil in the rows or hills where you plan to sow seeds. Dig soil when it is moist but not wet, because wet soil compacts and becomes difficult for seedlings to penetrate. Soil that crusts over is equally difficult for seedings to break through; solve the problem by adding more organic amendment before planting again.

• The seeds may have been planted too deep. Follow the directions on the seed packet; if there are no instructions,

plant no deeper than three times the diameter of the seed. It is especially important to avoid planting too deep in heavy clay soil.

• The seeds may have dried out. Never plant in very dry soil; water thoroughly, then wait a couple of days until the soil is just moist before you sow seeds. Plant at the proper depth, pat the soil firmly over the seedbed, and water with a fine spray. Until the seedlings emerge, water lightly whenever the soil surface has been dry for half a day. If your soil is drying out too quickly because it is sandy, add more organic soil amendment before planting again.

• The soil may be too cold. For the appropriate planting time for each crop, refer to the seed packet or a local planting calendar. A soil thermometer is useful. Seeds that are too cold often fall prey to disease (see damping-off, page 57).

• The seeds may be too old. Most vegetable seeds will germinate after two to three years if they have been stored in a cool, dry place. Some

seeds, including corn and onion, deteriorate after the first year. If you are unsure about the viability of any seeds, test them on a homemade seed dolly. Fold a paper towel crosswise into thirds, then arrange a row of 10 to 20 seeds of a single type along one short side of the resulting rectangle, stopping 1 inch from one end. Starting with the seed end, roll up the towel so that the seeds are in the center of the roll. Fasten the roll with two wire twist ties. Set the roll in a jar or tumbler so that the end that has no seeds is at the bottom of the container. Add water; it will wick up into the paper. Keep ½ inch of water in the bottom of the container for as many days as are normally required for the seeds to germinate, then unroll the paper towel and count how many seeds are growing. If fewer than 50 percent germinated, you are probably wise to discard the seeds. If 90 percent or more germinated, you know that the seeds are healthy. If the percentage falls between

Although many birds eat insects, some will peck to shreds young plants, such as this young brussels sprout plant.

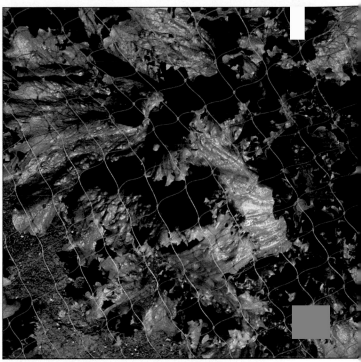

Plastic netting shields even tender lettuce plants from damage by birds.

those figures, plant the seeds but sow them more thickly than usual.

Sunburn

Transplanted seedlings develop light brown or dry, dead white areas on the leaves or stems. Sometimes, the entire seedling bleaches and dies. Rather than being diseased, the seedlings may be sunburned. This is a result of inadequate hardening off (see cold stunting, page 50), so that the seedlings aren't adjusted to outdoor light intensities. Even acclimated seedlings from a nursery may lose some of their resistance to bright sunlight if they are kept in a dimly lit place for several days or longer before being planted. If the transplants are only slightly burned, shield them from further damage. On the southwest side of each seedling place a board or a piece of brown paper fastened to two short stakes; set the shield at an angle to create the maximum length of early afternoon shadow. Discard severely sunburned transplants; they will

not recover quickly enough to produce a normal crop.

INSECT AND OTHER ANIMAL PESTS

Birds

Poor stands of seedlings result when birds peck out planted seeds. Birds nibble at seedling leaves making ragged edges, and they eat whole seedlings. They also peck at ripening corn and a wide variety of fruit, from cherry to strawberry. In addition, they eat ripening seeds you may have planned to save.

Some birds are in residence all year; others migrate, appearing in your garden only at certain times of year. Some birds feed in flocks; others are solitary feeders. Some prefer brushy areas near the garden, and others favor open, grassy areas. Certain types of birds feed mainly on insects and other pests; even birds that eat seeds and plants often eat many insects as well, especially when they are feeding their young in spring. Birds that feed on seeds devour many more weed seeds than they do crop seeds.

Although birds are generally beneficial, some types, including house sparrows, finches, starlings, crows, and pigeons, can cause considerable damage in a vegetable garden. Birds are easier to discourage before they have established the habit of eating in a particular place, so in a new garden watch closely and act before your garden becomes a regular feeding stop.

Barriers are the main way to control birds; a bird barrier doesn't have to be closed as tightly as an insect barrier, because birds are unlikely to crawl through partial openings. Creating an effective bird barrier may be as simple as making the area an unattractive landing place. In a small garden the surest barrier is plastic netting fastened over seedbeds.

A single string attached to two stakes and stretched the length of a planted row may discourage birds. Positioned a few inches off the ground, the

string may prove a more effective barrier if strips of aluminum foil or silvery Mylar are dangled from it. Small twiggy branches, poked into the ground throughout a seedbed, may also discourage birds from landing to feed.

Visual or noise repellents may be effective, but usually for only a short time. Birds soon learn that scary sights and sounds will not harm them. There are many bird-scaring products on the market, from balloons with painted eyes to inflatable snakes and owls. A product may work for you, or it may quickly lose its power to frighten.

A commercially available repellent consisting of 10 percent cayenne pepper, 4 percent garlic powder, and 86 percent powdered dolomite can be sprinkled on seedbeds to keep birds from eating seedlings for two to three weeks.

Cats

Although cats rarely nibble any crop except catnip, they ruin seedbeds and dig up seedlings when they carry out

Garden plantings need protection from cats until the plants grow big enough to cover the bare ground between them.

Cutworms, which feed at night and hide in soil crevices by day, sever seedling stems near the ground.

their normal practice of burying their excrement. Soil is pulled into a small pile, burying some seeds or seedlings and unearthing others.

Cats are attracted to bare soil; this is the condition that a kitty litter box tries to duplicate. How serious the damage is depends on the number of cats in your neighborhood, the amount of area they find suitable for their purposes, and the chance that your garden will become a favored site. (Because of the diseases that cat manure may carry, it is best not to add it to a compost pile. Dispose of any droppings away from edible plantings.)

The main methods of preventing cat damage to seedbeds are repellents and barriers. If there is only one cat and a large area in which it can roam, you may be able to discourage it quickly. But when there are many cats in the neighborhood and they favor your garden, more elaborate barriers may be in order.

Commercially available cat repellents are expensive to apply regularly over a large area, but they may be practical for

short periods to protect small seedbeds. Any material that visually changes the surface of the soil seems to repel cats. Even lawn clippings or cut weed leaves (remove the roots and seeds so that the weeds won't grow) scattered on the surface may be effective; renew the material every few days. A light straw mulch is another option, but don't put it directly over the seeds. Small brushy twigs, poked into the ground every few inches throughout the seedbed, may discourage cats.

If the problem is severe, you may need to cover seeded areas with window screening attached to small wood frames. Another solution is to build a large, walk-in enclosure for each planting area— or for the whole garden, if it is very small—made with fish net (the kind used to catch large bass) stretched over a wood frame.

Cutworms

Bean, corn, cabbage-family, and tomato seedlings are among the most commonly

damaged by these widespread insect pests. Another favorite target of cutworms is flower seedlings.

Seedlings are cut off near the ground and left lying on the soil surface. Plump, puffy caterpillars are found on the soil surface or just under surface debris. Most often gray, brown, or almost black, the caterpillars may be mottled or have other markings. The insects curl up tightly when disturbed. Some types of cutworms climb plants, devouring leaves and buds and eating into fruit.

Cutworms spend the winter as eggs, partly grown larvae, or pupae in the soil, in plant debris, or in clumps of grass. When the weather warms, they emerge from their hiding places at night to feed. Cutworm species that overwinter as partly grown larvae are particularly damaging in early spring, because they are already big enough to have a voracious appetite. When the cutworms are mature, they dig several inches beneath the soil surface and pupate for one to eight weeks or for the duration

of winter. The emerging adults are night-flying moths that have a wingspan of up to 2 inches. The wings are mainly brown or black with splotches or stripes of other neutral colors.

Avoid planting crops in an area that previously was a lawn or grassy field. If you decide to dig a vegetable patch in a lawn, till in late summer or early fall and then again one or more times before planting in spring. These fall and spring plowings will help reduce infestations by killing pupae and larvae or exposing them to predators.

Use barriers—either collars or stem wraps—to protect the stems of seedlings. Collars can be made from stiff paper, milk cartons, tin cans, or yogurt cups. Remove the ends of the containers and press them 1 to 2 inches into the ground; they should extend 2 to 3 inches up the stem. Stem wraps can be made from paper or aluminum foil; make sure that the wrap extends 1 to 2 inches above and below the

The pincers of the male European earwig, seen here, are larger than those of the female.

These western black flea beetles are ravaging a turnip leaf, leaving typical shot-hole damage.

soil surface. You may want to use a floating row cover to protect an entire bed of seedlings; leave the cover on until the plants are sturdy enough to withstand attack from the cutworms.

Although Bt will kill cutworms, spraying doesn't do much good because the caterpillars eat very little as they chew through the stems. However, the cutworms will feed on a bait made by mixing Bt wettable powder with apple pomace (the residue from making cider). Use 1 to 2 parts Bt to 100 parts apple pomace (for example, 1 to 2 ounces Bt to 6¼ pounds pomace). Wheat bran may be substituted for apple pomace, but it is not as effective. As an alternative, at planting time you can apply predatory nematodes to the soil at the rate of 50,000 per seedling (see page 42).

Earwigs

Common in all areas except the South and Midwest, where it is an occasional pest, the *European earwig* feeds on seedlings and on flowers, corn silk, and other tender parts of older plants. It is more destructive than native earwigs found in many areas of the United States. Like other earwigs the European earwig has an important redeeming quality: As a scavenger it helps gardeners by consuming decaying matter, insect larvae, and snails.

Damage to seedlings is obvious: The seedlings are nibbled or completely devoured. Look for a fast-moving dark brown insect, up to ⅘ inch long, with large pincers at the tail end of the body. You will find it feeding at night and hiding in plant crevices or soil debris during the day.

The insect overwinters as an adult. The female lays eggs just beneath the soil surface in early spring and watches over them until they hatch. She tends the young nymphs until they can feed on their own. Then she departs, often to lay more eggs. Earwigs eat tender seedlings as well as the leaves, flowers, and fruit of older plants.

Eliminate hiding places, such as woodpiles, empty flowerpots, and plant refuse. Search protected areas that can't be eliminated, such as just inside the drainage holes of flowerpots that are in use, and along the boards of a raised bed. Catch any earwigs that you find and destroy them. Despite their armored appearance, they are crushed easily by foot or hand if you move fast enough. Although menacing, earwigs are unlikely to use their pincers on gardeners. In spring you may find groups of young earwigs hiding in soil crevices. The nymphs are easy to crush, or they can be scooped into a plastic bag and discarded.

Trapping is a useful control. A rolled-up newspaper or a length of old garden hose will attract earwigs; this sort of trap must be emptied daily and the insects destroyed. Beer traps also work well. Sink shallow containers into the ground so that the rim is at soil level, and pour in about ½ inch of beer. Earwigs (and slugs) will fall in and drown. Empty the beer traps every couple of days.

A floating row cover is a practical way to protect seedlings, unless the plantings are very large or scattered. Parasitic flies are an effective control; they parasitize adult earwigs during the summer months. Insecticidal soap spray will kill earwigs in the unlikely event that you can score a direct hit. Rotenone dusted over plants may slow earwig damage.

Flea Beetles

Small circular holes, up to ⅛ inch in diameter, are eaten in leaves. Young seedlings may die if the damage is severe. Tiny black beetles, which jump like fleas when disturbed, may be visible on the plants. Although flea beetles also feed on older plants, they are particularly damaging to seedlings. Different types of flea beetles feed on different crops. (See *corn flea beetle*, under CORN, and *flea beetles*, under EGGPLANT.)

Pillbugs (left) roll up into a ball when disturbed, unlike sowbugs (right).

Cottontail rabbits, such as the one seen here, and the larger jackrabbits damage seedlings and older vegetable plants.

For general information about these beetles and how to control them, see *flea beetles* under EGGPLANT. Select sturdy seedlings that have been hardened off, and examine them often to catch damage early. Look for the insects on the tops and undersides of leaves. If flea beetles are common in your area, protect susceptible seedlings under a floating row cover until they are well established. For serious infestations dust with pyrethrum or sabadilla or spray with rotenone.

Pillbug and Sowbug

You may notice oval gray multilegged creatures up to ½ inch long and about half as wide feeding on seedlings and also on fruit that is on or near the ground. When these small crustaceans are disturbed, some of them roll up into a tight little ball, then uncurl when they have been left alone for a few minutes.

Related more closely to crayfish than to insects, pillbugs and sowbugs breathe through gills. They need a moist environment in order to survive. Although they look similar and may live together in the same garden, pillbugs and sowbugs are two different species. Here is the easiest way to tell them apart: Sowbugs have two taillike appendages; pillbugs curl up when disturbed. Both creatures mate in spring. The female carries the eggs and young in a pouch under her body for several weeks. An individual lives for up to three years.

Seedlings may be nibbled when there are large numbers of pillbugs and sowbugs and little other food is available, such as if you clear the garden of all decaying debris and then plant seedlings. Otherwise, pillbugs and sowbugs often inhabit a garden in great numbers without causing much damage to crops, because they feed primarily on decaying matter. They may nibble living plants near the end of the season, when the plants are declining and some decay is present.

Begin controlling these creatures by reducing the habitat that attracts them: Clean up organic debris and locate your compost pile away from crops. Keep the soil surface as dry as possible, perhaps by using a buried soaker hose or drip irrigation or watering only early in the day. If you reduce the creatures' habitat, you must also reduce their population so that they won't be forced to feed on crops. If practical, handpick them. You may be able to scoop them up by hand or trowel them into a plastic bag. Place the bag in the freezer, then discard it. As an alternative, wait two to three weeks after you clean up the garden before planting; this will encourage the pillbugs and sowbugs to seek food elsewhere.

Rabbits

Although rabbits feed all year, they are particularly hungry for fresh greens in spring. They chew seedlings off at the stem. They may also damage older plantings of lettuce, cabbage, bean, and other tender vegetables.

Exclude rabbits with a chicken-wire fence, either freestanding or attached to the bottom of an existing fence. The chicken wire should be buried 6 inches in the soil and extend 2 feet above the ground, with the top bent away from the garden. Dried blood meal may repel rabbits, but it must be renewed every few days during wet weather. Cats and dogs reduce the number of rabbits around a garden by chasing or killing them. Live traps are legal, although their effectiveness may be limited due to the high breeding rate of rabbits.

Seedcorn Maggot

This widespread insect feeds on seedlings of bean, beet, the cabbage family, corn, cucumber, onion, pea, and sweet potato. It also attacks potato sprouts and gladiolus corms.

A stand of weak, wilted, or substandard seedlings may be the work of the seedcorn maggot. If you search through the planting, you may find legless creamy white maggots from ¼ inch to ⅛ inch long feeding on seeds and stems. The maggots

Seedcorn maggots, the larvae of a small fly, have eaten into these corn seeds, killing them before they could grow.

Top: The gray garden slug travels on a slime trail.
Bottom: Slug eggs, seen here, and snail eggs are similar.

introduce decay bacteria, often causing damaged seeds and seedlings to rot.

The seedcorn maggot is the larva of a small fly that looks like a housefly. The insect overwinters as a ¼-inch-long dusty brown pupa. The adult fly emerges in spring and lays eggs on decaying organic matter or moist soil. In a few days the maggots hatch and begin feeding on the organic matter. They also feed on young seedlings or softened seeds that are about to germinate. There are three or more generations a year. The later generations are less damaging, because there are fewer germinating seeds later in the season.

Avoid planting in soil that contains a large amount of fresh animal manure or into which you have just turned green manure. Add manure in fall, so that it will have time to rot before you plant. Don't plant seeds too early or too deep; properly sown seeds grow quickly past their vulnerable stage. Plant extra seeds to allow for some loss. If practical, start seedlings indoors or protect seedbeds with a floating row cover.

Slugs and Snails

In addition to feeding on seedlings, slugs and snails eat tender parts of older plants, decaying organic matter, and paper. They make ragged holes in leaves, flowers, and fruit. On tomato, snails eat away the surface of the fruit, whereas slugs make deeper holes. Often, the shiny slime trails of both creatures are visible on the ground and on plants.

Slugs and snails are mollusks; slugs have evolved so that they have no shell or only an internal trace of a shell. Both creatures produce a mucous, or slime, on which they glide when they travel. They eat by rasping or scraping their food. Most slugs are between ¾ inch and 2 inches long, but some types may be as small as ¼ inch long or as large as 10 inches long. They are most often gray, usually with darker mottles or spots. Some types of slugs are light yellowish and others black. Not all slugs are garden pests, but several kinds are. These are usually more troublesome in high-rainfall areas. There are also many types of snails. The imported brown garden snail is a major pest on the West Coast and in parts of the South. Other snails are locally significant pests throughout the United States. The brown garden snail has a brown shell with darker markings; at maturity its shell is 1¼ to 1½ inches in diameter.

Depending on the climate and the species, slugs may overwinter at any stage of development. Some species can survive cold winters only as eggs, whereas others can survive as young or mature slugs. Some species live for three to four years. The brown garden snail continues to be active during winter; it takes two years to reach full size and can live for several more years. Both slugs and snails mate and lay eggs all year but probably more frequently during the warm season. The eggs, laid near the soil surface, look like a gelatinous mass of pearly white BBs. The brown garden snail is hermaphroditic; both sexes are able to fertilize and lay eggs. Slugs may be hermaphroditic, or they may go through a sex change as they mature: The youngest slugs are male, the oldest are female, and those in between have the capabilities of both sexes. All this means that the pests reproduce very efficiently.

The eggs hatch into tiny versions of the adults. Both slugs and snails are primarily nocturnal feeders. They also come out to feed on wet, overcast days, but not in heavy rain. On dry days slugs hide in moist debris on the soil surface, or they burrow 8 inches or deeper into the soil; they may not come out to feed every night. Snails spend dry days attached to a smooth, dry surface in a shady location. The brown garden snail is often found clinging to smooth, broad leaves, fences, house walls, or flowerpots. Snails close off their shell opening and hibernate for up to four years if conditions are too dry.

Imported in the 1800s as a food source, the brown garden snail has become a serious garden pest.

Slugs and snails often destroy smaller seedlings. Larger seedlings may survive damage.

The first line of offense against slugs and snails is to find and eliminate favorite habitats. Get rid of old boards and other debris, thickets of weeds and grasses, and piles of flowerpots. Any hiding places that can't be eliminated should be searched regularly. Destroy any slugs and snails that you find. If an ornamental planting near your vegetable garden attracts snails and slugs, consider replacing it with something less appealing to the pests.

Handpicking is an effective control for snails. Search known hiding places in the daytime, or hunt snails when they are active, such as early on wet mornings. You can drastically reduce the snail population by repeating this every day or two until the catch drops off, then maintaining a weekly hunt.

It is more difficult to handpick slugs, because they hide in less accessible places and may come out only every few nights. Still, it is worthwhile to hunt slugs. Look for them in moist crevices during the day and with a flashlight around plants after dark. Tilling the soil will kill many slugs and slug eggs or expose the eggs to the air so that they will desiccate. Crush any snails and slugs that you find and bury them in the soil, where they will act as fertilizer.

Barriers are commonly used to stop slugs and snails. Many barriers depend on rough or caustic substances heaped in a band 1 inch high and 3 inches wide. Although wood ash and diatomaceous earth are fairly effective, they do not work when they are wet. Copper or zinc strips or screening are a good alternative. These metals repel by reacting with the mucous secreted by slugs and snails and causing great discomfort to the pests. You can erect a low fence of copper, zinc, or galvanized screening; it has to be only 6 inches high, but burying it another foot in the ground will reduce entry by subterranean slugs. Bending the top edge outward and down will make the fence even more effective. Keep a cleared strip on each side of the fence so that the mollusks can't climb over plants to circumvent the barrier. Screening or strips of copper foil can also be wrapped around the sides of a raised bed or a cold frame. You can buy a copper foil strip with outward-bending flaps that has been designed for this purpose, but a plain copper band is reported to work just as well. Again, vegetation must not be allowed to grow over these barriers.

A floating row cover is a useful option for protecting particularly vulnerable seedlings. Basil, bean, lettuce, and very young cucurbit seedlings are among the most likely to be damaged by slugs and snails. If your garden plan allows it, clear a strip 1 yard wide around your vegetable patch to help prevent entry of slugs from adjacent weedy or landscaped areas. Till the strip frequently.

Natural enemies include birds, centipedes, earwigs, garter snakes, ground beetles, lizards, millipedes, rats, skunks, and toads. Domestic ducks and chickens eat snails; since the fowl themselves may damage plants, release them into the vegetable garden between crops. A predatory snail, the decollate snail, is sold to control the brown garden snail in some southern California counties, but it is illegal outside that area because of its possible negative environmental effects. Anyhow, the decollate snail is more useful in citrus groves than home vegetable gardens, since it is likely to eat seedlings and small plants.

Boards laid on the ground, overturned flowerpots, and black plastic sheeting make effective traps for snails and slugs; collect the trapped mollusks daily, or at least every other day, and destroy them. Traps baited with beer will often drown slugs, but they are ineffective against the brown garden snail. Different brands of beer vary in attractiveness to slugs. It may help to blend a little flour into the beer to make it sticky.

These spotted garden slugs and brown garden snails have been exposed in a favorite hiding place—under black plastic.

Tiny, but destructive, symphylans dwell in the soil and damage plant roots. Seedlings are particularly susceptible.

You can buy slug bait stations that use a bait based on malted grains. The bait ferments when it is mixed with water and slugs drown in it. The stations are covered so that rain won't dilute the bait.

Most of the commonly available commercial baits registered for use among food crops contain the active ingredient metaldehyde. Reserve this type of bait for situations in which the pests are out of control, and employ other methods to maintain control. Metaldehyde is relatively toxic to humans, domestic animals, and birds. It should not be used unless children and pets can be excluded from the treated area.

Use commercially available or homemade bait stations to keep the bait off the ground and dry during wet weather. A homemade bait station can consist of a small empty can placed on its side or a recyclable lidded plastic container with holes cut into the sides. Because slugs and snails will travel several feet to eat, place the stations where they will draw the pests away from, rather than toward, desirable crops. Position them near known hiding places but in an open area, so that immobilized slugs and snails will be exposed to the sun and will dehydrate. Lightly watering the area will increase the effectiveness of the bait, since the mollusks can move more easily across damp ground. Very wet weather will make the bait less effective, because the mollusks will not dehydrate after they are incapacitated. Replace the bait every three days and put the stations back in the same places.

Brown garden snails are edible, and you may want to try them as escargot. The usual practice is to pen them and feed them cornmeal for a few days to eliminate grit from their systems; just before cooking them, feed them fresh herbs for flavor. Be sure that no pesticides have been used in the area where you collect snails for eating.

Symphylan

Also known as the garden centipede, the symphylan is neither a true centipede nor an insect. A pest in warm-winter climates, it feeds on seedlings and mature roots of many vegetables and flowers. Affected plants may be stunted, or they may die. Tiny, fast-moving white creatures with many legs are visible in the soil. A mature symphylan is ¼ inch long and has 12 pairs of legs. To see the creature more clearly, drop small clumps of soil into a bucket of water; the symphylans will float to the top.

Symphylans live in moist soil that is rich in organic matter. Rarely seen on the soil surface, they mate and lay eggs 1 foot below the surface of the ground anytime between April and September. Although usually found in the first foot of soil, symphylans can flee very deep to escape unfavorable conditions—an ability that makes them difficult to control. They feed on plants whenever temperatures are mild, but they retreat to a deeper level during hot, dry weather.

Some soil-dwelling beetles prey on symphylans. Soil solarization does not control symphylans, because they just crawl deeper. Adding composted instead of fresh organic matter to the soil may help combat symphylans. If you are sowing the seeds in place, sow them thicker so that you can afford to lose some seedlings. Or, since symphylans prefer buckwheat roots to vegetable roots, use buckwheat as a trap crop. Start vegetable seeds indoors; two weeks before setting out transplants, sow a buckwheat crop in the garden. Clear small holes in the buckwheat planting for the vegetable transplants, then hoe the buckwheat as the crop plants grow.

DISEASES

Damping-off

This common disease can strike all seeds and seedlings. When it occurs before seeds come up, it is often referred to as seed rot. An entire or partial planting of seeds may fail to come up. If seedlings do emerge they develop sunken or dark areas at the base of the stem, and they wilt and die.

Top: Use good sanitation to prevent damping-off.
Bottom: Root rot is a hazard when garden soil is too moist.

Artichoke plants are small and unproductive when they are inadequately watered and fertilized.

Various soil-dwelling fungi can cause seeds or seedlings to decay. The problem is more severe when the soil is too cold for the type of seeds planted, when the seeds are planted too deep, when the planting is in heavy clay soil, or when the seeds are old and not very vigorous. Damping-off organisms are also encouraged by the addition of either fresh organic matter or compost made under anaerobic, or low-oxygen, conditions. This occurs when the materials being composted are too wet or in too tight a container for them to be turned sufficiently.

You can buy treated seeds—that is, seeds with fungicide already on them. In very cold, damp soil, treated seeds may mean the difference between the success and failure of a planting. If you prefer not to use treated seeds, there is no reason you can't succeed if you provide good growing conditions.

• Plant at the right time, in soil that is warm enough for the particular seeds.

• Plant at the right depth, following the directions on the seed packet.

• Allow adequate space between seeds so that seedlings are not overly crowded when they come up.

• Plant in well-drained soil amended with thoroughly composted organic matter; if your soil is very hard to work, consider planting in a raised bed.

• Avoid adding fresh or partially composted organic matter, such as uncomposted wood chips or green manure, right before planting. Fresh material can be dug under in fall or up to a couple of months before planting in spring.

• Be sure that your compost pile is well aerated, so that it ferments aerobically—that is, by microorganisms that work in the presence of oxygen.

• Don't presoak beans before you plant them. Although presoaking can hasten the germination of some seeds, it increases the chance of rot in bean seeds.

If damping-off has been a problem in the past, take the following extra measures.

• Use seeds that were grown for use this year instead of seeds that you saved from previous years.

• If you are growing a crop that transplants well, try starting seedlings indoors or buying nursery transplants. Often, older seedlings are able to combat the fungi that kill younger ones.

• Solarize your soil periodically to reduce the number of harmful organisms living in it (see page 30).

• If you grow seedlings indoors, use a sterile, soilless seeding mix; avoid excess warmth and moisture once the seedlings are up; and add nitrogen fertilizer only after the plants have true leaves.

ARTICHOKE (AND CARDOON)

PHYSIOLOGICAL PROBLEMS

Poor Production
The plant is disappointingly small and has sparse, undersized buds, although they are not misshapen. An artichoke plant will survive poor conditions—insufficient fertilizer and water—during active growth, but it will not grow large and produce many buds. If rain is infrequent during the growing season, be sure to irrigate regularly. Do not be too quick to cut back the plant when it finishes bearing. Remove the spent stalks and dead leaves, but don't cut back the old basal leaves until November in a cold-winter climate or until late spring in a mild-winter climate. The plant needs the leaves to store energy for next year's crop.

INSECT AND OTHER ANIMAL PESTS

Aphids
At least two types of aphids—the black or dark green *bean aphid* and the pale yellow to green *oleaster thistle aphid*—may infest artichoke plants. The oleaster thistle aphid is also found on elaeagnus, Russian olive, shepherdia, and various wild thistles.

Dark trails tunneled by artichoke plume moth larvae make artichoke buds unsightly and unappetizing.

Top: Oleaster-thistle aphids are a common pest of artichoke. Bottom: Plume moth larvae are small brown caterpillars.

For more information on aphids generally and the bean aphid specifically, see *aphids*, under BEAN.

Regularly check the undersides of artichoke leaves and the developing buds for aphids. In addition to spreading artichoke curly dwarf virus (see Diseases, at right), aphids weaken the plant. If not removed they may remain lodged under the bud scales through the cooking process.

If spraying with a strong stream of water doesn't knock the aphids off the plant, apply insecticidal soap. You can use pyrethrum or sabadilla to kill the aphids, but these are best applied before buds form.

If you suspect that harvested artichokes are harboring aphids or *earwigs* (see SEEDLINGS), aim a strong jet of water into the center of the buds before bringing them into the kitchen. To make doubly sure that you've dislodged the pests, agitate the buds in salty water, stem end down.

Artichoke Plume Moth

Usually discovered when the artichoke is being cleaned or eaten, plume moth larval damage consists of dark brown trails through the scales and into the heart of the artichoke. Sometimes these tunnels still contain larvae. If you look carefully you will see a brown entry hole in the base of an infested artichoke bud.

The moth, which is brown and has a 1-inch wingspan, lays eggs on the undersides of leaves or at the base of buds. The larvae feed first on the young leaves near the center of the plant. They may bore into the leaves or feed in the leaf folds. When buds develop, the larvae bore into them. The larvae pupate on the lower surface of older leaves and in leaf litter under the plant. In some regions there are three overlapping generations a year.

Remove all nearby wild thistles, especially bull thistle, since they are host plants. Clean up plant debris in fall; in mild-winter areas clean up at the end of the spring bearing season as well. Before the bud-bearing stalks emerge, search the center of the plants for black specks of insect frass, larvae, and larval damage. Remove any larvae or leaves tunneled by larvae whenever you see them.

Although the artichoke plume moth has many natural enemies, including brown lacewings and several ichneumon wasps, the enemies are unable to control large populations of the pest. Bt will kill plume moth larvae, but predatory nematodes have proved more effective as a control. Search the center of plants for larvae that have grown to about ¼ inch long. If you see larvae that size, use a pressurized sprayer to force a solution of nematodes (100,000 per plant) into the folds of the plant. Repeat three times, one week apart. The nematodes, which attack the pest only in the larval stage, work best on light infestations. Pheromones, or sex attractants, are used commercially to control plume moths by causing mass confusion among the insects; the pheromones may be available to home gardeners in the future.

Although artichoke plants do not need to be divided yearly, divide them often enough so that they don't become too large to search and to spray.

ADDITIONAL INSECT AND ANIMAL PESTS

Earwigs (see SEEDLINGS), another common stowaway under bud scales, may do minor damage to leaves and buds. Artichoke is also susceptible to various root-knot *nematodes* (see BEAN). *Slugs and snails* (see SEEDLINGS) often hide among the leaves of artichoke plants and eat them; they also rasp the surface of the buds, ruining their appearance although rarely causing serious damage. In addition, slugs may hide under bud scales.

DISEASES

Artichoke Curly Dwarf Virus

Although you may never encounter this virus, you should be on the lookout for it so that

As bean aphids feed on artichoke, they excrete honeydew, which ants eat. Wasps parasitize the aphids, leaving mummies.

The gray-green asparagus aphids are hard to see on asparagus. The round white droplets are aphid honeydew.

you can prevent its spread if it does appear. An infected artichoke plant is stunted, with small, often deformed, buds. The leaves may curl, and the plant may die. The virus is spread from infected host plants to healthy ones by sucking insects, such as aphids and leafhoppers. Host plants include artichoke, cardoon, chrysanthemum, milkthistle, stock, and zinnia.

Preventive measures include obtaining artichoke rootstocks from reputable sources, keeping aphid populations as low as possible (see *aphids,* page 58), and removing nearby milkthistles. As soon as you notice infected plants, get rid of them.

OTHER DISEASES

Artichoke is also susceptible to *southern blight* (see PEANUT) and *watery soft rot* (see *lettuce drop,* under LETTUCE). Avoid planting artichoke in soil infected with either disease.

ASPARAGUS

INSECT AND OTHER ANIMAL PESTS

Aphids

A European native, the *asparagus aphid* was first reported in New York and New Jersey in 1969. Since then it has spread across the South, Midwest, and Pacific Northwest, and it is beginning to appear in California.

The small (about $1/15$ inch long) light green pest attacks edible as well as ornamental asparagus species causing bushy, stunted new growth, sometimes called witches'-broom. An affected plant also takes on a bluish green cast.

The aphids overwinter as eggs on the foliage or the soil surface. In spring the eggs hatch and the young aphids feed on the ferny new growth. There are many generations of aphids throughout the summer. The aphids mate and lay eggs in fall.

Starve the newly hatched aphids by keeping asparagus plants from developing ferns during the harvest period and by pulling volunteer seedlings. In plantings too young to harvest, examine plants carefully for aphids as the ferns begin to appear.

Asparagus is also a host for the *bean aphid* (see *aphids,* under BEAN) and the *potato aphid* (see POTATO).

Common Asparagus Beetle

Also called the striped asparagus beetle, this widespread pest feeds on asparagus and wild relatives of asparagus. In early spring the adult beetles damage the tips of the emerging spears by eating holes in them and causing a brownish discoloration. The ¼-inch-long adult is easily identified by its wing covers: They are metallic bluish black with three orange to yellow spots and a reddish margin. Later, ⅛-inch-long dull gray larvae eat the tips of the spears and the foliage.

Adults spend the winter in garden debris, hollow stems, and tree bark, emerging when the first asparagus spears break through the soil. The beetles begin feeding and laying dark brown eggs singly or in rows of two to eight attached by one end to the tips of the spears. Later, they lay eggs on the leaves and stems. The eggs hatch in three to eight days; the larvae migrate to the plant tips, where they feed for two weeks, then crawl to the ground and pupate just beneath the soil surface. In one to two weeks, a second generation emerges. Depending on the climate there can be as many as five generations in one season.

Clean up plant debris and weeds in fall to reduce adult overwintering sites. Protect newly planted asparagus with a floating row cover. Keep beetles from multiplying by handpicking them when they begin to appear. In mature plantings cut spears frequently to prevent the eggs from hatching into larvae. Naturally occurring chalcid wasps and lady beetles may help with control. If handpicking is impractical, control the insects with a spray containing rotenone or a mixture of rotenone and pyrethrins.

Top: Common asparagus beetles are a widespread problem.
Bottom: Spotted asparagus beetles do not appear in the West.

Scaly pustules of asparagus rust develop first on the smaller stems and leaves of asparagus plants.

Spotted Asparagus Beetle

Found east of the Mississippi River, this pest feeds only on asparagus. It damages the crop by boring holes into the newly emerging spears and causing brown discoloration.

Slightly larger than the common asparagus beetle, this pest has reddish orange wing covers with six black spots on each. The ⅛-inch-long larvae are orange.

The adult beetle emerges in spring, usually later than the common asparagus beetle but often from the same hiding places. It feeds for about a month on the spears and the developing foliage, then lays eggs on the foliage just as the plant blossoms and begins to set berries. The greenish brown eggs are laid singly on their sides. The larvae hatch in a week or two and eat only the asparagus berries. Each larva destroys three or four berries before dropping to the ground to pupate. A second generation of the pest may appear before winter.

Clean up garden debris in fall, handpick beetles when you see them, and remove newly forming berries. Better yet, plant the recently developed male asparagus strains and avoid having any berries for the pest to feed on. 'Greenwich' and 'Jersey Giant' are male plants that are also resistant to asparagus rust and fusarium crown rot (see Diseases, at right). A spray containing rotenone or a blend of rotenone and pyrethrins will control the spotted asparagus beetle as well as the common asparagus beetle.

ADDITIONAL INSECT AND ANIMAL PESTS

The *harlequin bug* (see CABBAGE FAMILY) and the *Japanese beetle* (see CORN) may feed on asparagus. The plant is immune to the *cotton root-knot nematode* (see *nematodes,* under BEAN), and it may inhibit other kinds of nematodes (see page 151). Although asparagus visually does not show damage by root-knot nematodes, it may allow the pests to proliferate; for that reason it should not be regarded as an immune crop in a rotation.

Symphylans (see SEEDLINGS) may damage the roots of asparagus. When the *tarnished plant bug* (see BEAN) feeds on asparagus spears or young ferns, the part of the plant above the point of injury collapses and dies. This symptom, called tip dieback, is caused by a toxin in the saliva of the insect. The mature ferns do not show this symptom, however.

DISEASES

Asparagus Rust

After arriving from Europe in 1896, this fungus disease spread swiftly across the United States. It affects asparagus as well as onion, although garlic and leek appear to be immune. Reddish brown pustules appear first on smaller stems and leaves and then on the whole plant. When you touch the plant, the pustules burst to release dusty clouds of rust-colored spores. Later, black blisters appear and the plant turns yellow and then brown. The disease reduces the following year's crop. If this problem continues for several years, the plant may die.

Several generations of reddish spores form each summer. The black overwintering spores, which live in the tops of diseased plants, form in fall or after a dry spell. Dispersed hundreds of yards by wind and splashing water, the spores germinate in moist weather or after overhead watering.

Resistant varieties are the best way to control asparagus rust. Look for the newest varieties, since the fungus has become immune to some of the earlier ones. Some good bets are 'California 500', 'Seneca Washington', 'Waltham Washington', and the new male varieties, such as 'Greenwich' and 'Jersey Giant'.

Avoid planting in damp or low-lying areas, and refrain from overhead watering. Cut off the top of a plant as soon as the disease is apparent. Cut to the ground remaining asparagus plants in fall and pull volunteer seedlings in spring. Dust with sulfur three weeks after cutting stops and again one month later.

These asparagus rust pustules will release clouds of spores.

Bright yellow asparagus stems may indicate fusarium crown rot. Check the root crowns for reddish brown streaks.

Fusarium Crown Rot of Asparagus

Although the fungus disease fusarium crown rot attacks many crops, including cabbage and tomato, this strain infects only asparagus and is common in asparagus plantings. An affected plant may wilt or be stunted. Either the entire plant or individual stems turn bright yellow. The rootstock may be decayed or there may be reddish brown streaks in the tissue when it is cut open.

The fungal spores live in the soil and infect plants through the roots. You may introduce the disease into your garden by planting infected seeds or rootstocks.

Take preventive measures against the disease. Obtain seeds and rootstocks from reputable sources. 'Greenwich' and 'Jersey Giant' are resistant varieties. Since stressed plants are susceptible to the disease, avoid subjecting your planting to adverse conditions, such as drought, poorly drained soil, insect attack, or overly long harvests. Destroy affected plants as soon as you notice them. However, do not

remove all asparagus plants if only one appears to be infected; often, diseased plants are scattered among healthy ones. If your entire crop is affected, plant fresh crowns in a spot where asparagus has not grown for two to four years.

BEAN

PHYSIOLOGICAL PROBLEMS

Poor Pod Set

Few fully formed pods in an otherwise healthy plant can be caused by any of several factors: high temperatures, extremes in soil moisture, and failure to pick pods. When the maximum temperature is consistently over 85° F, flowers often fall (blossom drop) or deteriorate on the plant (blossom blast) without setting pods. Hot winds may contribute to both conditions. A plant tends to produce few pods when the soil is too wet or too dry or when the moisture level fluctuates widely. Also, leaving unpicked pods slows the production of new pods.

Avoid midsummer crops in areas where summer temperatures are very high or where hot, dry winds are common. Instead, plant beans in early spring and again in late summer. Water regularly, allowing the soil surface to dry out between waterings. When harvesting pods at the snap bean stage, don't forget to pick the oldest pods at the bottom of the plant.

For information on poor pod set caused by insect attack, see *green stinkbug* on page 64 and *tarnished plant bug* on page 66.

INSECT AND OTHER ANIMAL PESTS

Aphids

Troublesome throughout the United States, aphids attack almost every crop. Some types of aphids are limited to one particular crop, whereas others feed on many different crops. Bean is susceptible to attack by the bean aphid (see opposite page), *green peach aphid* (see SPINACH), *melon aphid* (see CUCURBITS), *potato aphid* (see POTATO), and

turnip aphid (see *aphids*, under CABBAGE FAMILY).

Aphids are small, soft-bodied, slow-moving insects that congregate on the tender parts of plants, often on the undersides of leaves or near the growing points. In a severe infestation aphids may cover most of the plant. Pear-shaped insects that are wider at the rear, aphids may be yellow, pink, green, gray, or black. Most are wingless, although some have two transparent wings. The pests suck plant sap, weakening and sometimes stunting the plant. When actively growing leaves, stems, or flowers are attacked, the result is often puckered or twisted growth. Also, the leaves may turn yellow.

Aphids excrete honeydew, a sticky substance consisting of partly digested plant sap, onto the plant. Sooty mold, a powdery black fungus, often grows on the honeydew deposits, blackening the plant. Although more common on woody ornamentals, sooty mold can appear on vegetables

Bean aphids on this lima bean pod include gray nymphs, black adults, and a winged adult. The white objects are shed skins.

Like other aphids, bean aphids have a teardrop-shaped body with two short protrusions, called cornicles, at the rear.

when an aphid infestation is allowed to build up.

Many species of ants feed on the honeydew. They may protect aphids by attacking predators when they approach. Some species of aphids, such as the *corn root aphid* (see *aphids,* under CORN), are actually dependent on ants for their survival, but most are not.

Aphids are among the insects most often responsible for spreading virus diseases among plants. They do it by feeding first on infected plants and then on healthy ones. Most aphid infestations don't result in a virus infection. However, when you know that a particular type of aphid is responsible for carrying a virus to a certain crop, you can be vigorous in controlling the aphid on that crop.

Depending on their species and the severity of the winter, aphids may overwinter as eggs or adults. Sometimes they switch hosts as the seasons change. Most of the aphids infesting plants are females that reproduce rapidly by live birth without mating. Since

each new aphid can begin reproducing in a week or so, there are many generations in a season. When a colony is overcrowded, the females give birth to winged aphids that fly to new plants. Fertile males and females are usually produced in fall; they mate and the females lay eggs.

Aphids are attracted to plants with succulent new growth produced by an excess of nitrogen fertilizer and to plants weakened by poor growing conditions. Deter the pest by meeting the cultural needs of your plants.

Trap flying aphids with yellow sticky traps (see page 37), or repel them with a mulch made of aluminum-coated construction paper, available in rolls from building suppliers. The reflection of the sky in the foil causes aphids and other small flying insects to lose their sense of direction. In hot weather remove mulch, since it may burn plants.

Neither yellow sticky traps nor aluminum foil mulch will

control wingless aphids. If you see just a few aphids, crush them with your fingers. If aphids are scattered over the plant, knock them off with a strong jet of water from a garden hose, being sure to hit the undersides of the leaves. To avoid damaging the leaves, hold your hand behind the plant or behind individual leaves. Repeat the process every three days, or as long as aphids are present.

Encourage native predators and other beneficial organisms in your garden (see page 38). Natural enemies of aphids include lady beetles, lacewings, aphid midges, soldier bugs, pirate bugs, assassin bugs, syrphid flies, spiders, braconid wasps, and various fungus diseases. Dead fuzzy brown or reddish aphids are evidence that a predatory fungus is at work; leave the dead aphids in the garden, where they will continue to release fungus spores. Also look for aphid mummies, bloated gray-brown aphid bodies parasitized by wasps; a round exit hole signifies that young parasitic wasps have emerged.

Probably the most effective predator you can buy is lacewings. Buying lady beetles for a small garden is usually impractical, since the insects tend to disperse over a large area when released.

Commercial plant-extract repellents are reported to be effective against aphids. Insecticidal soap, the most environmentally friendly of the chemicals that kill aphids, may prove to be sufficient to control the pest. A soap spray in combination with citrus oil or pyrethrum oil is more effective than the soap alone. Other chemicals effective against aphids include pyrethrum and pyrethrins, sabadilla, and rotenone.

The dark green to black *bean aphid,* about 1/16 inch long, feeds on bean, artichoke, asparagus, beet, cowpea, parsnip, pea, rhubarb, spinach, and Swiss chard. Other warm-weather hosts include many ornamentals, such as broom, dahlia, deutzia, English ivy, nasturtium, oleander, poppy,

Most common in the Southeast, bean leaf beetles damage not only the leaves but also the stems and roots of bean plants.

Green stinkbugs live up to their name by having a foul odor. They are among the insects known as true bugs.

weedy thistles, and zinnia. During the winter its hosts are evergreen shrubs, including euonymus and viburnum. The insect reproduces rapidly and congregates in large numbers on the leaves and stems of a host plant, weakening the plant and causing the leaves to turn yellow. It also spreads bean common mosaic virus and bean yellow mosaic virus (see *mosaic viruses,* page 71).

In warm-winter climates the bean aphid is active the year around. In colder areas it overwinters as an egg on evergreen shrubs and many other plants. When the temperature rises it moves to a warm-weather host. Try spraying winter hosts with a horticultural oil to kill the aphid eggs. When using oil on evergreen plants, test part of the plant and wait a few days to see if there is any damage before spraying the whole plant.

Bean Leaf Beetle
Usually confined to the eastern half of the United States, the bean leaf beetle is more prevalent in the southern part

of its range. The insect feeds on bean, cowpea, and pea, causing seedlings to yellow and wilt. It chews circular holes in the leaves and stems of older plants, and it may damage the pods. A weakened stem may break off when the plant is harvested or during strong winds.

The ¼-inch-long beetles are variable in color but are most likely to be reddish to yellowish. There is a black band around the outer edges of the wing covers and three or four pairs of dots down the center, where the wing covers meet. If you dig up a damaged plant, you may see among the roots slender, ⅛-inch white larvae with dark brown ends.

The adults overwinter in garden debris and weeds, emerge in spring, feed on the seedlings, then mate and lay eggs at the base of seedling stems. The larvae hatch in about two weeks and eat the underground roots and stems, sometimes killing young plants. After about 20 days of feeding, the larvae pupate in the soil. A month later another

generation of adults emerges and begins to feed on the aboveground plant parts. There may be only one generation a year in the North and up to four in the South.

Clean up debris in fall to discourage overwintering adults. Cover the seedbed with a floating row cover to prevent eggs from being laid on the seedlings. Apply beneficial nematodes at, or shortly after, planting time to control the larvae (see page 42). As soon as the seedlings are up, begin handpicking adults from the undersides of the leaves. When disturbed the beetles fall to the ground and play dead, so lay a cloth underneath and gently jiggle the plant. Gather up the cloth and shake the beetles into a container of soapy water.

Plants can tolerate 20 percent loss of leaf surface without a severe effect on yield, so chemical control is generally not recommended unless the infestation is severe. Adult beetles can be controlled with pyrethrum dust or rotenone

spray; be sure to coat the undersides of the leaves.

Green Stinkbug
A pest of bean, peach, and nectarine, the green stinkbug occasionally feeds on cabbage, corn, eggplant, mustard, okra, pea, tomato, turnip, and several ornamental trees. Various weeds are also hosts. Damage on bean includes fallen pods, deformed seeds, and brown spots on the leaves.

The foul-smelling, ⅝-inch-long, shield-shaped insect is bright green. The overwintering adults emerge in spring and begin laying eggs on the undersides of leaves when temperatures reach 70° F or higher. The females lay eggs in clusters; each female can lay as many as 300 to 500 eggs during a season. The young stinkbugs, called nymphs, are red with blue markings. More rounded than the adults, they mature into adults in about six weeks. New generations occur as often as every five to six weeks during the summer.

Reduce overwintering adults by keeping weeds under control and tilling the garden

Meadow mice are sometimes called voles. Shown here is a prairie vole, one of the species that damage gardens.

Top: Mexican bean beetles chew bean leaves to lace.
Bottom: Spined soldier bugs control Mexican bean beetles.

in fall. Handpick the stinkbugs and the eggs whenever you see them. Early in the day is the best time to pick adults, since they move more slowly in cool temperatures. Pyrethrum, sabadilla, and rotenone are effective chemical controls.

Meadow Mouse

This small rodent prefers to nest and feed in a dense, grassy environment. A pest of bean, cucumber, tomato, and other crops, it is likely to eat ripening fruit that is near the ground. There are three to nine mouse litters a year, and the populations often peak on a three- to six-year cycle.

A cat can be an effective control if the garden is its primary focus. However, if the cat has a larger area in which to hunt, it may not pay close enough attention to the garden to control the mice in it. Keep the weeds down to reduce cover. A cleared border at least 10 feet wide around a garden may help keep out meadow mice. The most effective barrier is a fence of ¼-inch wire mesh, extending 1

foot above the ground and 1 foot below the ground.

Mexican Bean Beetle

A common pest east of the Rocky Mountains, the Mexican bean beetle feeds on the undersides of bean and cowpea leaves, chewing them to lace. The damage may reduce pod production and even kill the plant. The ¼-inch, rounded coppery adult beetle has 16 black spots arranged in three rows. The ⅛-inch, legless larva is yellow to orange with many forked, black-tipped spines.

The adult spends the winter in garden debris, then emerges in spring to feed for a week or two before laying eggs. Look for yellow eggs clustered in groups of 40 to 60 on the undersides of leaves. These will hatch into larvae, which feed for two to five weeks, then attach themselves to leaves to pupate. When the young beetles emerge, they are yellow but they soon darken and acquire their characteristic spots. There are one to four generations a year.

There are likely to be fewer Mexican bean beetles during years with cold winters

and very hot, dry spells in summer. Gardeners in the South may escape the pest with an early planting, but gardeners in the North should not plant too early, since slow-growing plants are vulnerable to greater damage by early feeding. Gardeners in all areas can reduce next year's infestation by cleaning up debris immediately after harvest and by tilling the garden in fall. Planting a resistant bean variety, such as 'Logan' and 'Wade' snap beans and 'Black Valentine' lima bean, further reduces the chances of infestation. Cover the seedbed with a floating row cover to avoid early feeding by the pest. Handpicking is a good option if your planting is small. Begin picking adults early in the season, and crush any eggs that you find. Continue to pick adults as well as larvae that hatch from the eggs that you missed. Harvest pods promptly so that they present only a brief temptation to the beetles.

Several naturally occurring predators, including some types of lady beetles and the spined soldier bug, prey on the Mexican bean beetle. You can purchase spined soldier bugs and the tiny parasitic wasp *Pediobius foveolatus* for home garden use. Commercial bean growers start a few beans early as a trap crop and then release beneficial insects when the beetles arrive. Pyrethrum and rotenone are effective chemical controls; be sure to coat the undersides of the leaves when applying either insecticide.

Nematodes

Several kinds of root-knot nematodes infest bean. The *southern root-knot nematode* can occur in most areas of the United States but is most common in the warm, sandy soils of the South and Southwest. The pest attacks many ornamental and edible crops, including bean (especially lima bean), carrot, corn, cucumber, eggplant, okra, onion, pepper, sweet potato, tomato, and watermelon. It is a serious problem on peach. Peanut and strawberry are

Healthy bean roots bear nodules containing nitrogen-fixing bacteria. The nodules are loosely attached to the roots.

The swellings on these bean roots are galls caused by root-knot nematodes. Part of the root, they can't be knocked off.

immune and thus are useful in a rotation. Oat and crotalaria, both of which are immune, can be used as green manure in infested soil.

An affected plant grows more slowly and often wilts during the hottest part of the day. The leaves turn slightly yellow. Often the plant produces fewer and smaller fruit. Serious damage inflicted early in the season may kill the plant. The nematodes enter the root and feed inside it. The cells around the feeding pest react to nematode secretions by dividing many times and enlarging to form a gall. Although the galls may merge to become as large as 1 inch in diameter, more typically they are pea sized. Although the galls resemble nodules formed by nitrogen-fixing bacteria on legume roots, they cannot be rubbed off, as the nodules can. Some crops, such as asparagus, corn, and onion, may not form any galls.

After 15 to 30 days, each female nematode lays up to several hundred eggs that appear on the surface of the galls. These hatch into juvenile nematodes that can infest nearby plants. If you cut open a gall, you will be able to see one or more pinhead-sized white female nematodes.

Two other root-knot nematode species that are particularly common in the South also affect many ornamental plants and most vegetable crops. The *cotton root-knot nematode* infests bean, cabbage, cantaloupe, carrot, celery, corn, cucumber, lettuce, New Zealand spinach, okra, pepper, potato, radish, rhubarb, squash, sweet potato, Swiss chard, tomato, turnip, and watermelon. It is also a problem on grape. Asparagus, peanut, and strawberry are immune.

The *Javanese root-knot nematode* infests many vegetables, including bean, beet, cabbage, carrot, corn, cucurbits, eggplant, radish, and tomato. Peach as well as some ornamentals are susceptible. Pepper and strawberry are immune, and there are resistant varieties of peanut.

The *peanut root-knot nematode,* especially common in Florida, affects many crops, including bean, beet, cabbage, carrot, pea, peanut, pepper, potato, tomato, and some ornamental plants.

The *northern root-knot nematode* is more common in the North, although it can also appear in the South. In cold-winter areas it rarely builds to the population density of nematodes in the South. This nematode infests bean, cantaloupe, carrot, celery, cucumber, eggplant, escarole, kale, lettuce, mustard, parsnip, peanut, pepper, potato, and tomato. It is also a serious problem on blueberry, cherry, strawberry, and many ornamentals. Although onion and garlic are also attacked, they don't permit a buildup of the nematodes in the soil. Beet, cabbage, celery, corn, okra, sweet potato, and watermelon are immune.

Although you will be able to recognize root-knot nematodes in general, you won't be able to identify the specific type without a laboratory test. In any event, more than one type is likely to be present at the same time. Once you know which root-knot nematodes infest your soil, you can plan a sensible rotation. See pages 148 to 152 for ways to control nematodes.

In addition to root-knot nematodes, several other nematodes may attack bean. To identify these you will have to send a soil sample to a nematology laboratory.

Tarnished Plant Bug
Found throughout the United States, this pest feeds on many vegetables, including bean, beet, cabbage, cauliflower, celery, cucumber, lettuce, potato, Swiss chard, and turnip. Other hosts are apple, peach, pear, strawberry, and many flowers and weeds. The tarnished plant bug damages bean by causing blossoms and young pods to drop; older pods and seeds become pitted and unappealing.

The flattened, oval, ¼-inch-long adult is irregularly mottled with white, yellow, and black. If you can get a good look at this elusive bug, you will see a transparent yellow triangle with one black corner on the tip of each wing. The young bug, called a nymph, is

The tarnished plant bug will fly or run to the opposite side of the stem when you try to get a good look at it.

Top: Two-spotted mites cause stippled and yellowed leaves. Bottom: Barely visible, the mites are only 1/50 inch long.

tiny and yellowish green with four black dots just behind its head and a fifth dot farther back on its body.

The adults overwinter among weeds and under leaves, stones, and bark. They feed first on fruit tree buds, then move to other plants and lay elongated, curved eggs on leaves and flowers. These hatch into nymphs, which feed for three to four weeks. In warm-winter climates feeding and breeding continue all year. There are three to five generations a year in cold-winter climates.

In fall get rid of weeds as well as debris from susceptible crops. Till the soil to discourage overwintering bugs. Remove or mow weeds in spring before they get too large; otherwise, the tarnished plant bugs that were feeding on them will move to desirable crops. Destroy infested fruit and twigs on fruit trees, or control the pest on the trees in other ways. In early spring when the temperature reaches 60° to 65° F, use white sticky traps (see page 37) to catch adults before they lay eggs.

Tarnished plant bugs are too active to handpick. Coating them with a pesticide is also difficult. Use an insecticidal soap spray in the early morning, when the bugs are less active. If the infestation is serious, apply sabadilla dust.

Two-Spotted Mite

Bean, cucumber, melon, eggplant, and tomato are among the crops most likely to be infested by the two-spotted mite, one of the most common spider mites. This spider relative is so small that it is visible only as mealy, dustlike particles on the leaves. Usually, mites appear first on the undersides of leaves and near the veins. They multiply until they cover both sides of the leaves, which appear stippled, dirty, and yellowish. The mites form a very fine webbing, first on the undersides of leaves, then encasing the leaves or connecting them. Eventually, the entire plant may be enveloped in webbing. The plant is stunted and may die.

You may see moving particles that are usually pale yellow or greenish although sometimes red. You will need a magnifying lens to see the two spots on the pest's back. Unlike insects, which have six legs, mature mites have eight legs. For the best look without a magnifying lens, hold a white card under an infested leaf and tap the leaf. Mites will fall onto the card and will be visible as they crawl on it.

In warm-winter climates mites feed and lay eggs all year, slowing down only slightly in winter. In cold climates the mites overwinter as adults and hibernate in the soil, on tree bark, or on leaves of evergreen plants. In early spring they emerge and the females begin to lay eggs. Each female lays 100 to 200 eggs in three to four weeks. The eggs hatch into larvae in one to eight days. During warm weather the larvae can mature in as few as five days, so the mite population increases very quickly.

Keep plants adequately watered, since poorly watered plants are more susceptible to mite damage. Hosing plants off in dry weather can also reduce

the chance of mite infestation. Plants coated with dusty soil seem to fall victim to mite attack, so use a mulch to keep soil from blowing onto plants. Small populations of mites can be kept from increasing by directing forceful jets of water at the plant. Make sure that you strike the undersides of the leaves. Do this early in the morning, so that the plant dries before nightfall.

Predatory mites are an effective control. Ask a supplier for the species best suited to the temperature and humidity in your garden. Lacewings and certain naturally occurring lady beetles can also help in the battle.

Apply sulfur when you first see the pest, and repeat every 7 to 10 days for continuous control. As an alternative, apply insecticidal soap, preferably a formulation containing citrus aromatics. Spraying with pyrethrins or rotenone will also help to reduce the pest population. If the infestation is severe, consider pulling

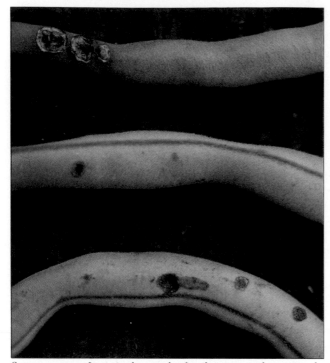

Corn earworms often enter bean pods after the corn crop has matured. Dimples on the pods show where the larvae entered.

When you see bean leaves that are yellowed, bronzed, or curled with brown edges, suspect the potato leafhopper.

up affected plants and discarding them. In the future try to avoid the pest by using better cultural practices or by catching infestations earlier.

ADDITIONAL INSECT AND ANIMAL PESTS

Blister beetles (see BEET) may feed on bean leaves. The *corn earworm* (see CORN) sometimes bores into bean pods. Since this is more likely to happen late in the season, plant early to reduce damage. Pick off infested pods. Spray plants with *Bt berliner-kurstake* as soon as you see the caterpillars or the damage.

The *cowpea curculio* (see COWPEA) feeds on snap and lima beans as well as cowpea, entering the pod and destroying the developing seeds. Since the larvae cannot be controlled once they are inside the pods, avoid problems by eliminating overwintering adults, planting late, and handpicking adults and eggs.

Cutworms (see SEEDLINGS) may sever the stems of bean seedlings, and the *European corn borer* (see CORN) may enter the stems and pods of bean

plants. Palestriped and potato *flea beetles* (see EGGPLANT) may damage bean leaves by chewing characteristic tiny round holes. The *harlequin bug* (see CABBAGE FAMILY) and the *Japanese beetle* (see CORN) may feed on bean plants as well.

The potato *leafhopper* (see POTATO), which is also called the bean jassid, is a serious pest of bean. Damaged leaves have brown edges that curl under. Bean varieties with hairy lower leaf surfaces are somewhat resistant, because the leaf hairs ensnare very young leafhopper nymphs. Still, control is often necessary. The threshold for chemical control in commercial bean fields is an average of one leafhopper nymph per three-leaflet bean leaf.

The serpentine *leafminer* (see BEET) occasionally tunnels in bean leaves. Bean seedlings are a favorite food of *rabbits* (see SEEDLINGS). *Slugs and snails* (see SEEDLINGS) feed on bean seedlings, sometimes killing them. On the West Coast, the imported

brown garden snail damages bean plants late in the season; the season's new hatchlings eat small holes in bean leaves.

Both *spotted cucumber beetles* and *striped cucumber beetles* (see CUCURBITS) damage bean. Spotted cucumber beetle adults, which chew the leaves of bean and corn, lay eggs at the base of host plants; the larvae, also known as the southern corn rootworm (see *corn rootworms,* under CORN), eat the roots and stems. Adult striped cucumber beetles begin feeding on bean, cucurbit, and pea leaves when the first generation of larvae matures in midsummer.

In mild-winter areas *symphylans* (see SEEDLINGS) may eat bean roots. Several kinds of *thrips,* including the onion thrips (see ONION) and the bean thrips, may infest bean as well as pea. The young bean thrips, called nymphs, are reddish yellow; the adults are dark gray with black and white wings. The thrips create whitish blotches by sucking plant sap from leaves. Remove prickly lettuce and sowthistle, which are alternative hosts.

Whiteflies (see TOMATO) may infest bean plants. Discourage attacks by keeping plants healthy. Examine the undersides of leaves often, so that you will be ready to control an infestation before it becomes serious.

DISEASES

Bacterial Blights of Bean

Two types of bacterial blight—bean common blight and bean halo blight—occur throughout the United States but are rarely found west of the Rocky Mountains. They are diseases of dry, lima, and snap beans.

Bean common blight produces small, water-soaked dark green spots on the undersides of leaves. Often a narrow lemon yellow margin surrounds the lesions, which may enlarge, turn brown, and merge to form large dead areas. Badly infected leaves may drop. Brown lesions, sometimes with a reddish margin, form on the stems and pods. Infected areas may have a yellow ooze or a whitish crust during wet or humid weather.

Halo blight lesions have a wide yellow or yellowish green halo, except on very hot days.

Top: Common blight lesions have a narrow yellow margin.
Bottom: Bean anthracnose pod lesions have light centers.

The first evidence of *bean halo blight* is small, water-soaked areas on the undersides of leaves. They remain small, turning brown. Often, they are surrounded by a broad greenish yellow halo, which is produced by bacterial toxin, but the halo may not be apparent during hot weather. Stem and pod lesions begin as water-soaked spots that become brown or reddish brown. Under moist conditions a cream-colored or silvery exudate appears on the stem and pod lesions.

In the case of both blights, the bacteria overwinter in infected seeds and plant residue. The diseases are spread by rain, irrigation water, and windblown particles of infected plant debris. The bacteria reproduce on the plant surface, building to high numbers before symptoms appear. Bean halo blight is favored by temperatures above 80° F and bean common blight by temperatures below 80° F. During wet conditions the bacteria enter the plant through wounds or natural openings. Symptoms appear in a couple of weeks.

In moist weather the lesions ooze bacteria, which can be spread to other plants by water, wind, or gardeners working among plants.

Use certified seeds, usually grown in disease-free parts of the West. Although this does not guarantee freedom from disease, it improves your chances considerably. There are a number of resistant varieties of dry beans. 'Redkote' kidney bean resists both blights; 'Isabella', 'Mecosta', 'Montcalm', and 'Redkloud' kidney beans have some resistance to bean halo blight in some areas. The great northern bean varieties 'Harris', 'Ivory', 'Sapphire', 'Star', and 'Valley' resist both blights. Most navy and small white bean varieties resist bean halo blight. The pinto bean varieties 'Olath', 'UI 111', 'UI 114', and 'WYO 166' have limited resistance to bean halo blight.

Since these diseases affect only bean, you can probably avoid the problem with a one- to three-year rotation of susceptible bean crops. Dig all bean debris under the soil surface in fall; the blight-causing bacteria will die if the debris decomposes rapidly. Destroy any volunteer bean seedlings, which can be a source of infection. Avoid overhead watering and working among wet plants. If halo blight has been a problem in the past, use a copper-based bactericide as a preventive when plants are four to six weeks old. Otherwise, apply the bactericide at the first sign of disease, repeating at 10- to 14-day intervals. The treatment may not be effective against all strains of the disease. Avoid injury to bean plants, since bacteria enter more easily through wounds.

Bean Anthracnose

The first evidence of this fungus disease is sunken brown to black lesions on the stems and seed leaves of bean (including broad, dry, lima, mung, snap, and scarlet runner) and cowpea seedlings. The fungus stunts or kills young plants. On older plants the most obvious symptoms are circular lesions, up to ⅜ inch or more in diameter, on the pods. Mature lesions are dark brown with a narrow reddish border. In moist weather the lesions ooze salmon-colored spore masses. Irregularly shaped brown or reddish brown spots also appear on the stems, leaves, and pods. Anthracnose spores are carried in bean seeds or they lurk in the garden on infected debris. Splashing water, tools, and gardeners may also spread spores from plant to plant.

This disease has been largely arrested by the use of seeds grown in western, anthracnose-free states. Still, outbreaks do occur in the central and eastern states, especially where there are cool to moderate summers and frequent summer rain. In all areas except the West, home-grown seeds invite disease unless you are absolutely sure that they are from healthy plants. As a precaution work in bean patches only when the leaves are dry. Remove infected plants immediately.

Bean rust spores are spread by gardeners on tools and clothing as well as by bean stakes from infected plants.

Cool nights and heavy dew favor downy mildew of lima bean.

Dry root rot causes reddish streaks on bean stems.

Turning the soil in fall will reduce the chance of the disease surviving. It is best to use a two- to three-year rotation for beans. The local cooperative extension office can tell you which varieties resist local anthracnose strains.

Chemical control is usually needed only when the climate favors the disease, susceptible varieties are planted, and rotations are short. Apply bordeaux mixture when you see flower buds forming and again during late flowering. If you are harvesting either dry or shell beans, spray a third time as the pods are filling out.

Stem anthracnose of lima bean, a closely related fungus disease, causes reddish steaks or blotches on lima bean plants, especially on the pods. Other susceptible plants are alfalfa, cowpea, lespedeza, soybean, and vetch. The life cycle and means of prevention and control are similar to those for bean anthracnose. The fungus can overwinter on a host plant whether it is present as a food crop, cover crop, or weed.

Bean Rust

A troublesome fungus disease throughout the United States, except in some arid regions, bean rust affects snap and dry beans. It is an infrequent pest of lima and scarlet runner beans. Small pale spots with dark centers, which turn into red or black blisters, appear on the undersides of leaves. Badly infected leaves turn yellow and drop.

The spores overwinter in bean debris and are blown to emerging plants. A new generation of spores is produced every 10 days. This fungus disease is favored by overcast, humid weather and a temperature of approximately 75° F.

Remove diseased plant material at the end of the season, and plan a three- to four-year rotation. Use new bean stakes each season. Avoid overhead watering, and try not to handle wet plants. Apply sulfur to upper and lower leaf surfaces, beginning when symptoms first appear and continuing weekly until the problem is eradicated. 'Dade', 'Genuine Half Dutch Runner',

'Green Lantern', 'McHarvest', 'Mountaineer', 'Old Dutch', 'Tenderlake', 'White Kentucky Wonder 191', and 'U.S. No. 3 Kentucky Wonder' are resistant snap bean varieties. The commonly planted 'Blue Lake' and 'Kentucky Wonder' are susceptible.

Downy Mildew of Lima Bean

Most prevalent in Middle and North Atlantic states, this fungus disease is very serious some years and minor other years. A downy white mold appears on lima bean pods, either in patches or covering the pods completely. When the fungus grows through the pod, the pod dies and turns black. Often, the leaves are distorted and the veins twisted and purplish. The spores are spread by splashing water and by bees and other insects.

Use western-grown seeds, and plan a two- to three-year rotation for lima bean. Applications of copper dust, begun a month or more before harvest or when the first signs

of the disease appear, can save the crop. 'Eastland Lima' is a resistant variety.

Dry Root Rot of Beans

This strain of the fungus disease fusarium affects only dry, lima, and snap beans. It is most serious on dry beans. An affected plant is stunted and may turn yellow, wilt, and die before it can mature. If you pull up the plant, you will see reddish brown streaks on the stem below the soil level and on the taproot.

The fungus can live in the soil and in infected bean refuse for many years. Since the disease is fostered by warm soil, it often develops late in the season.

Plant beans in well-drained soil and fertilize adequately. Use as long a rotation as possible between bean crops to try to prevent a buildup of the fungus. Remove any infected plants from the garden. Once the soil is infected, you may have to wait six years or longer before you can grow a satisfactory bean crop in that location.

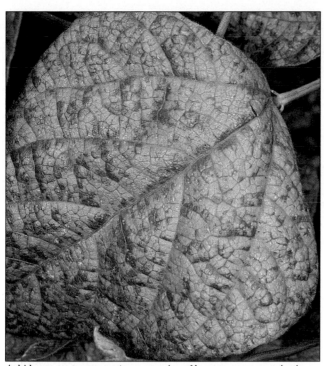

Aphids are a common vector, or carrier, of bean common mosaic virus, which causes a light yellow mottling on the leaves.

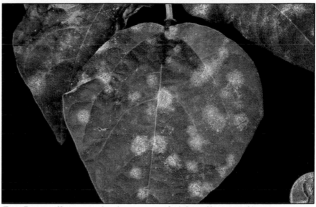

Top: Bean yellow mosaic virus causes bright yellow mottling.
Bottom: The grayish powdery spots are bean powdery mildew.

Mosaic Viruses

Three mosaic viruses—bean common mosaic, bean yellow mosaic, and cucumber mosaic—infect bean. All cause characteristic mottling of the leaves.

Bean common mosaic virus causes light yellow mottling of snap and dry bean foliage. Also, the leaves are crinkled and stiff and often the edges are curled down. On mature plants the symptoms may appear only near the top. Some strains of the virus cause sudden wilting and death of plants.

The virus is spread by infected seeds as well as by bean, cabbage, green peach, and turnip aphids. It can also be spread by gardeners working among the plants. The virus overwinters in white sweet clover.

Obtain certified seeds from a reputable source. Don't use white sweet clover as a cover crop near bean. Control aphids (see page 62), since they carry the disease. Because there is no cure, remove diseased

plants immediately and avoid touching healthy plants after having touched infected ones. Resistant dry bean varieties include 'Aurora', 'Midnight', 'Montcalm', 'Redkloud', 'Redkote', 'Ruddy', 'Seafarer', and 'T-39'. There are many snap bean varieties resistant to the virus.

Bean yellow mosaic virus causes bright yellow and green mottling on the leaves of bean, pea, clover, freesia, gladiolus, and sweet pea. It is transmitted by bean and pea aphids, not by seed. Avoid planting bean or pea near other host plants, and keep aphids under control. Since there is no cure, pull diseased plants as soon as you notice the infection. Snap bean varieties with some resistance include 'Bush Green Pod', 'Bush Wax', 'Extender', 'Harvester', 'Improved Tendergreen', 'Resistant Cherokee', 'Stringless Blue Lake', and 'Wade'.

Bean is susceptible to a strain of *cucumber mosaic virus* that is different from the one affecting cucurbits. This strain causes a two-tone

green mottling as well as curling and blistering of the leaves. The veins become rough and zipperlike. Although the symptoms are alarming, affected plants usually recover and resume normal growth. The disease may be transmitted by seed, but the main source of infection is aphids, which carry the virus from nearby weeds. To reduce incidence of the virus, control aphids. Also control weeds, particularly chickweed, clover, milkweed, and purslane.

Powdery Mildew of Legumes

A common sight in southern, Middle Atlantic, and West Coast states, this fungus disease affects dry, lima, and snap beans. It can spread from nearby field soybeans. Other vegetable hosts are cabbage-family members, carrot, and pea. Ornamental legumes affected are acacia, locust, lupine, and sweet pea. The fungus also attacks anemone, candytuft, calendula, California poppy, China aster, clematis,

columbine, dahlia, delphinium, erigeron, gardenia, geranium, hydrangea, honeysuckle, matrimonyvine, peony, and tulip tree.

A grayish powder coats the leaves and pods of affected bean plants. If the disease is not controlled, the leaves develop yellow spots and then drop. New growth is dwarfed and curled, and the pods are stunted and distorted. The problem usually develops on mature plants late in the season. Infected pods are inedible.

This disease is caused by the fungus *Erysiphe polygoni*, which overwinters in plant debris. Once the fungus appears in a garden, it spreads quickly from plant to plant. The spores can germinate in drier conditions than are usual for most fungus diseases. A shady environment with moderate temperatures encourages the disease.

Deter the fungus by planting in a sunny spot and providing good care. Dust or spray plants with sulfur at the first sign of the disease, and repeat every 7 to 10 days until the

White mold produces white cottony growth on bean.

From left to right, these beets show decreasing symptoms of boron deficiency. The beets on the right are healthy.

problem is under control. Sulfur does not cure diseased leaves, but it protects healthy leaves from infection.

A similar fungus, *Microsphaera diffusa,* also causes powdery mildew on dry, lima, and snap beans. Its alternate hosts are black locust, snowberry, and wolfberry, so watch for reservoirs of infection in these plants growing near the garden. Sulfur is effective in controlling serious outbreaks of this type of powdery mildew.

Other Diseases
In the West snap and dry beans may become infected with *beet curly top virus* (see TOMATO), which is spread by leafhoppers. Affected bean plants are stunted and the leaves are curled, yellowed, and dried. The virus *pea enation mosaic* (see PEA), which is spread by aphids, affects broad bean.

If you see watery spots on leaves, stems, and pods, followed in moist weather by a cottony white growth, your beans have *white mold* (see *lettuce drop,* under LETTUCE). Prevention is the best defense

against this fungus disease, which affects a wide variety of crops. On bean the most important measure is moisture control. Avoid overhead watering and don't irrigate for the last month of the season. Plant bush varieties that have an open habit, spacing them to allow good air circulation. Also, be sparing with nitrogen fertilizer.

BEET (AND SWISS CHARD)

PHYSIOLOGICAL PROBLEMS

Black Heart
Also called brown heart, this problem is most commonly seen on beets grown in the Southwest. The plant is stunted and the leaves have brown edges. Young, unfolding leaves may turn black and die. Damage to the edible root verifies that the problem is black heart. There are dark brown areas on the surface and inside the root, and the surface may be cracked and wrinkled. Also, there may be a hole in the middle of the root.

Black heart is caused by a deficiency or an unavailability of boron in the soil. This is most likely to occur in sandy and alkaline soils. A lack of moisture in the soil aggravates the problem.

As soon as you notice damage, add boron—but be aware that too much is as bad as too little. A solution of 1 teaspoon household borax in 1 gallon water is enough to treat a 30-foot row. If your soil is alkaline, lower the pH to between 6.0 and 7.0. (Get a soil test and follow the recommendations.) Add organic matter to sandy soil. All soils should be evenly watered. Next year, apply the borax solution soon after planting and repeat the application two to three weeks later.

INSECT AND OTHER ANIMAL PESTS

Blister Beetles
Several types of blister beetles feed on beet as well as many other crops. They derive their name from the painful blisters they inflict on anyone touching them.

The *black blister beetle,* also known as the old-fashioned potato bug or the yankee bug, is most troublesome in the East, although localized infestations occur throughout the United States. The pest chews irregular holes in the leaves of beet, Swiss chard, bean, cabbage, carrot, cowpea, eggplant, melon, onion, pea, pepper, potato, pumpkin, radish, soybean, spinach, sweet potato, and tomato. It also feeds on many kinds of flowers, particularly aster and Japanese anemone.

The slender black beetle, from ½ inch to ¾ inch long, has soft, flexible wing covers. There are several species of the pest, each with different markings and different hosts. The pest typically appears in swarms in June and feeds on garden crops well into the summer.

Adult beetles lay eggs in holes in the soil. The eggs hatch, and the active, strong-jawed larvae feed on grasshopper eggs and then spend the winter in a dormant state.

Top: Black blister beetles damage beets and other crops.
Bottom: A beet leaf has been cut to expose beet leafminers.

Female sugar beet cyst nematodes are white when young, then darken, die, and split open to release up to 600 eggs each.

Dormancy may last for several years, until one spring the larvae become active again briefly, then pupate and emerge as adults.

Handpick the beetles, being sure to wear gloves to prevent blisters. If the insects are present in large numbers, you may be able to sweep them up with a broom. Or apply rotenone or sabadilla dust, or spray with a blend of rotenone and pyrethrins.

Another eastern pest, the *striped blister beetle,* feeds on beet, Swiss chard, bean, corn, melon, pea, potato, radish, and tomato. The ½-inch-long adult is black with a yellow border and a yellow stripe on each wing cover. The similar *three-striped blister beetle,* found in the West, feeds on the same vegetables as the striped blister beetle. The controls for both pests are the same as for the black blister beetle.

Leafminers

Two types of leafminers damage beet by tunneling in the leaves. Beet crops in northern states are usually not as seriously affected as those in other regions.

The *serpentine leafminer* burrows into beet, Swiss chard, bean, cabbage, cowpea, pepper, potato, spinach, turnip, and watermelon leaves. It also mines nasturtium and sweet-pea leaves. Pale, narrow, winding trails disfigure the leaves, and dark frass and pupae are visible through the surface. Plants can usually outgrow the damage, although you will not want to eat affected leaves.

On the leaf surface the tiny adult fly lays eggs, which hatch into larvae that burrow into the leaves to feed. Then the insect pupates in the leaf mines or in the soil. The adult emerges and the cycle is repeated. There are several generations a year.

Kill overwintering pupae by tilling the soil in fall. If possible, grow beets in fall or early spring when the leafminer is less active. Plant Swiss chard as an early spring crop, and harvest before summer. Pick off infested leaves as soon as you notice the mines. Protect beet and Swiss chard plantings with a floating row cover, tucking the edges firmly into the soil. If you have a serious leafminer problem, leave the cover on until harvest. Often, naturally occurring parasitic wasps keep the pest under control. Once a miner is inside the leaf, it is beyond the reach of any chemicals registered for use on food crops.

A similar insect, the *spinach leafminer,* feeds in the leaves of beet, Swiss chard, and spinach. The damage begins as similar pale, winding trails, but later the larvae widen the trails, which join and become large blotches. A serious infestation reduces the leaf surface enough so that the plant becomes stunted. Control this pest as you would the serpentine leafminer. Also, eliminate nearby weed hosts, the most common of which are chickweed, lamb's-quarters, nightshade, and plantain.

Sugar Beet
Cyst Nematode

A potential problem in areas where sugar beet is grown, this nematode pest attacks sugar beet as well as beet, broccoli, brussels sprouts, cabbage, cauliflower, rhubarb, and spinach. Weedy plants that may be attacked include dock, mustard, shepherd's-purse, and wild radish.

On most hosts the first aboveground symptom of infestation is stunted top growth. However, beet leaves show no evidence of damage. All hosts suffer stunted roots; the damage typically begins in a limited area, which gradually enlarges.

Young nematodes enter the roots and migrate to food-conducting tissue, where they establish feeding sites. The females enlarge until they break through the root surface, forming lemon-shaped cysts that become visible four to six weeks after planting. At first, the females are white; later, they turn dirty white and then brown and leathery. The mature cysts are tiny—approximately ¹/₄₀ inch long. The eggs,

Red-rimmed spots mark cercospora leaf spot of beet.

The fungus has infected entire beet plants.

Beet curly top virus plagues the western sugar beet crop, and it also strikes garden beets and other vegetables.

which are enclosed in the protective brown cysts, can survive up to eight years. When the roots die the cysts fall loose into the soil. Cyst nematodes can move only a few feet a year on their own.

See pages 148 to 152 for ways to control nematodes. Since there are no varieties resistant to the sugar beet cyst nematode, crop rotation is very important. A one-year rotation isn't sufficient to keep the pest from increasing; it is better to grow a susceptible crop every third year.

Beet is also susceptible to the *Javanese root-knot nematode* and the *peanut root-knot nematode* (see *nematodes*, under BEAN), as well as other nematodes whose damage lacks definite symptoms.

ADDITIONAL INSECT AND ANIMAL PESTS

Many types of *aphids* feed on beet and Swiss chard. Among the most common are the bean aphid (see *aphids*, under BEAN), the green peach aphid (see SPINACH), and the melon aphid (see CUCURBITS). The

beet leafhopper (see TOMATO) sucks plant sap from beet and Swiss chard, and it spreads beet curly top virus to both crops. Include beet and Swiss chard plantings when checking for the webbed feeding places of the *celery leaftier* (see CELERY); pick off infested leaves. You may see the shot-hole damage of palestriped and potato *flea beetles* (see EGGPLANT) on beet and Swiss chard leaves, or you may find the *harlequin bug* (see CABBAGE FAMILY) feeding on the plants of either crop.

The *onion thrips* (see ONION) removes chlorophyll from the leaves, leaving a typical whitish pall. The *tarnished plant bug* (see BEAN) causes deformed leaves on beet and Swiss chard. In mild-winter areas the *vegetable weevil* (see CARROT) may eat beet and Swiss chard leaves. Some species of *wireworms* (see POTATO) bore into beet roots.

DISEASES

Cercospora Leaf Spot of Beet

More serious east of the Rocky Mountains, this fungus disease affects beet, Swiss chard, and spinach. Small circular gray-brown spots with dark reddish borders appear on the leaves. The center may drop out of the spots, leaving holes. The older leaves, which are affected first, may turn yellow and die. The damage is usually restricted to the foliage and doesn't affect the roots.

Splashing water, wind, tools, and insects spread the disease from infected plants and debris to healthy plants. The spores enter plants through natural openings. Warm, humid weather favors the disease. You probably won't have a serious problem with this fungus if you water and fertilize adequately, dig plant debris under in fall, and rotate susceptible crops on a three-year basis. Avoid overhead watering, and try not to work among wet plants. Mulching may reduce splashing of fungal spores. Pick off

damaged leaves as soon as you notice them, and destroy seriously infected plants.

OTHER DISEASES

Beet curly top virus (see TOMATO) stunts the tops and roots of beet and Swiss chard. The leaf margins roll upward and are brittle. The veins develop small wartlike growths on the undersides of the leaves. Cover the planting to protect it from the beet leafhopper, which spreads the virus. Fasten cheesecloth or a floating row cover to a low cage or frame placed over the planting. It is important to shield the plants during the period of greatest leafhopper activity, usually May and June.

Potato scab (see POTATO) is widespread on beet. The scabbing is similar to that on potato, but more bulging. Rotation offers the best control. Reducing the soil pH is not a viable control, since a pH lower than 6.5 is considered too acidic for beet. Beet is also susceptible to *verticillium wilt* (see TOMATO).

Top: *This curled broccoli leaf hides a mass of cabbage aphids.*
Bottom: *Cabbage aphids are a powdery, waxy gray-green.*

Top: *Cabbage loopers travel inchworm fashion.*
Bottom: *The adult looper is a mottled brownish gray moth.*

CABBAGE FAMILY (Broccoli, brussels sprouts, cabbage, cauliflower, Chinese cabbage, collards, cress, horseradish, kale, kohlrabi, mustard, radish, rutabaga, and turnip)

INSECT AND OTHER ANIMAL PESTS

Aphids

Several kinds of aphids feed on the cabbage family. The *cabbage aphid* is the most damaging to the widest range of cruciferous crops. The insect is particularly bothersome in the South, although it makes its presence felt in other regions. Obvious symptoms are general dwarfing of the plant and cupping and curling of the leaves. A heavy infestation may kill seedlings.

Masses of small gray-green aphids with a powdery, waxy covering congregate on leaves, buds, and flower heads. Like other aphids, the cabbage aphid prefers the undersides of leaves. The insect may also

mass on the tops of leaves, curling them by their feeding to form protected chambers. If the aphids get into the heart of a developing cabbage head, they can make it inedible. It is difficult to dislodge the aphids once they gather between broccoli buds. When the insects get into brussels sprouts, you must peel away several layers before cooking the sprouts.

In northern regions the cabbage aphid overwinters as a small black egg on the stems and leaves of mature cabbage-family plants. In southern regions it reproduces the year around without mating. Inspect young transplants carefully and crush any aphids that you find. Pick off and destroy any leaves holding a large colony. For additional information about aphids and ways to control them, see *aphids*, under BEAN.

The *turnip aphid* is a special pest of mustard, radish, and turnip, although it may feed on other members of the cabbage family. You are most

likely to encounter this insect in the South. It is pale green and it lacks the waxy covering of the cabbage aphid. The winged form has black spots and a black head.

The *green peach aphid* (see SPINACH) may attack any cabbage-family crop, and the *potato aphid* (see POTATO) feeds on turnip.

Cabbage Looper

A common pest of all cabbage-family crops, this destructive caterpillar also feeds on beet, celery, lettuce, parsley, pea, potato, spinach, and tomato. In addition, it attacks many flowers.

The cabbage looper feeds on the undersides of leaves, chewing ragged holes between the veins. The larger caterpillars are able to bore into cabbage heads, eating their way through as many as six layers of tightly wrapped leaves. Since the looper consumes more foliage than the imported cabbageworm or the diamondback moth larva (see page 77), it is more troublesome.

The cabbage looper grows up to 1½ inches long and is

light green with a light stripe along each side and two more down the back. It has three pairs of legs near the head and three additional legs, called prolegs, near the rear. The pest gets its name from its habit of humping up its middle when it walks, a trait called looping.

The insect survives the winter only in southern climates. In other areas infestations are due to migrating adult moths. Depending on the weather and wind patterns, the moths reach northern regions from early July to mid-August. The mottled grayish brown moth, with a wingspan of about 1½ inches, has a small white figure eight in the center of each forewing. It flies mainly at night, but you may see it resting on the undersides of cruciferous leaves during the day. It lays eggs singly on the upper surfaces of the leaves. The size of pinheads, the round eggs are off-white at first and mature to yellow. The caterpillars

Top: Pull damaged plants to verify the presence of maggots.
Bottom: Plants damaged by cabbage maggots wilt or fall over.

Top: Diamondback moth larvae eat from leaf undersides.
Bottom: The adult moth sports a diamondlike design on its wings.

hatch in three to six days, feed for two to four weeks, and then form pupae. There may be one or two generations a year in the northern part of the insect's range and three or more generations in the southern part.

'Mammoth Red Rock', 'Savoy Chieftain', and 'Savoy Perfection Drumhead' are cabbage varieties resistant to both the cabbage looper and the imported cabbageworm. Examine susceptible plants and crush any eggs that you find. Also, handpick the loopers. Natural enemies are moderately effective in controlling this pest; they play a greater role in warm climates, where the looper survives the winter. Enemies of the looper include beetles, true bugs, and spiders, which eat the eggs, as well as wasps and tachinid flies, which parasitize the caterpillars. Before the caterpillars hatch you can release trichogramma wasps, which parasitize the eggs. Polyhedrous granulosis viruses sometimes kill loopers in late summer. Infected loopers are yellow or brown. If you see any, leave

them alone; when they die they release more virus to infect other loopers.

Young loopers are susceptible to *Bt berliner-kurstake* and Javelin® (see page 19). Pheromone traps will let you know when active male moths have arrived and egg laying is about to begin. Spray plants as soon as you see that the loopers are feeding on them, and repeat every two to three days while loopers are active. The loopers are also susceptible to pyrethrum, sabadilla, and rotenone. If you decide to apply an insecticide, don't delay: The smaller the caterpillars the easier they are to kill. Thorough coverage is essential, since the caterpillars are adept at avoiding treated parts of a plant that has been sprayed unevenly.

Cabbage Maggot

Found mainly in northern climates, the cabbage maggot feeds on the roots of many cabbage-family crops. Affected plants wilt on warm days; although they may appear to recover overnight, they are

stunted and may eventually turn yellow and die. If the plant is dug up, legless, wormlike white larvae from ¼ inch to ⅓ inch long can be seen tunneling in stem and root tissue just below the soil surface. On Chinese cabbage the maggots eat into the stem at the base of the head. In severe cases the plant falls over. In addition to inflicting direct harm, the cabbage maggot sometimes infects plants with blackleg (see page 79).

After overwintering in the soil as a brown pupa, the insect emerges as a ¼-inch gray fly; this occurs in April in mild climates and as late as June in colder climates. The adult lives for five to six weeks. Before dying the female lays furrowed white eggs near the stems of host plants. The eggs hatch in 3 to 10 days and the young maggots begin to feed on the stem and roots. After two to three weeks, the maggots enter the soil to pupate and the cycle is repeated. There are usually three or four generations in a season. The later generations cause a second wave of damage in late

summer, although mature plants are often able to withstand this attack.

Once the maggot enters the stem, there is no cure. Destroy infested plants. Also clean up and destroy crop residue after harvest. Tilling the soil is not an effective deterrent, because hatching flies can crawl up through a foot of soil to infest spring crops. Avoid following one crop of crucifers with another, since the pupae will still be in the soil.

Improve the soil; plants grown in a fertile, well-aerated soil will be stronger and better able to withstand infestation. If possible, plant after the first wave of damage—from late May to early July, depending on the climate. Or, if your area is warm enough, plant early to avoid the first spring hatching.

Use barriers to prevent flies from laying eggs near susceptible plants. A traditional barrier for transplants is a 6- to 8-inch square of tar paper slit to accommodate the stem. A newer method consists

Top: Tiny holes in radish leaves were made by flea beetles.
Bottom: Harlequin bugs damaged this horseradish leaf.

The harlequin bug, which has the typical shield shape of a true bug, is strikingly marked in black and red.

of wrapping the stem twice with paper extending 1 to 2 inches above and below the soil. Another successful barrier is a ring of sawdust mulch 1 to 1½ inches deep and 4 to 6 inches in diameter.

The best protection for Chinese cabbage is to grow it under a floating row cover. This is also a good preventive measure for radish, rutabaga, and turnip, since it is impossible to make individual barriers for these crops. Another way to protect root crops is to sow seeds on the soil surface and mulch with sawdust 1 inch deep and 4 inches beyond the planting. As an alternative to barriers, introduce predatory nematodes into the soil before sowing seeds or transplanting (see page 42).

Diamondback Moth Larva

When you search for insects on cabbage-family crops, you may encounter this relatively minor pest. Small (less than ⅛ inch long) green caterpillars mine the leaves. They chew small irregular holes in the lower surface, often leaving the upper surface intact. The larvae can damage cabbage

heads severely if they get into the heart of the forming head; on plants that have already headed, the caterpillars usually stay on the outer leaves. When disturbed, the caterpillars wiggle vigorously and fall from the plant, hanging by a thread.

A diamond pattern appears on the folded wings of the ⅓-inch-long adult moth; looking down on the moth, you will see a row of three diamond-shaped yellow markings on the brown wings. The moth lays tiny eggs that hatch in 5 to 10 days; the caterpillars feed for 10 days to 4 weeks before pupating. There are four to six generations a year. The moths are believed to migrate northward from southern states in midspring.

Control cabbage-family weeds and get rid of debris from cruciferous crops after harvest. Damage is rarely severe enough for extensive control measures, but you can crush any diamondback moth caterpillars that you see. Many

natural enemies, including ground beetles, true bugs, syrphid fly larvae, lacewing larvae, spiders, and a parasitic wasp, help control this pest. Spray *Bt berliner-kurstake* on the undersides of leaves when larvae are feeding. The pest is also susceptible to sabadilla.

Flea Beetles

Several kinds of flea beetles feed on cruciferous plants. A widespread pest, the *striped flea beetle* makes tiny, round shot holes in leaves, especially on young plants. The 1/12-inch-long shiny black pest has a crooked yellow stripe on each wing cover. Populations of striped flea beetles tend to build up later in summer.

Its life cycle is the same as that of the potato *flea beetle* (see Eggplant), also an occasional cabbage-family pest, except that the adult striped flea beetle gnaws small cavities in a plant stem and lays its eggs there. The larvae are especially damaging to turnip and radish roots. Use the same controls as recommended for the potato flea beetle. If your climate permits two successive

plantings yearly of cruciferous crops, dig under the debris from the first planting right after harvest and don't plant the second crop in the same location.

Another pest, the *sinuate striped flea beetle*, resembles the striped flea beetle but has different habits. It lays eggs on the leaves of cabbage, radish, and turnip. The larvae mine the leaves instead of living on the roots. Control is the same as for other flea beetles. In addition, pick off mined leaves or remove badly infested plants.

The *horseradish flea beetle* feeds on horseradish and mustard. The ⅛-inch-long pest is black with a yellow stripe on each wing cover. It lays eggs on the leaf stems, and the hatching larvae burrow inside to feed.

Harlequin Bug

A problem in the southern half of the United States, the harlequin bug prefers to feed on cruciferous plants, although it sometimes wanders over to asparagus, bean, corn,

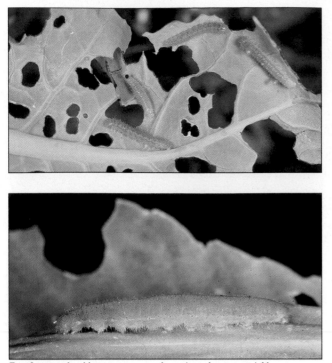

Top: Imported cabbageworms can do serious damage quickly.
Bottom: The green larvae are hard to see against the leaves.

The adult imported cabbageworm is the cabbage white butterfly,
among the few butterflies that are garden pests.

eggplant, lettuce, okra, potato, squash, and sunflower. It may also feed on many ornamental plants as well as citrus, cherry, grape, plum, and other fruit plants.

The flat, shield-shaped, ⅜-inch-long adult, which is black with red markings, damages plants by sucking the sap. The plant wilts and the leaves turn brown. A seriously affected plant may die.

Adults spend the winter around old cabbage stalks and other garden refuse. In spring females lay distinctive eggs, which look like rows of tiny white barrels with black hoops, on the undersides of the leaves. In four to seven days, the eggs hatch into round, wingless black and red young bugs, called nymphs. There are usually three generations a year.

See page 146 for a list of resistant varieties. Clean up plant debris and control weeds after harvest. Twice weekly, inspect cruciferous plants; crush any eggs and handpick any bugs that you see. If the infestation is severe, apply insecticidal soap, pyrethrum, or sabadilla.

Imported Cabbageworm

A general pest of edible as well as ornamental and weedy plants in the cabbage family, the imported cabbageworm is damaging only in the larval stage. The caterpillars chew ragged holes in the leaves of host plants. Sometimes they bore into the base of cabbage heads, leaving piles of green frass on the plants. Young crucifers may be so badly damaged that they are stunted or even killed.

The slow-moving velvety green caterpillar, up to 1¼ inches long, may have alternating light and dark stripes along the length of its body. When disturbed it may exhibit a characteristic waving of the head from side to side, or it may not move much at all. You may mistake a caterpillar for part of a leaf, since it is the same color as cabbage leaf midribs.

This is one of few butterflies whose larvae are pests. The adult has white wings with yellowish undersides. The forewings have black tips and one or two additional black spots. The females, which have two black spots, lay elongated yellow eggs singly on the undersides of lower leaves. The eggs hatch in three to seven days. The larvae feed for two to three weeks and then pupate on a leaf, usually some distance away from the plant on which they were feeding. The insect overwinters as a pupa. There are two or three generations in the North and as many as six in the South.

'Mammoth Red Rock', 'Savoy Chieftain', and 'Savoy Perfection Drumhead' cabbage varieties resist both the imported cabbageworm and the cabbage looper. Twice a week inspect cabbage-family crops; handpick caterpillars and crush any eggs that you find. Protect young plants under a floating row cover. In warm-winter climates the caterpillars can be active all year, except perhaps in the middle of winter. In all other areas, growing cruciferous crops in fall, winter, and early spring may offer some relief.

Natural enemies of the imported cabbageworm include ground beetles, the spined soldier bug, spiders, lacewing larvae, and syrphid fly larvae. Two tiny naturally occurring parasitic wasps and several tachinid fly larvae are also useful in controlling the pest. Polyhedrous granulosis viruses (see *cabbage looper,* page 75) take their toll when the cabbageworm population is large.

The pest is susceptible to *Bt berliner-kurstake*. Spray a plant as soon as you see the caterpillars feeding on it, and repeat every two to three days while the caterpillars are active. Be sure to spray the undersides of leaves. The imported cabbageworm is also susceptible to pyrethrum, sabadilla, and rotenone. After the crop is harvested, destroy remaining stalks and till the soil.

Regularly search cruciferous plants for cabbage loopers as well as imported cabbageworms, diamondback moth larvae, cutworms, slugs,

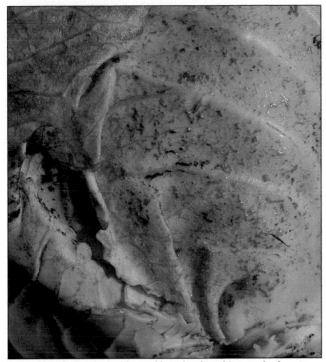

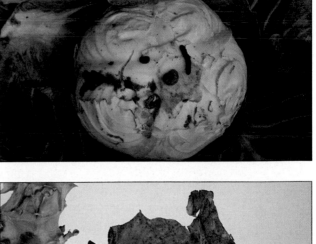

Once onion thrips are inside a cabbage head, nothing can be done to stop the infestation.

Top: Cutworms can eat into the surface of a cabbage head. Bottom: Blackleg damages cabbage leaves and stems.

snails, and aphids. Handpicking is a useful control for all these pests if your planting is small. If you have too many plants to handpick, you can use Bt to kill the caterpillar pests. See individual pest entries for other controls.

Onion Thrips

Although this insect can inflict serious damage on cabbage, there is a good chance your crop will escape infestation. For a complete list of host crops, a description of the pest, and its life cycle, see ONION. On cabbage, onion thrips create silvery patches dotted with small specks of black frass. These damaged areas spread until the whole plant looks silvery. At that point it is likely to turn yellow, then brown, and collapse.

Cabbage harvested before late spring may be out of the garden before the onion thrips becomes active. If cabbage is in the ground after this time, check plants for developing infestations. On young plants, thrips first appear on the

undersides of leaves. Use a hand lens to search for early damage and immature thrips. Be sure to search just before the leaves begin to fold over in the center to form the head. As the head forms, search by lifting back the outermost leaves. Once the thrips are in the head, there is no cure. You may as well pull up the plant and discard it.

See ONION for a list of natural enemies of the onion thrips. A floating row cover may help protect cabbage transplants in late summer and early fall. A strong spray of water may dislodge thrips from young plants. If an infestation is minor and only on the surface of the head, wash off the thrips or agitate the cabbage head in salty water.

ADDITIONAL INSECT AND ANIMAL PESTS

As they march through a garden, hordes of fall *armyworms* (see CORN) may attack cruciferous crops. Black *blister beetles* (see BEET) feed on cabbage and radish. In addition to damaging seedlings, *cutworms* and *earwigs*

(see SEEDLINGS) may eat holes in the leaves of larger cruciferous plants. Cutworms may bore into cabbage heads, and earwigs may hide in the leaves by day and feed on them by night. The *green stinkbug* (see BEAN) occasionally feeds on cabbage, mustard, and turnip. The serpentine *leafminer* (see BEET) may riddle cabbage, cress, and turnip leaves.

The cabbage family may be damaged by root-knot *nematodes* (see BEAN). All crucifers are vulnerable to the Javanese root-knot nematode and the peanut root-knot nematode; turnip may be attacked by the southern root-knot nematode. All cabbage-family crops may also be injured by the *sugar beet cyst nematode* (see BEET) and the closely related cabbage cyst nematode; the latter affects edible and ornamental crucifers. The cabbage family is susceptible to several other nematode species as well.

Rabbits (see SEEDLINGS) feed on seedlings and tender leaves of older plants. *Slugs*

and snails (see SEEDLINGS) may seriously damage young crucifers, and they occasionally injure larger ones. The *tarnished plant bug* (see BEAN) may feed on cabbage-family crops. The *vegetable weevil* (see CARROT) attacks cruciferous plants, and *wireworms* (see POTATO) may tunnel into turnips.

DISEASES

Blackleg

A problem east of the Rocky Mountains, this fungus disease affects all members of the cabbage family, although it is most common on cauliflower, broccoli, brussels sprouts, and cruciferous flowers, including stock and sweet alyssum.

The disease can strike plants at any stage of growth. It can be recognized by an oval brown depression at the base of the stem. The canker enlarges until it encircles the stem. Gray-brown spots develop on the leaves, and soon black dots appear in the stem canker and on the leaf spots. When enough of the stem is destroyed, the plant topples and dies.

V-shaped yellow or brown areas at the leaf edges are a symptom of black rot of cabbage family.

Cabbage yellows causes yellowing of the plant and often curving of the leaf midribs; leaves then die from the base.

Fungal spores quickly spread the disease to other susceptible plants in the garden. The spores are carried by splashing water and by gardeners working among the plants. The spores can live in plant debris for at least three seasons. The disease is also carried on and in seeds; any plant growing from an infected seed is infected too.

Since infected plants cannot be cured, prevention is the key. Obtain seeds—preferably western-grown seeds—from a reputable source. If you doubt the quality of the seeds, soak them for 30 minutes in 122° F water (see page 32). In some areas certified seedlings may be available. Inspect susceptible plants, especially during the rainy season, and remove infected ones at the first sign of disease. Avoid overhead watering and try not to work among wet plants. Clean up plant debris in fall. A three- to four-year rotation is usually enough to control this disease.

Black Rot of Cabbage Family

A problem everywhere except the West, this bacterial disease is most serious on cabbage, broccoli, brussels sprouts, cauliflower, and turnip. Other hosts include collards, kohlrabi, radish, and rutabaga. Infected plants show V-shaped yellow or brown areas at the margins of the leaves, and the veins are blackened. Infected leaves turn yellow and fall off, often leaving a bare stem with only a small tuft of leaves on top. Plants growing from infected seeds are stunted. Plants infected later may show symptoms on only one side of the plant. If you cut across the stem, you will see a black ring. Although black rot infection is dry and odorless, diseased plants often develop soft, foul-smelling secondary decays.

The bacterium causing black rot is spread by seed, infected plant debris, soil, and water. It survives much better in plant debris than in soil. The disease is favored by warm, humid conditions and is less likely to spread during dry weather.

Controls are the same as for blackleg (see page 79). Cabbage seeds should be soaked for 25 minutes, and broccoli, cauliflower, and collard seeds for 18 minutes in 122° F water. Resistant cabbage varieties include 'Blueboy', 'Blue Vantage', 'Custodian', 'Defender', 'Genesis', 'Green Cup', 'Guardian', 'Lariat', 'Regal Red', 'Solid Blue Brand', and 'Supermarket'. 'Emperor', 'Shogun', and 'Sprinter' are resistant broccoli varieties, and 'White Contessa' is a resistant cauliflower variety.

Cabbage Yellows

Also called fusarium yellows wilt, this fungus disease may be the most destructive pest of susceptible crucifers in the Midwest and perhaps elsewhere. Race 1 strikes cabbage, kale, and kohlrabi more severely; broccoli, brussels sprouts, and cauliflower are fairly resistant. Race 2 affects radish.

Diseased plants take on a lifeless yellow-green cast, which is often more obvious on one side of the plant. The stem or the midribs of lower leaves may develop a pronounced curve. Starting at the base the plant turns yellow and then brown. The yellowing begins at the base of the leaves and not in the margins, as is typical of black rot (see at left). The plant may die, although sometimes cool weather prompts a partial recovery. Once a plant is infected, it rarely makes a good crop. Cutting across the stem or leaves reveals darkened water-conducting tissue.

This fungus disease is caused by a fusarium variety that is closely related to the ones that affect tomato, bean, and other crops (see *fusarium wilt of tomato,* under TOMATO; and *dry root rot of beans,* under BEAN.) The fungal spores causing this disease can live in the soil for many years in the absence of a host plant. The fungus grows most actively when soil temperatures are 80° to 90° F. Soil moisture and pH have little effect on its growth, but a potassium

These cauliflower roots show typical evidence of clubroot. Before buying or planting seedlings, check for symptoms.

Yellow streaks on this cabbage lower leaf are caused by cabbage black ring spot virus, which is spread by aphids.

deficiency is thought to favor infection. The disease is spread by spores on tools and by infected transplants, soil, and plant debris. It is not transmitted by seed.

Grow your own seedlings or purchase certified seedlings if they are available. Make sure that plants receive adequate fertilizer, particularly potassium. Resistant varieties are the best control once the fungus has entered your soil. See page 146 for a list of resistant cabbage varieties. Resistant radish varieties include 'Dandy', 'Fancy Red', 'Far Red', 'Fuego', 'Red Pak', 'Red Prince', and 'Scarlet Knight'. The only other hope of escaping infection is to grow susceptible crops when soil temperatures are cool.

Clubroot

This common fungus disease affects cabbage and most other cruciferous crops. Turnip and radish tend to be resistant. Since there are many races of the disease, crops may respond differently in different locations.

The roots of affected plants are thickened, in some cases becoming grotesquely club shaped. Eventually, the roots rot. Usually, the first noticeable symptoms are wilting on a warm day and some yellowing leaves. By this time the roots are severely damaged. Young plants become stunted and may die. More mature plants may survive, but they will not produce a harvestable crop.

The fungal spores can survive in soil for at least seven years, germinating best in acid soil. The spores are spread by contaminated soil, manure, water, and tools. The disease is not transmitted by seed.

Grow your own seedlings or purchase certified seedlings if they are available. If not, check the roots for abnormal thickening before buying plants. Don't bring in soil or manure from infected areas. Plant in well-drained soil. Get rid of mustard-family weeds and other plants known to harbor the disease. Raise the pH of infected soil to 7.2, using both ground limestone and

hydrated lime, since limestone alone will not prevent the disease. Obtain a soil test and ask for recommendations for changing the pH of your soil.

Look for resistant varieties. Because there are so many strains of the fungus, you may have to find locally resistant varieties. Plan as long a rotation as possible for cruciferous crops. If clubroot infects your soil, a rotation that separates susceptible crops by seven years may be necessary. Dig up infected plants carefully, getting as much of the root as possible, and destroy them.

OTHER DISEASES

Cruciferous plants are susceptible to *beet curly top virus* (see TOMATO), which is spread by leafhoppers. Aphids transmit several viruses to cabbage-family crops. Perhaps the most serious is *cabbage black ring spot,* also known as turnip mosaic virus. Yellow and green mottling and leaf distortion may occur anywhere on brussels

sprouts, cauliflower, Chinese cabbage, mustard, radish, and turnip. On cabbage these symptoms may occur only on the lower leaves. Black spots may appear in cabbage heads or anywhere on cauliflower and brussels sprouts. These spots may not be present on cabbage heads at harvest but may appear as long as two to five months into storage. To control the virus you must contain cabbage and green peach aphids (for general information on controlling aphids, see page 63) and remove diseased plants from the garden. Also control cabbage-family weeds, since they serve as reservoirs for this and other viruses.

Radish, rutabaga, and turnip are susceptible to *potato scab* (see POTATO), which is best controlled by rotation away from susceptible crops. Do not lower the soil pH as much as you would for potato; lower than 5.5 is considered too acidic for radish and turnip, and lower than 6.0 is too acidic for rutabaga. *Powdery mildew* (see BEAN) may damage cabbage-family plants.

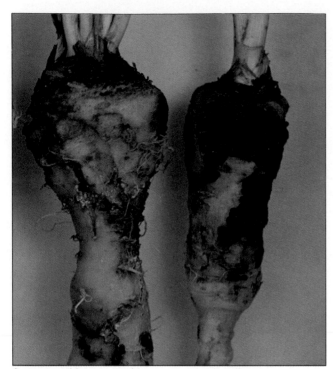

Carrot weevil larvae tunnel in carrot roots primarily near the soil surface.

Top: Carrot rust fly larvae damage carrot roots.
Bottom: Parsleyworms are the larvae of a striking butterfly.

White rot, caused by the same fungus that induces *lettuce drop* (see LETTUCE), attacks cabbage, Chinese cabbage, and other crucifers. Look for the typical cottony white mold followed by hard black spore capsules on the dead leaves.

CARROT

INSECT AND OTHER ANIMAL PESTS

Carrot Rust Fly
This insect is particularly destructive in the Northeast and on the West Coast. The larvae feed on carrot, celery, celeriac, parsley, and parsnip. They also attack carrot-family weeds, including Queen-Anne's-lace and wild parsnip.

The larvae feed by tunneling in the roots. The tunnels may be completely inside the roots or they may run along the surface. A rust-colored frass is visible in the tunnels, and you may see narrow, legless cream-colored larvae, up to ⅓ inch long. The roots may decay due to secondary infection by soilborne diseases.

The insect overwinters in the soil as a small brown pupa. In late spring tiny flies emerge and lay eggs in the soil next to susceptible plants. The eggs hatch in 7 to 10 days and the larvae begin to feed on the root. An infestation may kill young carrots or leave them forked and misshapen. After feeding for approximately a month, the insect spends the next month as a pupa. A second generation of the pest inflicts damage in late summer.

Deter the pest by controlling carrot-family weeds. Till the garden in fall and early spring and don't leave carrots in the ground over the winter. Schedule carrot plantings to avoid the egg-laying periods of the fly. In cold-winter areas sow seeds after the first egg-laying period and harvest early, before the second generation of adults lays eggs. In mild-winter areas plant in late winter and harvest before the first flies emerge, or plant in late summer after the second generation of flies has laid eggs. If the crop is in the ground during an egg-laying period, protect it by growing it under a floating row cover. If you are planting when the pest is likely to be active, apply predatory nematodes (see page 42) at seeding time.

Carrot Weevil
A pest from New England to Georgia and west to Colorado, this beetle feeds on carrot, dill, celery, parsley, carrot-family weeds, dock, and plantain.

The larval form of the insect is the most destructive, making zigzag tunnels in the upper part of the root. The tunnels are wider than those made by the carrot rust fly (see at left). You may see stout, legless white larvae feeding in the cavities.

The adult carrot weevil hibernates in grass and debris, emerging in April or May to feed. The insect is slightly longer than ¼ inch and has a snout and a dome-shaped back that is brownish with black spots. After minor feeding on leaves and stems, the adults lay eggs on the stems. After hatching, the larvae move to the roots to feed for two to four weeks. Then they pupate

in the soil and emerge as adults in July. The adults lay eggs to begin a second generation, which survives in all regions except those with very short summers. The adult generation that survived the previous winter also continues to lay eggs until mid-August, so that all stages of the insect are usually present during the summer.

Contain the pest by rotating susceptible crops, controlling host weeds in and near the garden, and removing infested debris. If the weevil has been a problem in the past, apply predatory nematodes to the soil at planting time (see page 42), or protect young carrot plantings under a floating row cover. Be sure to tuck the edges well into the soil.

Parsleyworm
Although a minor pest the parsleyworm can cause alarm when found feeding on carrot, celery, dill, parsley, and parsnip. The 2-inch-long, smooth-skinned caterpillar has clearly defined bands of black and yellow. When disturbed it sticks out two forked orange

Top: The vegetable weevil is a night-feeding insect.
Bottom: Both the adult and larva, shown here, eat foliage.

Alternaria lesions begin on older carrot leaves.

Cercospora lesions appear on carrot leaves and stems.

horns and emits a sickeningly sweet smell. The insect feeds on leaves, occasionally stripping plants.

The caterpillar is the larva of the black swallowtail butterfly, a yellow and black insect with black lobes, or swallowtails, projecting from the rear of the wings. The adult lays eggs singly on plants. After hatching, the larvae feed for 10 days to several weeks. The adult butterflies survive the winter in the South; in colder climates the pest overwinters as pupae on host plants.

Handpicking is usually sufficient control. In the unlikely event that the pest requires large-scale control, spray Bt when the larvae are small.

Vegetable Weevil

A problem in California and the Gulf states, this night-feeding beetle attacks mainly carrot, potato, spinach, tomato, and turnip. It may also feed on beet, cabbage, cauliflower, lettuce, mustard, onion, radish, Swiss chard, and dichondra.

Both adults and larvae damage plants by chewing the

leaves. There may be small holes in the leaves, or the entire plant may be defoliated. The ⅜-inch-long adult, which has a downturned snout, is buff with a V-shaped lighter marking at the end of the wing covers. The larva, also ⅜ inch long, is green and legless.

Originally from Brazil the pest is active in winter and dormant in summer. The adult rests in debris or under tree bark from late April or early May until early fall. It feeds and lays eggs through the winter except during the coldest weather.

Infestations take hold gradually and spread slowly because the insect is slow moving and rarely flies. Persistence pays off in efforts to control the pest. During daytime in fall and winter, handpick any adults or larvae that you find on the ground or in debris. Dig deep after harvest to destroy pupae in the soil, and rotate susceptible crops with nonsusceptible ones. Eliminate hiding places in summer by cleaning up garden debris. Apply predatory nematodes (see page 42) in

fall when temperatures are still warm and larvae begin to appear on crops. An old recipe for controlling the vegetable weevil is a bait consisting of 1 pound wheat bran mixed with a scant ⅓ cup molasses; this is enough to treat one-third acre. If the pest is numerous, apply pyrethrum or rotenone.

ADDITIONAL INSECT AND ANIMAL PESTS

The *aster leafhopper* (see LETTUCE) siphons sap from the leaves, transmitting the virus disease aster yellows as it feeds. The black *blister beetle* (see BEET) chews irregular holes in the leaves. Both palestriped and potato *flea beetles* (see EGGPLANT) feed on carrot.

Carrot is susceptible to many types of root-knot *nematodes* (see BEAN). In the North the northern root-knot nematode is a particularly serious pest on carrot crops, especially those grown in muck soils. Damage is scattered throughout the planting. Affected plants are stunted, the leaves

are pale and often wilted, and numerous galls appear where nematodes penetrated the root. Above the galls the carrot typically forms clumps of hairy roots. Often, the edible root is forked, knobby, and misshapen. Masses of soil cling to the roots when they are pulled. Rotate carrot, growing resistant crops for at least two years to break the cycle.

DISEASES

Blights of Carrot

Carrot is subject to two types of blight: alternaria leaf blight, which affects carrots and parsley, and cercospora leaf blight, which affects only carrot. Both are fungus diseases.

Alternaria leaf blight usually attacks older leaves. The disease causes the leaf margins to turn brown, and these lesions spread into irregular shapes. Often, the leaves shrivel and die. There may be dark brown to black areas of firm, shallow decay on the edible carrot root.

Cercospora leaf blight usually attacks younger leaves

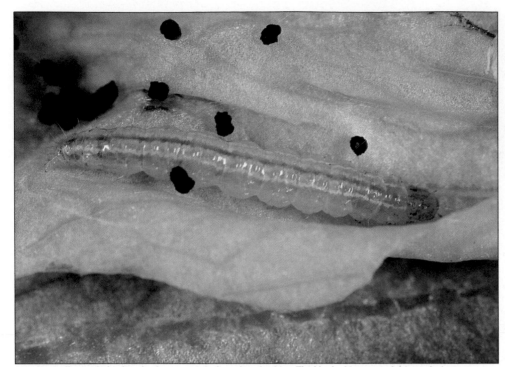

If you unroll a curled celery leaf, you may find a celery leaftier. The black objects are the insect's frass.

Celery is among the many crops damaged by the cabbage looper.

first. Lesions appear on the leaf margins, sometimes causing the leaves to curl. Roughly circular tan to black spots soon appear on the leaves and stems. Although cercospora leaf blight may kill the foliage, it does not affect the root.

The spores of both blights are spread by seed and infected plant debris. Alternaria leaf blight, which is favored by cool weather, is most severe in fall. Cercospora leaf blight is favored by hot, humid weather and thus is likely to appear in mid- to late summer.

Obtain carrot seeds from a reputable source. If you have any doubt, soak the seeds for 20 minutes in 126° F water (see page 32). Use a three-year rotation for carrot crops and plant resistant varieties. 'Chancellor', 'Chantenay', 'Chantenay Andina', and 'Red Core Chantenay' resist both blights. Alternaria leaf blight is less likely to attack if carrots are well fertilized; a booster application of nitrogen fertilizer when the crop is partly grown may impede the disease. Avoid overhead

watering and try not to work among wet plants. Remove diseased leaves or plants and dig under any debris after the fall harvest. Spraying with a fixed copper fungicide may prevent blight.

OTHER DISEASES

In carrots *aster yellows* (see LETTUCE) causes dwarfed yellowish leaves usually arranged in a tight rosette. The root is deformed and covered with many hairlike roots; it has a bitter taste. Resistant carrot varieties include 'Chantenay', 'Hicolor 9', 'Royal', and 'Scarlet Nantes'.

Potato scab (see POTATO) can also mar carrot roots. Rotation away from susceptible crops is an effective control. Lowering the soil pH is not a practical control, since carrot grows best in slightly acidic soil—between pH 6.0 and 6.5. When carrot is infected by *sclerotinia rot* (see *lettuce drop* under LETTUCE), the leaf stems turn dark brown and collapse. Under moist conditions a cottony

white mold appears on the infected parts. The infection usually spreads to the root and continues to develop in storage. Oval black sporing bodies grow in the cottony mold on stored carrots.

CELERY (AND CELERIAC)

INSECT AND OTHER ANIMAL PESTS

Celery Leaftier

A major pest of celery, this destructive caterpillar also attacks bean, beet, cabbage, cucumber, kale, lettuce, parsley, pea, and spinach. It feeds on many ornamentals, including ageratum, chrysanthemum, ivy, nasturtium, rose, sweet pea, and snapdragon.

The celery leaftier is the larva of a night-flying moth, which lays eggs on the undersides of leaves, usually near the ground. The larva begins as a pale green caterpillar, then turns yellow with a green and white stripe down the back. It chews holes in leaves and tunnels in the stalks. The insect earned the name

leaftier from its habit of folding and tying leaves together with webbing. It hides inside and feeds on the leaf. When disturbed the caterpillar wriggles in its web or drops to the ground. The celery leaftier completes its life cycle in about 40 days, and there may be as many as six generations a season in warm-winter climates.

Handpick the occasional leaftier, tied leaf and all. If the pest is numerous, use Bt; it is most effective when sprayed on young caterpillars. Dust heavily infested plants with pyrethrum, then repeat in one hour. The first application will flush the leaftiers from their webs, and the second application will kill them. After an infestation dig under the plant debris.

ADDITIONAL INSECT AND ANIMAL PESTS

Aphids, particularly the green peach aphid (see SPINACH), are serious pests of celery. They suck plant sap from the stalks and the undersides of the

Top: Early blight of celery causes rounded brown leaf spots.
Bottom: Celery late blight spots are brown with black dots.

Pink or white cottony growth on decayed tissue at the base of a celery plant indicates pink rot.

leaves, and they spread virus diseases.

The *cabbage looper* (see CABBAGE FAMILY) may damage the leaves but usually does not injure the stalks directly. Still, heavy infestations can reduce plant vigor. Since the caterpillar is more susceptible to Bt and insecticides when it is young, the timing of sprays is important.

The *carrot rust fly* and the *carrot weevil* (see CARROT) may cause serious damage to celery. Both feed on celery roots, stunting and sometimes killing the plant. The potato *flea beetle* (see EGGPLANT) chews tiny holes in celery leaves, and the potato *leafhopper* (see POTATO) spreads the virus disease aster yellows to celery.

Among the *nematodes* (see BEAN) that may damage celery are the cotton root-knot nematode and the northern root-knot nematode. Celery is also vulnerable to many other nematodes, whose identification requires help from a nematology laboratory.

The *onion thrips* (see ON-ION) may damage celery, leaving unsightly whitened areas on the stalks. The *parsley-worm* (see CARROT) is an occasional pest of celery. The toxic saliva of the *tarnished plant bug* (see BEAN) will kill celery stalk tissue—a condition known as black joint of celery. *Slugs and snails* (see SEEDLINGS) often damage plants by gouging out channels in the stalks, and the *two-spotted mite* (see BEAN) causes harm by sucking sap from celery leaves.

DISEASES

Blights of Celery
Two types of fungal blights—*early blight of celery* and *celery late blight*—affect celery and celeriac. Also known as cercospora blight, early blight of celery produces small round yellow-brown spots first on the older leaves and then on the stalks. Celery late blight, also called septoria blight, produces light yellow spots that turn grayish brown with black dots; the leaves may turn dark brown and rot.

The spores of both blights are transmitted by seed and infected plant debris. Wind, water, and gardeners spread the spores rapidly from infected plants to healthy ones. Early blight is favored by warm, moist weather and late blight by cool, moist weather.

Use seeds more than two years old, since any disease spores will have died by then. As an alternative, soak seeds for 30 minutes in 118° F water (see page 32). As soon as you notice symptoms on growing plants, remove the infected plants or spray with a fixed copper fungicide. Rotate crops and plant resistant varieties. 'Early Belle', 'Emerson Pascal', and 'June Belle' resist early blight; 'Emerson Pascal' resists late blight.

OTHER DISEASES
Celery is susceptible to *aster yellows* (see LETTUCE), a virus disease that causes yellowed leaves and twisted, malformed new growth. Resistant varieties include 'Florida Golden', 'Forbes Golden Plume', and 'Michigan Golden'.

Pink rot (see *lettuce drop*, under LETTUCE) is caused by the same fungi that produce white mold of bean and a host of other diseases. In celery, water-soaked spots form at the base of the stalks, followed by cottony white to pink growth. The stalks rot and taste bitter. In moist conditions, tiny black structures grow in the mold.

CORN

INSECT AND OTHER ANIMAL PESTS

Aphids
Of the several aphids that may feed on corn, the corn leaf aphid and the corn root aphid are the most damaging.

Although widespread, the *corn leaf aphid* is more prevalent in the South. Small bluish green aphids feed in masses on the leaves and the upper part of the stalk and tassel of corn. In the tassel the honeydew produced by the aphids interferes with pollination and attracts the corn earworm moth (see page 87). For more information about aphids

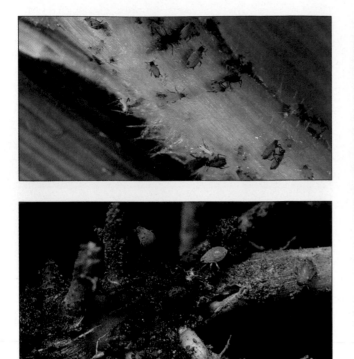

Top: The corn leaf aphid feeds in tassels as well as leaves.
Bottom: Corn root aphids are captured and tended by ants.

The armyworm travels in large numbers, feeding on corn and grass. It spends nights in the soil at the base of plants.

and ways to control them, see *aphids* under BEAN. Generally, the best way to combat the corn leaf aphid is to plant early and provide good growing conditions.

The *corn root aphid* feeds on the roots of corn, beet, and carrot. Other hosts include clover, cotton, grasses, smartweed, and some annual and perennial flowers. Affected plants turn yellow, stop growing, and wilt on sunny days. If you look at the roots, you will see many tiny, powdery bluegreen aphids. Usually, ants are present.

The corn root aphid depends on ants for its survival. The ants collect the aphid eggs in fall and store them in their nests. In spring they carry the eggs to smartweed or grass roots and allow the aphids to complete two or three generations. Then they carry the aphids to corn roots for the summer. When any winged aphids appear, the ants capture them and carry them underground.

The best way to suppress the corn root aphid is to control ants. Set out a boric acid

bait, such as Drax®, in a covered container. For an effective homemade bait station, dribble some bait into a soft drink can and lay it on its side.

Armyworms
Several types of armyworms march through gardens and cornfields, devouring corn and other crops in their line of march. Among the most destructive of these insects are the fall armyworm and the armyworm (*Pseudaletia unipuncta*).

A common pest east of the Rocky Mountains except in extreme northern areas, the *fall armyworm* prefers grasses; its second choice is corn. Of other crops it is most likely to injure lettuce and the cabbage family. It may also feed on bean, cowpea, cucumber, peanut, and tomato.

The fall armyworm acts much like the corn earworm (see opposite page), feeding in the leaf whorls and later eating into ears of corn. It enters the ear from the side as well as the tip, whereas the corn earworm enters only through

the tip. Several fall armyworm larvae may be present in a single ear, whereas only one corn earworm larva usually feeds in an ear.

Although feeding in the leaf whorls can damage or kill the growing point, corn usually outgrows the damage inflicted by the fall armyworm. The 1½-inch-long caterpillar has light green and black stripes and a black head with an inverted white Y. It feeds primarily at night and hides in the plant during the day.

The fall armyworm is so named because it doesn't reach the northern part of its range until fall. It overwinters as a pupa in the South, then migrates northward as an adult. The adult is a night-flying grayish brown moth with a 1½-inch wingspan. One moth lays fifty to several hundred eggs.

The pest is more numerous in years with a cold, wet spring. At these times they may converge in hordes, or armies, and injure many kinds of crops. Because they begin feeding near the ground, they may escape notice until damage is severe. After feeding for

1 to 2 weeks, the caterpillars fall to the ground and pupate for 10 days to 2 weeks. In the North, where pupae are killed by frost, there may be only one complete generation; in the South there may be several generations.

Control grassy weeds, since infestations most often start there. In cold-winter areas early plantings may escape the pest. Farmers usually take action when more than 15 percent of young plants show damage in the leaf whorls. Granular and liquid forms of Bt, particularly Javelin®, will kill the larvae, but it must be applied during the two- to three-week period when the caterpillars are young and feeding actively. In the South turn over the soil after harvest to expose pupae to their natural enemies.

A widespread pest that is more damaging east of the Rocky Mountains, the *armyworm* appears periodically, especially during years with a cold spring. It has a stronger

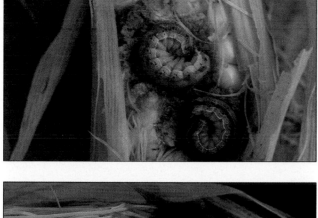

Top: More than one fall armyworm commonly feeds in an ear.
Bottom: An ear usually contains only one corn earworm.

The corn earworm adult is a yellowish brown moth. A night flier, it is attracted by lights left on near the garden.

preference than the fall armyworm for corn and grains, so that other crops are not as endangered by this pest. The caterpillar is smooth, about 1½ inches long, and greenish with stripes down the back. There are two or three generations a year in the North. Since the armyworm overwinters in northern climates, its larvae hatch earlier there than do the larvae of the fall armyworm. The first generation often demolishes small corn plants. Unlike the fall armyworm, the armyworm hides in the soil during the day.

Control measures for both insects are similar: Get rid of grassy weeds, apply Bt, and turn over the soil after an infestation. Natural enemies of the armyworm include tachinid flies, wasplike egg parasites, birds, skunks, and toads.

Dig a furrow or ditch to hinder both types of caterpillars. The ditch should be at least 6 inches deep, with the steeper side toward the plot that you are protecting. Keep a layer of loose soil on the surface of the ditch, so that the worms will have trouble

crawling out. Handpick and crush the worms.

Corn Earworm

This caterpillar is a serious pest of corn and tomato; when it appears on tomato, it is known as the tomato fruitworm. The insect also injures bean, cabbage, eggplant, okra, pea, peanut, pepper, pumpkin, squash, and sunflower. Nearby alfalfa, cotton, and tobacco crops may harbor the pest.

The corn earworm is most often discovered near the tip of a mature corn ear, eating kernels of corn. Earlier in the season the earworm feeds in the center of the plant, eating young leaves. The caterpillar is about 1½ inches long at maturity and is green, brown, or pink with light stripes on the sides and back.

Pupae, which overwinter 2 to 6 inches below the soil surface, usually survive only in the southern half of the United States. A night-flying yellowish brown moth with mottled wings emerges in spring and lays yellow eggs

singly on the undersides of the leaves and on the corn silks. In 2 to 10 days the eggs hatch into caterpillars, which feed on the silks and then the kernels. Usually, there is one caterpillar per ear. The moths migrate northward in the summer and lay eggs on corn in northern states.

Some home gardeners ignore the earworm; they plant extra corn and cut the ends off damaged ears. However, there are many ways to control the pest. In warm-winter areas till the soil in fall to kill the pupae or expose them to predators. Avoid the pest by planting as early as possible in the North and in other areas where pupae have been killed. Where the earworm survives the winter, early and late plantings are vulnerable, but there may be a window of reduced predation.

Don't leave lights on at night near the corn patch, because these will attract the moths. Controlling the corn leaf aphid (see page 85) will also help, since the honeydew produced by the aphid attracts earworm moths.

You can attach a clothespin or rubber band to the top of the ear after the tips of the silks have turned brown to close off entry to the earworm, or you can plant a variety with a naturally tight husk. These include 'Calumet', 'Country Gentleman', 'Golden Security', 'Iona', 'Seneca Scout', 'Silver Cross Bantam', 'Silvergent', 'Staygold', and 'Victory Golden'. Corn varieties with purple silks will give you a clearer view of the eggs and help you time treatments.

Mineral oil is another effective preventive. Inject 20 drops of oil into the tip of each ear, three to seven days after the corn silk has formed or when the tip of the silk has begun to turn brown. Don't use the oil when the temperature exceeds 90° F. Timing is critical: Applied too soon the oil will interfere with pollination; applied too late, the worm will already be inside.

Pheromone traps will tell you when moths have arrived

Top: Southern corn rootworm larvae, not adults, feed on corn.
Bottom: Corn flea beetles spread bacterial wilt of corn.

Rotation of corn controls northern corn rootworms (top) and western corn rootworms (bottom). The adults are shown here.

and egg laying is about to begin. You can release trichogramma wasps and lacewings, which prey on earworm eggs. Bt will kill young caterpillars; apply a dust form to the silks as soon as the first silks appear and repeat every few days until all the silks have turned brown.

If you begin to see frass, indicating that earworms have already entered the ears, you can inject predatory nematodes into the husks with a garden syringe. The nematodes will kill earworms within 48 hours of application.

Corn Flea Beetle
The shiny black corn flea beetle feeds only on corn. It inflicts direct damage early in the season, when plants are small and growing conditions are poor. This direct damage is minor compared to the beetle's role in spreading bacterial wilt of corn (see page 91). When corn flea beetles emerge from hibernation, as many as 20 percent of the insects are carriers of the disease. Once a healthy beetle feeds on an infected plant, the beetle becomes a carrier too.

Although palestriped and potato *flea beetles* (see EGG-PLANT) and the *sweet potato flea beetle* (see SWEET POTATO) may feed on corn, they do not spread bacterial wilt.

Corn Rootworms
Several kinds of corn rootworms, also called spotted cucumber beetles when they feed on cucurbit crops, attack corn. They are found in various regions of the United States.

The *southern corn rootworm* is a pest east of the Rocky Mountains, although it is most common in the South. The larva injures the roots and stems of corn and bean; it also feeds on grass roots. The adult beetle feeds on the leaves of many plants but not corn. The larva bores into the crown (where the stem and root meet) of young corn plants, causing the central bud to die. The plant either falls over or becomes stunted and yellowed. Larger plants lean at the base.

Rotate corn and bean together, and control nearby wild grasses. Plant early, so that the corn plants develop an extensive root system before the rootworm begins to feed. Fertilize and water adequately. Pyrethrum, sabadilla, or rotenone, applied weekly beginning when the seedlings emerge, will help control the pest. Adding predatory nematodes to the soil when you plant will reduce the numbers of larvae (see page 42). If a corn plant is injured despite your efforts, pile soil around the base to keep the plant upright until harvest.

The *northern corn rootworm*, a similar pest from New York to Colorado, is a particular problem in the Upper Mississippi Valley. The ¼-inch-long beetle resembles other corn rootworm and cucumber beetle adults. The young adult starts out pale cream or light brown and turns an overall yellowish green. The larvae live only on corn roots, then pupate in the soil. In late July and August, the new generation of adults emerges and feeds on corn silk

and the pollen of many other kinds of plants. The beetles lay eggs in the cornfields and die with the first frost. Rotating corn with any other crops will reduce damage, since this rootworm must complete its life cycle on corn. Controls for the southern corn rootworm are also effective on this pest.

The *western corn rootworm* is a major pest of corn in the High Plains area, from the northern panhandle of Texas to the Dakotas. Recently, it has spread eastward to Ohio and Michigan. The adult beetle is yellow with black stripes on each wing cover. The stripes are variable, ranging from thin streaks to bands so wide that they cover nearly the whole wing. Overwintering eggs hatch in late May or June. The larvae feed on corn roots until early July, then pupate in the soil. The adults, which emerge from mid-July until September, feed on the silks, tassels, pollen, and leaves of corn as well as on the pollen of cucurbits. As summer ends, the

Unlike corn earworms, which enter the ear only at the tip, European corn borer larvae can enter at any point.

A European corn borer larva is feeding in the tassel.

Shred cornstalks to kill European corn borer pupae.

adults lay eggs under the soil. As with the northern corn rootworm, rotating corn is an effective control. The controls for the southern corn rootworm will also work on this insect.

Two other similar pests, the *striped cucumber beetle* and the *western striped cucumber beetle* (see CUCURBITS), feed on the leaves and pollen of corn but do not damage corn roots. The adults eat corn, bean, and pea leaves as well as flowers and pollen from these and other plants. The larvae of these beetles live only on the roots of cucurbits.

European Corn Borer

A pest throughout the United States, except in Florida and the Far West, this insect prefers sweet corn, although it also feeds on bean, beet, celery, eggplant, lettuce, pepper, potato, tomato, many flowers, small-grain crops, and weeds.

Usually the first sign of damage is a shot-hole pattern in the leaf whorls of early corn crops, followed by boring into the leaf midrib or the stalk. Later in summer, the damage is mainly from boring into the cornstalk, tassel, ear shank, and ear. Ears may fall off or the entire plant may collapse. You will see entry holes with sawdustlike frass at the openings. A stalk damaged by the European corn borer usually breaks partway up rather than near the base, as does a stalk damaged by corn rootworms (see opposite page).

The larval stage of the corn borer does the damage. Up to 1 inch long, the larva is a pale pink or brown caterpillar with rows of small brown spots and a brown head. The caterpillar spends the winter in corn stubble and pupates in spring. Depending on the strain of insect, there may be one, two, or three generations. The first-generation adults are most likely to emerge from late May through early June, and this strain produces a second generation in August. The caterpillars that hatch from eggs laid by the second generation feed for a while, then overwinter to become the adults of the first generation

in spring. In July the single-generation strain emerges as adults and lays eggs; after hatching, the caterpillars feed, bore into the stalk, overwinter, pupate in spring, and emerge as adults the following July. The adult is a mainly night-flying yellowish brown moth with a 1-inch wingspan.

The adults lay egg masses mainly on the undersides of corn leaves. The eggs, which hatch in four to nine days, start out white and turn cream, then orange-tan. Finally, they darken as the dark heads of the caterpillars become visible through the shells. The black head stage indicates that the eggs will hatch in about 36 hours. The first-generation caterpillars feed only on corn leaves and stalks; later generations feed on pollen, stalks, and ears. Unlike the corn earworm (see page 87), which enters the ear only through the tip, the European corn borer may enter from the base, side, or tip.

Shred and dig under all of last year's cornstalks in fall or early spring. Although this will kill many larvae, it won't

reduce infestations if there is a nearby reservoir of overwintering caterpillars. Controlling spring and summer weeds will reduce the food supply for first-generation caterpillars and provide less cover for egg-laying moths.

Consult the local cooperative extension office to find out which strain of European corn borer you have, when they usually emerge, and which corn varieties are most resistant in your area. Schedule plantings to avoid damage. Corn planted in mid-May is often unaffected when first-generation adults emerge in late May to early June, since the moths prefer taller corn. Caterpillars that hatch on corn less than 16 inches high (measured from the ground to the top leaf held upright) often languish. If you are planting corn after the first wave of moths, plant a short-season variety that will mature before the second wave begins.

Several naturally occurring predators will kill eggs and caterpillars. A tachinid fly

If Japanese beetles destroy the corn silks before the corn is fertilized, kernels won't form.

Silky webbing and sawdustlike frass indicate where common stalk borers have entered corn stems.

parasitizes the larvae. Among the purchased controls are lady beetles and trichogramma wasps, which feed on the eggs. Lacewings feed on the eggs and very young larvae.

Begin to search for first-generation caterpillars when the corn is 16 to 22 inches high (measured from the ground to the top leaf held upright). When most of the eggs have hatched and shot-hole feeding has begun, apply *Bt berliner-kurstake* bait granules. Be sure to get the bait into the base of the leaves. As an alternative, spray with ryania, making sure to coat the undersides of leaves and any crevices. Generally, two applications of either control must be used on second- and third-generation caterpillars. Begin applications when the eggs hatch and caterpillars are visible on the leaf axils. Repeat in a week if more eggs are seen.

Once a caterpillar has bored into the stalk or ear, it is protected from predators and insecticides, although handpicking is an effective control in a small garden. Slit the stalk lengthwise just below the entry hole and remove the caterpillar.

Japanese Beetle
A pest from southern Maine to Georgia and west to the Mississippi River and Iowa, the Japanese beetle is highly destructive in both the larval and adult stages. The larvae feed on the roots of many vegetable crops, including corn, asparagus, bean, beet, onion, and tomato. The adults feed on aboveground parts of deciduous ornamentals and vegetables, particularly corn, asparagus, bean, okra, and rhubarb. They chew on the silks and leaves of corn.

You are most likely to see the adults, which feed by day and are most active during warm, sunny weather. The beetles are just under ½ inch long and are oval and bright metallic green with coppery wing covers. They feed from approximately late June to October, peaking in numbers in July. Toward the end of summer, they lay eggs under

lawn grasses. The larvae, up to 1 inch long and usually found in a curved position, are grayish white with a brown head. They feed on grass roots until the weather turns cold, then dig deeper to avoid freezing. In spring they resume feeding, then pupate in May or June.

If only a few adult Japanese beetles are present, handpick them. Do it early in the day, before they are active. If you use pheromone traps, place them well away from your garden or your neighbors' gardens, or they will attract more beetles than they kill. Pyrethrum dust and rotenone spray are effective controls for adult beetles.

Milky spore disease, which you can purchase and apply to a lawn in spring or fall, offers long-term control by infecting and killing larvae. Not completely effective the first year, it works best if neighbors cooperate and apply it to lawns throughout the area. Predatory nematodes, applied in mid-spring or late summer, are another good way to combat larvae (see page 42). Use 50,000 nematodes per foot of

garden row or square foot of lawn.

Stalk Borers
A pest east of the Rocky Mountains, the *common stalk borer* prefers corn and giant ragweed but will feed on any plant with a large, soft stem. Among the vegetables it may attack are asparagus, pepper, potato, rhubarb, and tomato.

The larvae, caterpillars up to 1 inch long, chew a ragged pattern in corn leaves, often curling or distorting them. Affected plants do not produce ears. The caterpillars also bore into stems, leaving a silky webbing and sawdustlike frass in the entry holes. When very small seedlings are infested, the symptom is often a wilting of the two center leaves. The young caterpillar can be recognized by a dark brown or purple band around its midsection. When fully grown it is an overall gray or light purple.

The eggs overwinter on weeds, especially giant ragweed. After hatching, the caterpillars feed on corn leaves and enter the stalk, burrowing

Raccoons often knock over corn plants in the process of pulling off the ears and eating the kernels.

Although bacterial wilt can arise from infected seeds, it is much more likely to be spread by corn flea beetles.

upward. They come out of the stalk, form pupae, and fall to the ground. In late summer and early fall, grayish brown moths emerge and lay eggs on weeds and grasses.

Control nearby weeds, especially giant ragweed and other weeds with large, soft stems. Check corn seedlings for signs of damage and remove infested plants. You may as well remove the plant once the caterpillar is inside the stalk, although it is sometimes possible to slit the stem, remove the pest, and bind the stem back together with plastic garden tape or old nylon stockings. Lady beetles and ground beetles are the most important native predators, and several fly and wasp parasites may also attack the caterpillars.

The *lesser cornstalk borer,* a similar pest in the southern and Middle Atlantic states, is a bluish green caterpillar with brown stripes. Controlling its favorite weed host, Johnson grass, will help reduce the borer population. The insect may also attack bean, cowpea, pea, peanut,

turnip, crabgrass, and wheat. It injures corn by feeding on the leaves, then entering the stalk about 2 inches above the ground and feeding for about three weeks. One caterpillar can damage or kill several plants. There are two or more generations a summer. A plant is usually a lost cause once the borer enters the stalk, although you can try to slit the stem and extract the insect. Winter plowing may help to reduce the population of this pest.

ADDITIONAL INSECT AND ANIMAL PESTS

Blister beetles (see BEET) may chew holes in corn leaves. *Earwigs* (see SEEDLINGS) not only feed on leaves and silks, they use corn as a hiding place for nightly forays to nearby plants. Other insects that may harm corn include the *green stinkbug* (see BEAN) and the *harlequin bug* (see CABBAGE FAMILY).

The roots of corn may be injured by several root-knot

nematodes (see BEAN), including the cotton root-knot nematode, the Javanese root-knot nematode, and the southern root-knot nematode. Corn is also susceptible to damage by many other nematode species that require laboratory identification. Symptoms of nematode damage include wilting at midday and production of fewer, smaller, poorly filledout ears. Alternate peanut crops with corn crops, since the major nematode pests of corn do not build up in peanut. A one-year rotation is not enough to wipe out the problem; the length of time that peanut should be planted depends on the nematode population level in your soil. Give corn the best possible growing conditions to help it tolerate nematode damage. Nematodes may be easier to combat if the corn is grown in beds that have been double dug. (Consult any good basic gardening book for instructions on double digging.)

The *raccoon* is renowned for its love of ripening corn. Schemes for discouraging raccoons include covering each

ear of corn and leaving radios on at night in the corn patch. But raccoons are intelligent and they learn to avoid deterrents. One effective obstacle is a temporary electric fence, which you can buy in kit form. *Wireworms* (see POTATO) may damage corn seeds and roots.

DISEASES

Bacterial Wilt of Corn
Also known as Stewart's wilt, this disease is common everywhere except the West. It is worse on sweet corn than field corn. Pale green or yellow streaks with wavy margins form on corn leaves, and later the streaks turn pale brown. They may be quite short or travel the length of the leaves. An affected plant may be stunted or wilted. Yellow bacterial slime oozes from cut stalks.

The bacteria overwinter in adult corn flea beetles (see page 88), which infect corn plants by feeding on them. Unaffected beetles soon get the bacteria from infected corn and spread it to healthy

Once northern corn leaf blight appears in a corn patch, it can spread quickly through the planting.

Top: Common smut (left) and head smut (right) disfigure ears. Bottom: Common smut affects stalks, leaves, and even tassels.

plants. The bacteria can survive in corn seeds, although only about 2 percent of infected seeds will produce infected plants. However, healthy plants soon succumb when the flea beetles are present.

Plant resistant varieties; see the chart on page 141. Generally, late-maturing varieties are less susceptible than early-maturing varieties. Control corn flea beetles early in the season. Remove plants that show wilt symptoms and clean up infected debris.

Corn Leaf Blights

Two types of fungal leaf blights affect corn east of the Rocky Mountains. A problem from Minnesota to Florida, *northern corn leaf blight* is more severe in areas with warm, rainy summers. Affecting field and sweet corn as well as grasses, the blight shows up as elliptical gray-green to tan lesions on the leaves. A lesion may measure up to 2 inches wide and 6 inches long. If several appear on the same leaf, the leaf may die. Although lesions also

appear on the husks, they do not grow through to the kernels.

The fungus overwinters in corn residue. In spring, spores are blown by the wind onto new plantings. Once in a field the disease can spread to healthy plants from infected ones.

Plant resistant varieties; see the chart on page 141. If northern corn leaf blight still appears, either the variety does not have resistance bred into it properly or perhaps a new race of the fungus has appeared. Contact the local cooperative extension office for advice.

Southern corn leaf blight, a similar disease caused by a related fungus, occurs throughout the South and into Illinois. It is more common on field corn than sweet corn. The leaf lesions are also elliptical, but they measure only ¼ inch wide by ¾ inch long. Resistant varieties are the main control for this disease; see the chart on page 141.

Corn Smut

A common fungus disease affecting sweet corn more than field corn, *common corn smut* shows up as irregularly shaped greenish to silvery white galls on cornstalks, leaves, ears (among the kernels), and tassels. The galls enlarge, then burst open, releasing a blackish powder. Galls on the stalk stunt the plant. Young seedlings may die, although this rarely happens.

Spores released by galls overwinter on or in the soil, in crop refuse, and in manure. Viable for up to seven years, the spores germinate on corn during moist conditions. Galls form where the spores germinate, and the infection is confined to that area of the plant. Infection is more likely to occur when the soil is high in nitrogen or when plants have been injured by hail, blowing sand, or cultivating tools. Spores released from galls early in the season can infect other plants.

Resistant varieties include 'Apache', 'Golden Nectar', 'Honeycomb', 'Lukon', 'Northern

Bell', 'Seneca Scout', 'Seneca Star', 'Style Pak', and 'Sugar Loaf'. Resistance is not foolproof: Some varieties may show symptoms during a hot, dry summer. Destroy galls before they can open and release spores. Do not compost infected plant debris. If all the gardeners in a neighborhood remove galls two or three times a season, the amount of corn smut in an area will decrease considerably over several years. Another way to get rid of common corn smut is to boil or fry the young, immature galls and eat them. Considered a delicacy, the galls are served in gourmet restaurants.

Head smut makes similar galls on corn, but they appear only after the ears and tassel are formed. Common on the ear and tassel, they rarely form on leaves. Smutted ears are short and rounded and they lack silk. The kernels and cob are replaced by smut. Plants with this disease may be stunted and they may form several small ears in the same

The cowpea curculio, which lays eggs in cowpea and bean pods, is a type of long-snouted beetle.

Seek resistant cowpea varieties to avoid infections by viruses. This plant has cowpea chlorotic mosaic virus.

location. Infection is by spores in the soil. Unlike common corn smut, this disease grows throughout the plant. It has been spotted in states from Washington to New York, including most of the corn-belt states. If you think your corn has it, contact the local cooperative extension office for assistance. Unlike common corn smut, head smut is not an edible delicacy.

COWPEA (black-eyed pea, southern pea)

INSECT AND OTHER ANIMAL PESTS

Cowpea Curculio

Common in the South Atlantic and Gulf states but found as far north as Iowa, this destructive insect feeds on cowpea as well as snap and lima beans. The seeds inside the cowpea or bean pods are eaten into and may contain ⅓-inch-long whitish larvae with yellowish heads.

The adult is a hard-shelled, humpbacked black beetle, nearly ¼ inch long, with prominent round dimples on the back and a slender snout. The adult feeds on the pods, leaving wartlike scars. It also deposits eggs in holes eaten through the pods. After hatching, the larvae feed on the seeds. The adults overwinter in nearby weedy borders.

Where feasible, remove the weeds broomsedge and bluestem from the garden edge to reduce overwintering sites. Till the soil in fall to disturb or kill adults. Plant as late as possible, since early plantings are most severely attacked. Handpick adults and crush any eggs that you find. Remove infested pods and destroy them. The pest is resistant to many insecticides, although rotenone and pyrethrins may provide some control. Begin spraying when the plants are blooming, and repeat at five-day intervals. There is no way to control the larvae, since they are inside the pods.

ADDITIONAL INSECT AND ANIMAL PESTS

Aphids (see BEAN) commonly feed on cowpea. You may see the bean aphid, which is dark green to black, or the cowpea aphid, which is slate gray when young and shiny black with white legs when mature. The cowpea aphid also feeds on laburnum, locust, and other bean-family ornamentals as well as deutzia and grape. Control both kinds of aphids to keep them from spreading virus diseases to cowpea.

The *bean leaf beetle* (see BEAN) and the black *blister beetle* (see BEET) may feed on cowpea leaves. The serpentine *leafminer* (see BEET) may mark cowpea leaves with winding trails. The *lesser cornstalk borer* (see *stalk borers,* under CORN) may damage cowpea by boring into the stalk, although early plantings are less likely to be attacked. The *Mexican bean beetle* (see BEAN) commonly eats from the undersides of cowpea leaves, chewing them to lace.

Among the root-knot *nematodes* (see BEAN) that may injure cowpea are the Javanese root-knot nematode, the peanut root-knot nematode, and the southern root-knot nematode. See the list of resistant varieties on page 146.

DISEASES

Cowpea is susceptible to many diseases, most of which affect bean as well. A sulfur spray will control *bean anthracnose* and *bean rust* (see BEAN) on cowpea. Apply the sulfur no later than the first bloom, and repeat every five to seven days. A strain of the soilborne fungus disease *fusarium wilt* affecting only cowpea causes yellowing, leaf drop, and eventual death of the plant. If you cut the stem lengthwise near the soil line, you will see the typical brownish discoloration of conducting tissue. 'Mississippi Purple' and 'Mississippi Silver' are resistant varieties.

Cowpea is vulnerable to several *mosaic viruses* (see BEAN), including bean yellow mosaic, cowpea chlorotic mosaic, and cucumber mosaic. The first two mosaics produce

A heavy infestation of melon aphids can cause serious malformations, such as this misshapen watermelon leaf.

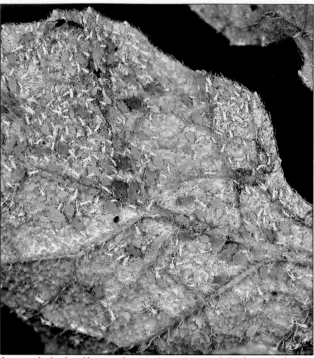

Inspect the backs of leaves, the growing points, and the flower buds for incipient melon aphid infestations.

light and dark green mottling, whereas the third shows up as bright yellow blotching of the leaves. All are spread by sucking insects, such as aphids and leafhoppers, and by infected seeds. 'Corona', 'Pinkeye Purple Hull', 'White Acre', and 'Worthmore' resist cowpea chlorotic mosaic virus. 'Mississippi Purple' and 'Mississippi Silver' are generally tolerant of viruses. Cowpea is also susceptible to *verticillium wilt* (see TOMATO).

CUCURBITS (Cucumber, gourd, melons, pumpkin, squash, and watermelon)

PHYSIOLOGICAL PROBLEMS

Bitter Flavor
The bitter-tasting compounds found in most wild cucumbers are present in varying amounts in domestic plants. They are usually confined to the leaves, stems, and roots, but occasionally they enter the fruit. Why this happens is not

completely understood, but it seems to be related to poor growing conditions. Some cucumber varieties are more susceptible than others. Often, poorly filled out or misshapen fruit is bitter. Diseased plants may also produce bitter fruit.

Avoid the problem by growing a variety known to produce bitter-free fruit. Among the best are 'Ashley', 'County Fair 87', 'Eversweet', 'Lemon', 'Saticoy', 'Sunnybrook', and the new long hybrids, such as 'Burpless Tasty Green', 'Green King', and 'Sweet Success'. Provide good growing conditions. Often, bitterness is only skin deep, although it may be extend deeper into the fruit at the stem end. Peel the cucumber, going deeper at the stem end. Contrary to popular belief, peeling in a certain direction or rubbing the cut end has no effect on bitterness.

INSECT AND OTHER ANIMAL PESTS

Melon Aphid
A widespread pest that is particularly troublesome in the South, the melon aphid

may attack cucumber, melon, pumpkin, and squash in all parts of the United States. Gourd is somewhat less susceptible. In Florida the melon aphid is a serious pest of watermelon. The insect may also feed on asparagus, bean, beet, eggplant, okra, spinach, sunflower, and many flowers as well as weeds. It distorts twigs and generally weakens citrus plants. The pest is also known to attack strawberry.

The leaves of infested cucurbit plants wilt and curl. Ants, bees, wasps, or flies may be present; they feed on the honeydew excreted by the aphids. Careful examination of the undersides of the leaves will reveal tiny aphids. Most are dark green, although variations in color range from pale yellow to almost black. The melon aphid transmits cucumber mosaic and other viruses, so that symptoms of these diseases may appear on infested plants. (See *cucumber mosaic virus*, page 100.)

For general information about aphids and ways to

control them, see *aphids* under BEAN. The melon aphid is a greater pest in warm-winter climates. In the North it overwinters as an egg, but in the South it reproduces by live birth the year around. Southern gardeners must contend with 25 or more generations yearly. The population multiplies rapidly, because each female gives birth to about 80 offspring. During most years predators keep the pest under control. When spring is particularly cool and wet and summer unusually hot and dry, the aphid population can get out of hand.

To reduce the transmission of viruses among cucurbits, spray twice a week with a fine mist of 4 percent mineral oil solution (sold as citrus soluble oil). Spray a small area of the plant; complete the spraying after 48 hours if the plant shows no sign of damage. This treatment is more effective on young plants, since complete coverage is difficult on older, larger plants.

The *green peach aphid* (see SPINACH) may also attack cucurbit crops.

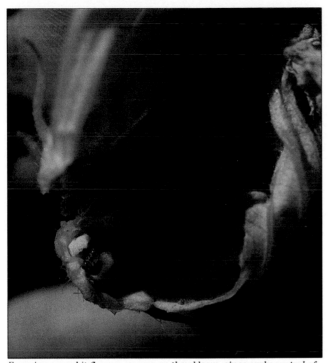

Examine cucurbit flowers as soon as they bloom, since early control of pickleworms will reduce fruit damage later.

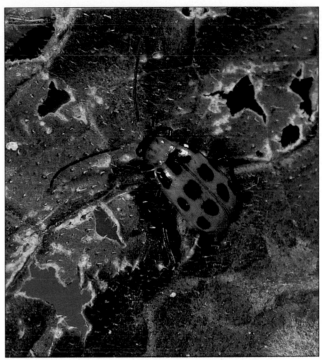

The spotted cucumber beetle, which is the southern corn rootworm adult, eats holes in cucurbit leaves and fruit.

Pickleworm

This caterpillar survives the winter in southern Florida and Texas and spreads northward late in the season. Its summer range extends through the southeastern part of the United States, extending as far north as Connecticut and as far west as Kansas. The pickleworm may seriously injure cucumber, muskmelon, and squash. It rarely damages watermelon and is not likely to harm pumpkin.

In the southern part of the range, the insect overwinters as pupae in rolled-up leaves. In mid- to late spring adult moths, with 1-inch-wide light yellow wings with a yellow-brown margin, emerge, mate, and lay eggs. The young caterpillars, which are light yellow with rows of black dots and a dark brown head, eat squash blossoms and feed on the terminal buds and stems of squash and other susceptible plants. The mature caterpillars, up to ¾ inch long, lose their dots and turn a uniform green or copper. They enter the ripening fruit, ruining it. Sawdustlike green frass protrudes from the holes, and the damaged fruit rots. A single mature caterpillar may enter several fruits. After feeding for two to three weeks, the caterpillars pupate in rolled-up leaves; in a few days a new generation of adult moths emerges and mates. There are several generations a summer, even in the northernmost part of the range. The population may increase to disastrous proportions by August. In the southernmost part of its range, the pest is active all year.

Clean up garden debris in fall and dig under any scattered leaves that may bear overwintering pupae. Use resistant varieties, such as 'Blue Hubbard', 'Boston Marrow', 'Buttercup', 'Butternut 23', and 'Summer Crookneck' squash; and 'Ashley', 'Colorado', 'Princess', and 'Slicemaster' cucumber. Plant as early as possible, so that plants will be ready for harvest before the insect builds up to damaging levels. Plant squash as a trap crop; early in the season the pickleworm will feed on squash blossoms in preference to other cucurbit crops. Remove the squash plants along with the caterpillars, and continue to replant every two weeks for a continuous supply of squash blossoms to attract the insect.

Release trichogramma wasps or lacewings to coincide with the beginning of the egg-laying season. Spray weekly with Bt, beginning when caterpillars first appear on the flowers and buds. Rotenone is also an effective control.

Spotted Cucumber Beetle

A destructive pest east of the Rocky Mountains, this insect is more common in the South. It does not survive winters in the North and must migrate each spring to reach the northern part of its range.

Both the larva and adult are harmful. The caterpillar injures the roots and stems of corn and bean, and it also feeds on grass roots. (When found on corn the caterpillar is known as the southern corn rootworm; see *corn rootworms*, under CORN.) The adult beetle eats the foliage of cucurbits, asparagus, bean, beet, cabbage, eggplant, pea, potato, and tomato. The adult also feeds on the foliage and flower petals of ornamental plants; it is especially fond of petals of late-season, light-colored flowers, including aster, calendula, canna, chrysanthemum, coreopsis, dahlia, impatiens, rose, Shasta daisy, sweet pea, and zinnia.

The spotted cucumber beetle damages cucurbits by eating holes in the leaves and the rinds of fruit. As it feeds it spreads bacterial wilt, often causing plants to wilt and die. The adult beetle is slender, approximately ¼ inch long, and yellowish green with a black head, black legs, and 12 black spots on the wing covers. It spends the winter among weeds or garden plants. In spring when the temperature nears 70° F, the beetles become active, mate, and lay eggs just below the soil surface near bean, corn, and grass plants. The eggs hatch

West of the Rockies the western spotted cucumber beetle adult damages many crops and the larva eats corn roots.

Top: Young squash bug nymphs are green and red.
Bottom: Older nymphs become gray with darker legs.

into ½-inch- to ¾-inch-long, slender, wrinkled white larvae with brown heads. The larvae tunnel into the roots and stalks of host plants and feed for two to six weeks, then form pupae in the soil. Soon, the adults emerge and feed on aboveground parts of host plants. There are two or three generations a year.

The spotted cucumber beetle is difficult to control well enough to prevent the loss of cucurbit crops. It takes very little feeding by a beetle contaminated with bacterial wilt to infect and kill a plant. Although an insecticide may drastically reduce the beetle population, it may not save the crop.

Look for resistant varieties. Among cucumber varieties 'Ashley', 'Chipper', and 'Gemini' are resistant and 'Pixie' is moderately resistant; 'Crispy', 'Explorer', and 'Frontier' are more resistant as seedlings than as mature plants. Among squash varieties 'Blue Hubbard' is resistant; 'Green Hubbard', 'Summer Crookneck', and

'Summer Straightneck' are more resistant as seedlings than as mature plants. 'Crimson Sweet' and 'Sweet Princess' watermelon resist attack. 'Stono', 'Fletcher', and 'Niagara' cucumber and 'Hearts of Gold' muskmelon are reported to show resistance to both the spotted cucumber beetle and the striped cucumber beetle (see page 98).

Another approach is to plant extra seeds and thin out all but the most vigorous plants. As an alternative, plant pumpkin seeds to emerge a week before the main cucurbit crops; the pumpkin seedlings will attract spotted cucumber beetles and allow you to determine whether to expect the pest. If you plant the pumpkins in containers, you can easily throw out the plants with any beetles or eggs that they attract.

Protect cucurbit seedlings with a floating row cover, or make small cone-shaped

covers from window screening. Keep the row cover in place until the plants begin to bloom. Remove the cones before the plants touch the screening. Handpicking the beetles is difficult, because they drop to the ground and hide in the soil when disturbed.

Natural enemies don't usually keep the beetle population low enough to prevent crop losses. If you see spotted cucumber beetles feeding on nearby trees and shrubs before cucurbit plants are up, you may be able to reduce the number of beetles that will attack your vegetable garden by treating these plants with pyrethrum, sabadilla, or rotenone. If the host plants are blooming, use pyrethrum in ways that minimize damage to bees (see page 45).

Predatory nematodes added to the soil at planting time will destroy some larvae, but they may not be effective in a small garden, since adult beetles will continually fly in from surrounding areas. Pyrethrum, sabadilla, or rotenone, applied weekly from the first emergence of cucurbits, will

help control larvae by killing adults before they are able to lay eggs.

The *western spotted cucumber beetle* is a similar pest west of the Rocky Mountains. The adult is slightly smaller than the eastern species, and its spots are somewhat larger. The larvae feed on the roots of corn, sweet pea, and native grasses. When the grasses dry in spring, the beetles may descend on gardens and orchards, feeding on most plants except conifers.

Squash Bug

A widespread pest, the squash bug prefers squash and pumpkin. Its next favorite crops are gourd and melon, but it may attack any cucurbit.

The leaves of affected plants wilt due to loss of sap from the feeding of the squash bug. A toxin in the insect's saliva causes the leaves to turn black and die. These symptoms, known as anasa wilt of cucurbits, closely resemble those of bacterial wilt (see

Squash bug adults feed in swarms on ripening fruit. Trap them under boards at night, then handpick them.

Top: Striped cucumber beetles are feeding on a pumpkin. Bottom: A western striped cucumber beetle rests on a flower.

page 100). Young plants may die; larger ones may only lose some of their runners.

The adult squash bug is about ⅝ inch long, flat backed, and dark brown to black, sometimes with gray or light brown mottling. Although it emits an unpleasant odor when crushed, it is not among the insects classified as stinkbugs. In addition to the adult, you may see small wingless larvae, called nymphs. When young they are green with a red head and red legs. Older nymphs are grayish white with dark legs. Both the adults and nymphs harm plants.

Adults overwinter in moist, protected areas, such as in garden plant debris or under boards or rocks. They emerge in late spring and fly to gardens, apparently locating cucurbits by scent. They mate and lay masses of brick red or golden brown eggs on the undersides of leaves. The eggs hatch in one to two weeks; the hatchlings take four to six weeks to mature into adults. The nymphs from a single egg mass feed together at first. Later, as fall approaches, large

groups of adults may feed on the sunny side of fruit. Usually, there is only one generation a year.

Clean up garden debris in fall to eliminate winter hiding places. Use a two-year rotation, and be sure to grow cucurbits as far as possible from where they were grown the previous year. Crush the egg masses and handpick the bugs whenever you see them. Lay roof shingles or boards flat on the ground at the base of squash plants and look for squash bugs under them early every morning. Use a dense mulching material, such as sawdust or compost, rather than straw or another loose mulch that offers hiding places. Because there is only one generation a year, you can greatly reduce numbers by making the plants unavailable when the adults arrive to lay eggs. Do this by protecting young plants with a floating row cover until they begin to bloom. After harvest remove the plants from the garden.

Resistant squash varieties include 'Butternut', 'Early Golden Bush Scallop', 'Early Prolific Straightneck', 'Early Summer Crookneck', 'Improved Green Hubbard', 'Royal Acorn', and 'Table Queen'.

If used, chemical controls should begin when the vines are beginning to run. Rotenone kills squash bug nymphs, and sabadilla is more effective on squash bug adults.

Squash Vine Borer
A pest east of the Rocky Mountains, the squash vine borer feeds only on cucurbits. Host plants, in order of preference, are squash, pumpkin, gourd, cucumber, and muskmelon. The symptoms of borer infestation are runners that suddenly wilt and masses of greenish yellow frass protruding from holes in the stems. If you make a lengthwise slit in the stem near a hole, you will see a 1-inch-long, wrinkled white caterpillar with a brown head.

The adult is a clearwing moth with a 1-inch to 1½-inch wingspan. The forewings are iridescent copper green and the back section of the body is

orange and black. The moths emerge when the squash vines begin to run, and they lay flat, oval brown eggs singly on the stems and leaf stalks. In about a week the eggs hatch into caterpillars, which tunnel into the stems to feed. Later in the season they often feed on fruit as well as stems. The caterpillars feed for four to six weeks, then enter the soil to spend the winter.

In northern climates there is only one generation a year. Farther south some larvae pupate right after feeding on the plants; the emerging adults give rise to a second generation of larvae during August and September.

In fall and again in spring, till the soil deeply to kill any caterpillars and pupae. Grow resistant varieties, such as 'Butternut' and 'Butternut 23' squash and 'Green Striped Cushaw' pumpkin. Rotate cucurbits together, growing them as far as possible from where cucurbits were grown the previous year. Plant early so that

Squash vine borer larvae feed in cucurbit stems, causing plants to wilt. Slit the stem and remove the borer.

The adult squash vine borer, which appears when the vines begin to run, lays eggs on the stems and leafstalks.

the plants will be sturdier and better able to withstand attack during the egg-laying period, which occurs from late June through July. As an alternative, plant late and protect seedlings with a floating row cover during the heaviest egg laying; when blooming begins remove the cover so that pollination can take place. Grow a few summer squash plants as a trap crop among less vulnerable cucurbits. When the squash plants become infested, remove them from the garden. To avoid damage by borers, harvest cucurbit crops as soon as they are ready.

Although cultural controls are effective against this pest, regular applications of pesticide may help prevent entry into plants. As soon as vines begin to run, dust weekly with rotenone or pyrethrum. Use pyrethrum in the evening when bees are less active, and apply it below the blossoms, where borers, but not bees, are likely to congregate.

Once borers are in the stem, they are difficult to control. If you notice the holes

before the vine has been killed, you have two choices: Inject nematodes into the stem, or manually remove the insects. Using a hypodermic needle designed for plants, inject nematodes at the rate of 5,000 nematodes per injection every 4 inches into the lower 3 feet of stem. (Follow dilution instructions on the package of nematodes.) If manually removing the insects, slit open the stem with a razor or sharp knife and remove the borer; mound soil over the slit part of the stem to encourage the formation of new roots at the burial point.

If the squash vine borer is a serious problem in your garden, remove all dead vines to interrupt the life cycle of any borers still inside.

Striped Cucumber Beetle

This insect is the most serious pest of cucumber east of the Rocky Mountains, particularly in the Northeast. It also damages melon, pumpkin, squash, and sometimes watermelon. The larva is a caterpillar that

injures the roots; the adult beetle chews on the leaves, flowers, and rinds of the fruit. In addition to harming cucurbits, the adult also feeds on the leaves of bean, corn, and pea and on the flowers of other plants.

Cucurbit plants may wilt and die, not only from direct damage to roots and young shoots, but also because the adult beetle spreads bacterial wilt (see page 100). A plant that survives both of these problems may become distorted and unproductive because the beetle has infected it with cucumber mosaic virus. The adult is about ⅕ inch long and yellowish green with a black head, black legs, and three longitudinal black stripes on the wing covers. Look for beetles at the base of a plant and on the undersides of leaves.

Adults overwinter in nearby woodlands, especially where wild species of goldenrod and aster grow. When the temperature rises above 55° F in spring, the beetles emerge to feed on pollen, flowers, and leaves of host plants, including

apple, buckeye, elm, hawthorn, lilac, wild plum, and willow. As soon as cucurbit seedlings are up, the beetles descend on the garden; sometimes they attack seedlings before they poke through the soil surface. The adults lay orange eggs in or on the soil at the base of cucurbit plants. These hatch into ⅛-inch-long, slender white larvae with brown ends. They feed on the roots of cucurbits for two to six weeks, often killing the plants. After feeding the larvae pupate in the soil; adult beetles emerge in midsummer and feed on cucurbits as well as corn, legumes, and possibly other crops. This may be the only generation in the North, but in the South there are up to four generations a year.

The controls for the striped cucumber beetle are the same as for the spotted cucumber beetle (see page 95). 'Stono', 'Fletcher', and 'Niagara' cucumber and 'Hearts of Gold' muskmelon reportedly show resistance to both the striped

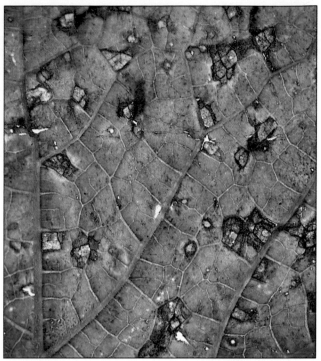

Top: Sowbugs may damage squash late in the season.
Bottom: Check cucurbit leaf undersides for whiteflies.

Angular leaf spot is most common on cucumber, but there are resistant varieties.

cucumber beetle and the spotted cucumber beetle. Resistant squash varieties include 'Butternut 23', 'Early Prolific Straightneck', 'Golden Bush Scallop', 'Marine Black Zucchini', 'Royal Acorn', and 'Summer Crookneck'.

The *western striped cucumber beetle* injures the roots and tops of cucurbits west of the Rocky Mountains. It also feeds on the leaves and flowers of bean, beet, pea, and sunflower.

ADDITIONAL INSECT AND ANIMAL PESTS

When the *beet leafhopper* (see TOMATO) sucks sap from cantaloupe, cucumber, and squash, it is likely to spread beet curly top virus to those plants. *Blister beetles* (see BEET) may feed on melon and other cucurbit leaves. Palestriped and potato *flea beetles* (see EGGPLANT) occasionally chew tiny circular holes in the leaves. The palestriped flea beetle feeds on melon and pumpkin, and the potato flea beetle feeds on cucumber, melon, and pumpkin. Squash may be injured by

the feeding of *harlequin bugs* (see CABBAGE FAMILY). You may see the winding trails of the serpentine *leafminer* (see BEET) on watermelon leaves. When the ripening fruit of cucumber is near the ground, the *meadow mouse* (see BEAN) will gnaw on it.

Expect damage to cucurbits from the Javanese rootknot nematode, the cotton root-knot nematode, and the southern root-knot nematode, if any of these *nematodes* (see BEAN) are present in the soil. Watermelon is immune to the northern root-knot nematode, but other cucurbits may be attacked.

The *onion thrips* (see ONION) may feed on cucumber, melon, and squash. Poorly developing fruit of summer squash is a favorite delicacy of *pillbugs and sowbugs* (see SEEDLINGS); summer squash with the skin chewed away is likely the work of these garden crustaceans. The *seedcorn maggot* (see SEEDLINGS) often feeds on cucumber

seedlings. The *tarnished plant bug* (see BEAN) may attack cucumber. Forestall damage by the *two-spotted mite* (see BEAN) by providing adequate soil moisture and hosing off early infestations. *Whiteflies* (see TOMATO) may infest any cucurbit crop.

DISEASES

Angular Leaf Spot

A common bacterial disease, angular leaf spot is most prevalent on cucumber, although it is also found on muskmelon and summer squash. It occasionally attacks other cucurbits.

Angular, irregularly shaped, water-soaked spots appear on the undersides of leaves. The spots turn light brown, and milky droplets may be visible in them during humid conditions. Eventually, the spots become dry, and infected tissue drops out, leaving jagged holes in the foliage. Small, circular, water-soaked spots appear on the fruit; they enlarge and become covered with a white crust. The infected fruit may be curved or otherwise deformed, and it is

vulnerable to rot from other invading decay organisms.

The bacteria live from year to year on seeds and infected plant debris. Warm, moist weather favors development of the disease, which is spread rapidly by wind, splashing water, and gardeners working among the plants. The bacteria enter plants through natural openings and wounds.

Buy seeds or transplants from a reputable source. As a preventive measure use at least a two-year rotation for cucurbits. For resistant cucumber varieties see the charts on pages 142 and 143. Use a dense mulch to prevent windblown sandy soil from injuring crops. Avoid overhead watering, and try not to work among wet plants. Clean up plant debris after harvest.

Apply a liquid copper fungicide at the first sign of the disease, and repeat weekly. Although the fungicide will not eliminate the disease, it will slow its spread. Before spraying, test a small area of the

Bacterial wilt is spread by cucumber beetles. Avoid it by controlling the beetles.

Remove plants with zucchini yellow mosaic virus to prevent further spread of the disease by aphids.

plant to make sure that it does not have an adverse reaction to the fungicide.

Bacterial Wilt of Cucurbits

Also known as cucumber wilt, this bacterial disease is troublesome in the north central, midwestern, and northeastern states. The disease affects cucumber and muskmelon primarily; it is less common on pumpkin and squash, and it is unlikely to attack watermelon.

Young plants wilt and die rapidly. On older plants wilted leaves may recover at night, at first. A single shoot may be affected or the entire plant may wilt and eventually die. To find out if bacterial wilt is the problem, cut a stem near the base and squeeze both cut ends, watching for a milky exudate. Touch the cut ends together and slowly draw them apart. Look for a fine thread stretching between them. If you don't see a fine thread, test further by putting a bit of cut stem in a glass of water; strings of ooze will flow into the water if the disease is present.

The disease is transmitted by spotted cucumber beetles (see page 95) and striped cucumber beetles (see page 98). The overwintering beetles emerge from hibernation already carrying the bacterium that causes the wilt. As the beetles feed on plants, they spread the disease. The bacteria do not survive on infected plant material from season to season.

Control cucumber beetles. Pull up infected plants and remove them from the garden, bury them, or compost them. Weakened or dead plants continue to be a source of infection. Removing just the diseased runners will not eliminate the infection from diseased plants. 'County Fair 83' and 'Saladin' are resistant cucumber varieties. 'Acorn', 'Buttercup', 'Butternut', 'Ebony', and 'Table Queen' winter squash resist the disease. Although not resistant, the following cantaloupe varieties consistently produce satisfactory crops even when infected:

'Burpee Hybrid', 'Dixie Jumbo', 'Earlisweet', 'Early Delicious', 'Early Sugar Midget', 'Roadside', 'Super Hybrid', and 'Supermarket'.

Bordeaux mixture has some ability to prevent bacterial wilt, but at best it will reduce it by only one third. Controlling cucumber beetles and using resistant varieties are the most effective tactics.

Cucumber Mosaic Virus

A widespread problem, this virus disease strikes cucumber, melon, and squash. Different strains of the virus infect bean, pepper, spinach, and tomato. The disease also infects many flowers, including aster, chrysanthemum, geranium, gladiolus, larkspur, marigold, petunia, phlox, and zinnia. Many weeds harbor the disease.

Infected seedlings turn yellow and die. In older plants the virus causes general stunting as well as yellow and green mottling, distortion, and downward curling of the leaves. White blotches among raised dark green blisters appear on diseased cucumber

fruit; the fruit tastes bitter and becomes soggy when it is pickled. Infected summer squash is knobby and distorted. The fruit of muskmelon and winter squash rarely shows symptoms, but it may be off-color and taste bitter. Usually, infected watermelon plants are not as stunted or mottled as cucumber and muskmelon plants.

The virus overwinters in the roots of susceptible plants and in greenhouses. The disease is transmitted primarily by aphids, although it can be spread by spotted and striped cucumber beetles and by gardeners working among susceptible plants.

Restrict weeds in and around cucurbit plantings. Control aphids (see *aphids*, under BEAN), spotted cucumber beetles (see page 95), and striped cucumber beetles (see page 98). Pull out infected plants as soon as you notice them, and either remove them from the garden or compost them thoroughly. Resistant varieties are probably the

Top: *Cucumber mosaic virus caused mottling on the melon leaf.*
Bottom: *The same virus makes cucumber fruit lumpy.*

Top: *Papaya ring spot virus causes shoestring leaves.*
Bottom: *Downy mildew spots affect both sides of leaves.*

best defense for cucumbers; see the charts on pages 142 and 143.

Cucurbits are vulnerable to other similar mosaic viruses. *Papaya ring spot virus,* formerly called watermelon mosaic virus race 1, infects only cucurbits. Although more common in the South and the West, it has been found as far northeast as New York. *Watermelon mosaic virus race 2* affects cucurbits, legumes, and some weeds. Both diseases cause general stunting as well as bumpy, sometimes mottled fruit and leaves. Leaves of affected plants often have deep notches between narrow lobes. Aphids are the primary transmitters of these diseases, although leafhoppers may participate as well.

Zucchini yellow mosaic virus, also transmitted by aphids, was first identified in Europe in 1981 but has now spread to New York and California and across the South. All cucurbits are susceptible. Infected plants are stunted; the leaves are mottled in shades of green or yellow-green, and the fruit is lumpy and distorted.

Downy Mildew

A problem in the Atlantic Coast and Gulf states, this fungus disease severely affects cucumber and muskmelon. It also occurs on gourd, pumpkin, and squash but rarely strikes watermelon.

Angular yellow spots appear on the upper surfaces of the leaves, usually on the oldest leaves first. The spots are angular because they are limited by the small veins of the leaves. On the undersides of the leaves, the spots are brown. In humid weather a fine grayish mold also develops on lower leaf surfaces. Later, entire leaves wither then die. The fruit is stunted and has an off-flavor.

The fungus spores survive the winter in Florida and blow northward in spring. They also survive in greenhouses. The disease reaches the northernmost limit of its range, New York and New Jersey, by July or August. Rainy, humid weather with temperatures between 60° and 72° F encourages the disease, whereas hot, dry weather suppresses it.

See the charts on pages 142 and 143 for resistant varieties of cucumber and muskmelon. Start your own seedlings or obtain them from a reputable source. In mild-winter areas clean up plant debris after harvest. Apply liquid copper fungicide or bordeaux mixture as a preventive when the disease is expected, and repeat every five to seven days when plants show symptoms. Before spraying the entire plant, test a small area to make sure that the plant does not have an adverse reaction to the fungicide.

Powdery Mildew

A widespread problem, this fungus disease affects cucumber, gourd, muskmelon, pumpkin, and squash and is less common on watermelon. Okra is susceptible to infection, as well. The disease is caused by the fungus *Erysiphe cichoracearum,* a different strain of which infects many flowers but not cucurbits.

The first symptoms appear in midsummer. Circular whitish spots usually appear first on the lower surfaces of older leaves but soon spread to the upper surfaces as well. Then a white or gray powder covers the affected leaves and leaf stems and eventually blankets most of the plant. Growth slows and the plant turns yellow and may die. The fruit is not attacked, but it may sunburn when the leaf cover is lost. Fruit production stops when the infection is severe.

The main source of infection is fungal spores carried by the wind. The spores may also come from crop debris and weeds. The disease spreads rapidly from plant to plant. The spores germinate best at 82° F. Water isn't necessary for infection to begin, but the infection rate increases in high humidity.

Plant resistant varieties; see the cucumber and muskmelon charts on pages 142 and 143. Squash varieties that tolerate the disease include 'Butternut', 'Crookneck', 'Early Summer Prolific', 'Table Queen', 'Yellow Summer Crookneck',

White powdery mildew spots spread rapidly until the whole plant is covered with dusty white spores.

The leaves and fruit of this spaghetti squash plant show symptoms of scab of cucurbits.

'White Bush', and 'Zucchini Select'. The disease tends to adapt to resistant varieties and fungicides. If possible, choose a planting site with good air circulation and low humidity. Inspect plants regularly and remove leaves as soon as spots appear on the undersides. Never remove more than half of the leaves at one time; if the disease is that severe, you may as well pull up the plant. In mild-winter areas remove the infected leaves from the garden. (It is not necessary in the North, since this fungus does not survive the winter.) Some plant scientists believe that washing early spores from the leaves will reduce the spread of the disease. If plants are affected when they are young, they generally do not recover; you may as well pull them up and replant.

Although a tiny gray and brown mottled lady beetle feeds on the spores, it does not provide adequate control. Use liquid lime sulfur or a copper fungicide. Make two applications, the first when there are up to five mildew spots per leaf on the undersides of leaves near the top of the plant and the second when mildew again reaches that degree of severity. Before spraying the entire plant with either chemical, test a small area to make sure that the plant does not have an adverse reaction. Refrain from using sulfur when the temperature is above 80° F, and never use it on muskmelon.

A similar disease, sometimes called *S-type powdery mildew,* is caused by the fungus *Sphaerotheca fulginae.* It affects cucumber, muskmelon, pumpkin, and winter squash. Diseased plants show the same symptoms, except that the powder on the leaves is rusty brown. Use the same control measures as are recommended for powdery mildew.

Scab of Cucurbits

This fungus disease is found in the north central and northeastern states. Although potentially most damaging to cucumber, scab is rarely seen on that crop because of resistant varieties. Summer squash is the next most susceptible crop, followed by pumpkin, winter squash, and gourd. Watermelon is highly resistant, although it may show slight symptoms.

Sunken gray spots, about ⅛ inch in diameter, appear on the fruit. As the spots age they become darker, wider, and deeper. A sticky substance may ooze from them. In humid weather a layer of velvety dark olive green spores may cover the spots. Other rot organisms may enter the scab lesions on the fruit, causing foul-smelling decay. Water-soaked pale green areas appear on the leaves. The spots, which turn brown, may be surrounded by a pale halo. Dead tissue may fall out, leaving ragged holes.

The fungus overwinters in crop debris and can also infect seeds. In spring the fungus produces spores, which are spread by wind, insects, and gardeners working among the plants. High humidity and temperatures between 70° and 75° F encourage the disease. Scab of cucurbits is most common after midseason, when the weather is favorable and plants are growing slowly.

Control measures consist of obtaining seeds from a reputable source, using a rotation that includes cucurbits only once in three years, planting resistant varieties (see the charts on pages 142 and 143), choosing a well-drained planting site with good air circulation, and removing infected plants from the garden. Chemical control is difficult once the fungus appears.

Other Diseases

Beet curly top virus (see TOMATO) may affect cucumber, melon, pumpkin, and squash. It causes older leaves to turn yellow and leaves and stems near the tips of runners to turn dark green and bend upward. When *Sclerotinia* fungus (see *lettuce drop,* under LETTUCE) infects cucurbits, it most often causes *stem rot,* although it may attack leaves and fruit. A cottony white growth appears on the infected tissue. When the main stem is diseased, the plant gradually turns yellow and

The white growth on this pumpkin stem is sclerotinia fungus. The black structures allow the fungus to reproduce itself.

Top: This eggplant leaf was riddled by flea beetles.
Bottom: Spider mites produced stippled leaves and webbing.

dies. Cutting open the stem where the white mold appears reveals pea-sized black fungal structures.

Verticillium wilt (see TOMATO) affects all cucurbits, although cantaloupe, honeydew, and watermelon may escape serious damage. Of the melons, Persian, casaba, and crenshaw are very susceptible. Avoid planting cucurbits in soil seriously infected with the fungus, and include cucurbit crops in a rotation intended to combat the disease.

EGGPLANT

PHYSIOLOGICAL PROBLEMS

Poor Fruit Set
Little or no fruit forms on the plant; fruit that does set may be misshapen or rough skinned. Cool weather during pollination is responsible for poor fruit set. Pollination can't take place when nighttime temperatures are below 58° F, so blossoms drop without forming fruit. A flower that has been partly fertilized will form fruit, but it will be imperfect. Discard malformed

fruit because it slows down the production of later fruit. The plant will bear normally when nights become warmer. Avoid planting too early in spring. Use a row cover or other protective covering to warm the air around plants early in the season.

INSECT AND OTHER ANIMAL PESTS

Flea Beetles
Of the several flea beetles that feed on eggplant, the most damaging to the widest range of crops is the *potato flea beetle*. It feeds on other tomato-family plants (pepper, potato, and tomato) as well as bean, beet, cabbage, carrot, celery, corn, cucumber, lettuce, melon, pumpkin, radish, rhubarb, spinach, sunflower, and sweet potato. It also attacks tomato-family ornamentals, such as petunia. Additional hosts include many other ornamentals as well as weeds.

Damaged leaves have a shot-hole effect: They are riddled with holes measuring ⅛ inch in diameter. A young

plant may be so badly damaged that it dies. A plant injured by flea beetles is more susceptible to *tomato anthracnose* (see TOMATO). Flea beetles may also carry potato virus diseases. If you look at the tops and undersides of leaves, you may see tiny (⅟₁₆ inch long), oval shiny black beetles that leap like fleas when they are disturbed.

The adult beetles overwinter in the soil and in garden debris. In early spring they begin to feed on weeds and sometimes tree leaves. As soon as eggplant and other tomato-family crops appear in the garden, the beetles swarm in and feed on them. They lay eggs in the soil; after hatching, the legless gray larvae eat plant roots. There are usually two generations a year.

Till the soil in fall or early spring to disturb overwintering adults. Control weeds in and around the garden. Watch for characteristic feeding holes and flea beetles on weed hosts. White sticky traps (see page 37) will help you monitor flea beetles; they can also be used to trap large numbers of

the pest. Plant large, sturdy, well-hardened seedlings and examine them often to catch damage early. If the potato flea beetle is common in your area, protect eggplant and other susceptible seedlings with a floating row cover until they are well established. For serious infestations dust with pyrethrum or sabadilla or spray with rotenone. In summer add predatory nematodes to the soil (see page 42) to prey on flea beetle larvae.

Other flea beetles common on eggplant are the *eggplant flea beetle,* which resembles the potato flea beetle but feeds on eggplant only, and the *palestriped flea beetle,* which also feeds on bean, beet, carrot, corn, lettuce, melon, parsnip, pea, peanut, pumpkin, radish, tomato, turnip, alfalfa, clover, grasses, pear, strawberry, and many weeds. The palestriped flea beetle has a broad white stripe down each pale to dark brown wing.

Southern gardeners are wise to seek eggplant varieties that resist the damage of eggplant fruit rot.

On eggplant, verticillium wilt causes leaf discoloration, including V-shaped brown lesions at the edges.

ADDITIONAL INSECT AND ANIMAL PESTS

Aphids that commonly feed on eggplant include the green peach aphid (see SPINACH), the melon aphid (see CUCURBITS), and the potato aphid (see POTATO). The black *blister beetle* (see BEET) may chew irregular holes in the leaves. Among the insects most injurious to eggplant is the *Colorado potato beetle* (see POTATO), which may defoliate plants. The *green stinkbug* (see BEAN), the *harlequin bug* (see CABBAGE FAMILY), *hornworms* (see TOMATO), and the potato *leafhopper* (see POTATO) may attack eggplant. The crop is also vulnerable to attack by *nematodes* (see BEAN), especially the Javanese root-knot nematode, the northern root-knot nematode, and the southern root-knot nematode.

When the *tomato russet mite* (see TOMATO) is numerous, it may infest eggplant. Although a plant can survive a serious infestation, its leaves are usually distorted and crinkled. There may be some russeting of eggplant varieties that have small glandular hairs on the surface of the leaves. The *two-spotted mite* (see BEAN) commonly attacks eggplant. The *whitefly* (see TOMATO) may feed on eggplant.

DISEASES

Eggplant Fruit Rot

Also known as phomopsis blight of eggplant, this widespread fungus disease is particularly troublesome in the South. Circular gray to brown spots, up to 1 inch in diameter, form on the leaves; black dots may develop in the center of the spots. Infected leaves turn yellow and die. Constrictions or light gray lesions appear on the stems. Large tan to brown sunken spots with concentric rings of black dots form on the fruit. Eventually, the fruit decays or shrivels.

The fungal spores, which overwinter on seeds and in contaminated soil, are spread by splashing water. High temperatures and wet weather favor the development of the disease.

Obtain seeds from a reputable source. If you doubt the quality, treat the seeds for 30 minutes at 122° F (see page 32). Look for resistant varieties, such as 'Florida Beauty', 'Florida High Bush', and 'Florida Market'. Avoid overly wet conditions in the seed-starting medium and in the garden after you transplant the seedlings. Try not to splash water on the leaves. A four-year rotation for eggplant may clean up contaminated soil.

OTHER DISEASES

The beet leafhopper transmits *beet curly top virus* (see TOMATO) to eggplant. Rotate eggplant with other members of the tomato family as part of a program to prevent *early blight of tomato and potato* (see TOMATO) and *late blight* (see POTATO). *Tobacco mosaic virus* (see TOMATO), which is most commonly spread by smokers, often kills eggplant; resistant eggplant varieties include 'Black Bell', 'Blacknite', 'Dusky', 'Epic', and 'Imperial'. If you have *verticillium wilt* (see TOMATO) in your soil, you have another reason to rotate eggplant with other crops in the tomato family.

LETTUCE

PHYSIOLOGICAL PROBLEMS

Tipburn

A widespread problem occurring more frequently on head lettuce than leaf lettuce, tipburn appears first as small dark brown spots at the edges of the leaves. The spots enlarge and may decay, turning black and slimy. Tipburn often occurs when damp, foggy weather is followed by warm, bright days.

Tipburn results from a sporadic supply of calcium caused by fluctuating soil moisture. Prevent the problem by watering evenly and growing varieties that are either resistant to tipburn or tolerant of warm weather. Some of the best varieties are 'Canasta', 'Dark Green Boston', 'Floricos 83', 'Great Lakes', 'Ithaca', 'Kagran Summer', 'Ruby', 'Slobolt', and 'Summer Bibb'.

Top: There are tipburn-resistant lettuce varieties.
Bottom: Slugs feed on and hide among lettuce leaves.

Yellowed and twisted central leaves are an indication that lettuce is infected with aster yellows.

INSECT AND OTHER ANIMAL PESTS

Aster Leafhopper

Also known as the six-spotted leafhopper, this common pest feeds on lettuce, broad bean, carrot, celery, endive, New Zealand spinach, onion, parsnip, parsley, pea, potato, and tomato. It also infests many flowers and weeds. Although the aster leafhopper weakens plants by removing sap, it inflicts the greatest damage by spreading a disease called aster yellows (see at right).

The ⅛-inch-long insect is gray-green with six black spots arranged in two rows of three just behind the head. It overwinters as an egg on perennial weeds and flowers. The insect feeds and reproduces throughout the summer, completing several 40-day cycles before winter.

Control weedy hosts, including chicory, dandelion, fleabane, horseweed, plantain, perennial sowthistle, pineappleweed, ragweed, thistle, and wild carrot, growing in and near the vegetable garden. For other controls see *leafhoppers,* under POTATO.

ADDITIONAL INSECT AND ANIMAL PESTS

Any of several *aphids* (see BEAN), including the green peach aphid (see SPINACH) and the turnip aphid (see aphids, under CABBAGE FAMILY), may feed on lettuce leaves. The green peach aphid is the aphid most commonly responsible for spreading lettuce mosaic (see page 106). The fall *armyworm* (see CORN) may eat holes in lettuce leaves. Suspect *birds* (see SEEDLINGS) if the ends of young as well as older lettuce leaves have been nibbled. At their worst, birds prune lettuce to a ragged rosette of leaf bases.

The *cabbage looper* (see CABBAGE FAMILY) may chew holes in leaves. Palestriped and potato *flea beetles* (see EGGPLANT) may riddle the leaves. The *harlequin bug* (see CABBAGE FAMILY) may harm lettuce by sucking sap. Tunneling by the serpentine *leafminer* (see BEET) makes lettuce leaves unappetizing.

Several *nematodes* (see BEAN), including the cotton root-knot nematode and the northern root-knot nematode, may damage lettuce. When attacked by root-knot nematodes, head lettuce forms small, poorly filled-out heads, and leaf lettuce is stunted.

Rabbits (see SEEDLINGS) find tender lettuce leaves appealing. *Slugs* (see SEEDLINGS) feed on the leaves by night and hide by day at the base of plants. Lettuce is among the crops most likely to be seriously injured by *symphylans* (see SEEDLINGS), which feed on the roots. The *tarnished plant bug* (see BEAN) may harm lettuce by sucking sap. *Whiteflies* (see TOMATO) may infest lettuce plants.

DISEASES

Aster Yellows

Also called lettuce yellows, this common, viruslike disease is spread by the aster leafhopper (see at left). It affects the same plants that host the leafhopper. Diseased plants are stunted, the leaves are distorted, and either the veins or entire leaves become yellow. On lettuce the central leaves are small, thickened, and yellow or white; the outer leaves are twisted and yellow. A gummy light brown or pink substance appears on diseased leaves.

Aster yellows is caused by a mycoplasma, an organism as tiny as a virus but with some traits of bacteria. The aster leafhopper egg is free of the disease, but the insect picks it up from infected plants as it feeds on them. The leafhopper must harbor the disease for 10 days to 3 weeks before it is able to infect plants. This means that aster yellows is most often spread by leafhoppers that have caught the

Big vein symptoms are most dramatically visible when lettuce leaves are held up to the light.

Top: Look for black fruiting bodies in lettuce drop fungus.
Bottom: Remove plants that exhibit lettuce mosaic.

disease early in the season from weeds or from winter or early-spring crops.

Control the aster leafhopper. Protect later plantings by removing diseased plants. Dig any plant debris well under the soil surface.

Big Vein

Most common in fine-textured, wet soils, big vein is a disease affecting only lettuce. It is caused by a soilborne virus or viroid (a type of infectious nucleic acid) transmitted to the plant by a water mold, a fungus that infects the plant roots. A band of tissue on either side of the veins becomes pale, making the leaf look as if it has wide veins. The leaves are abnormally upright and ruffled. The disease, which can survive in the soil for 8 to 10 years, is most active when the temperature is between 42° and 60° F. During warmer weather the leaf symptoms diminish. Avoid planting in heavy, wet soils early in the season.

Lettuce Drop

A problem in the northeastern, north central, and southern states, lettuce drop is a disease caused by the fungi *Sclerotinia sclerotiorum* and *S. minor*. When these or related fungi infect other crops, the disease is called white mold, white rot, cottony rot, pink rot, sclerotinia rot, and watery soft rot. The same or related fungi also cause stem rot of cucurbits, okra, pepper, and tomato, as well as damping-off in seedlings. The fungi are active in cool, wet weather.

On lettuce the older leaves wilt and fall flat on the ground. The center leaves remain upright, but these soon collapse into a soggy mess. In moist weather a cottony white mold forms on the plant and pea-sized black pellets develop in the mold.

On celery there is a cottony pinkish mold with hard black structures embedded in it. In all cases, the black structures contain dormant bits of fungus that survive in the decaying plant tissue and can live in the soil for many years. In spring you may see another stage of fungus growing on the ground: cup-shaped brown structures, up to 1 inch across and borne on stalks, release spores into the air.

Beware of borrowed tillers or other garden equipment that may have been used in infected soil. Avoid close planting in poorly drained soil. Remove any infected plants along with any black structures. If signs of the disease have appeared in your garden, corn may be the only nonsusceptible crop that you can plant in that area the following year. In clear, warm-summer climates, soil solarization is effective in controlling the disease (see page 30).

Lettuce Mosaic

A widespread virus disease, lettuce mosaic affects lettuce and many weeds, including wild lettuce and groundsel. The leaves of diseased plants are deformed and mottled light green and yellow; the edges may be ruffled or curled inward. The plant may be stunted, and a heading variety may not form a head. The disease is more evident in cool, overcast weather.

The virus is spread by the green peach aphid and other insects, by plants touching in a crowded planting, and by gardeners handling the plants. It is also transmitted by seed.

Obtain seeds from a reputable company. 'Nancy', a variety of Boston lettuce, is resistant to the disease. Inspect lettuce regularly and pull any diseased plants as soon as you notice them; discard them and don't handle healthy plants until you have washed your hands. Control the *green peach aphid* (see SPINACH).

Cucumber mosaic virus (see CUCURBITS) may also infect lettuce, causing symptoms so similar that both diseases are usually lumped together as lettuce mosaic.

Corn earworms may not affect much of the okra crop, but remove any affected pods to keep the earworm population in check.

Planting time and onion variety are the factors that may cause onion plants to form seeds prematurely.

OKRA

INSECT AND OTHER ANIMAL PESTS

Many types of *aphids,* particularly the corn root aphid (see CORN) and the melon aphid (see CUCURBITS), may feed on okra. The *corn earworm* (see CORN) bores holes in pods; often, the injury is minor and late in the season, requiring no action other than discarding damaged pods. Other insects that may damage okra include *flea beetles* (see EGGPLANT), the *green stinkbug* (see BEAN), the *harlequin bug* (see CABBAGE FAMILY), and the *Japanese beetle* (see CORN).

Root-knot *nematodes* (see BEAN) are among the worst pests of okra. If the cotton root-knot nematode and the southern root-knot nematode are present in the soil, they will attack okra. Knots on okra roots are among the largest inflicted by root-knot nematodes—up to an inch in diameter. A three- to four-year rotation with less susceptible crops is the best control. Only

one variety, 'Annie Oakley', is tolerant of the pest.

The *striped cucumber beetle* (see CUCURBITS) may feed on okra leaves. The *two-spotted mite* (see BEAN) and the *whitefly* (see TOMATO) may infest okra plants.

DISEASES

Powdery mildew (see CUCURBITS) caused by the fungus *Erysiphe cichoracearum* may infect okra. The crop is also susceptible to *southern blight* (see PEANUT). The fungi that cause *lettuce drop* (see LETTUCE) and a host of diseases in other crops produce a *stem rot* in okra. *Verticillium wilt* (see TOMATO) may severely affect okra plants.

ONION (AND CHIVE, GARLIC, LEEK, AND SHALLOT)

PHYSIOLOGICAL PROBLEMS

Going to Seed

The onion sends up a tough stalk, and a flower head forms at the top. Once the stalk

begins to form, the bulb is inferior; by the time seeds form, the bulb has dried up.

An onion plant is a biennial, meaning that it completes its life cycle in two years. It produces foliage and forms a bulb the first year, and it blooms and sets seed the second year. It may go to seed the first year if it is exposed to cold temperatures when the stem near the ground is thicker than a pencil. Onion varieties differ in the amount of cold required to stimulate flowering.

Plant onion varieties recommended for your area, and schedule plantings so that onions do not experience excessive cold weather at the wrong time. If you are planting sets, or small bulbs, pick small ones; large sets are more likely to produce flower stalks. Do not plant onions sold as food in the grocery store. They have already grown for a year and are ready to go to seed as soon as they are planted.

INSECT AND OTHER ANIMAL PESTS

Onion Root Maggot

Of all onion and related plants, shallot seems to be the most susceptible to this primarily northern pest. Onion is quite vulnerable as well. Garlic and leek are relatively resistant, although they may be attacked. Infested plants wilt and may turn yellow and die. On pulled plants you will notice entry holes in the bulb. Feeding inside are ⅓-inch-long, legless creamy white larvae that are tapered toward the head. If eggs were laid just before harvest, maggots may hatch and infest the bulbs while they are in storage.

Chestnut brown pupae, also ⅓ inch long, overwinter 1 to 4 inches beneath the soil surface. Beginning in late spring the adult flies emerge over a period of about a month and lay eggs at the base of host plants. The larvae, which hatch in two to seven days, immediately enter the stem and feed for two to three weeks. A single maggot may

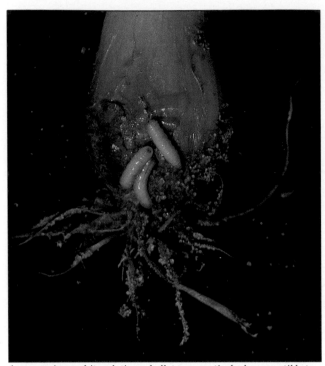

Among onion and its relatives, shallots are particularly susceptible to attack by the onion root maggot.

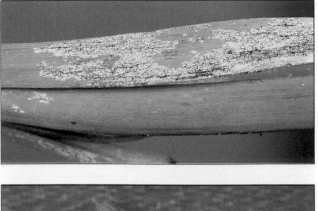

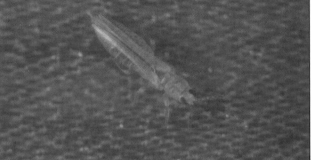

Top: Onion thrips cause white blotches and sometimes death.
Bottom: Thrips are identifiable only with a hand lens.

injure several plants in a close planting. Fully developed maggots crawl into the soil to form pupae. A second generation emerges in midsummer; a few more adults may emerge for a partial third generation in late summer.

Rotate onion and its relatives with crops that are unrelated to reduce attacks by first-generation maggots. Certain kinds of Japanese bunching onions show some resistance. Some gardeners report that red bulb onion varieties fare better than white varieties. Till the garden in fall to expose and destroy pupae. Eliminate nearby weedy areas, which offer cover to the adult flies. Onion-related weeds, in particular, attract the pest. Space plants farther apart, so that maggots can't easily crawl from bulb to bulb. Pull infested plants and remove them from the garden, and clean up debris after harvest. If you are planting while the adult flies are active, protect the seedbed or transplants with a floating row cover,

making sure that the cover is at least 6 inches from the plant stems.

Natural enemies include predatory beetles, which eat both the eggs and the maggots, and predatory flies and birds, which eat the adult flies. A parasitic wasp helps control the first-generation maggots, and a parasitic fungus infects adult flies during cool, moist weather in spring and fall. Flies infected with the fungus are driven to attach themselves to vertical objects before they die. This is probably when the ¼-inch-long, bristly gray-brown adult flies are most noticeable; once infected with the fungus, they become swollen and yellowish. Although the fungus is favored by cool, moist weather, most of the other natural enemies are active during warm, dry weather. As a result, the maggot is less troublesome during warm, dry years.

Apply predatory nematodes (see page 42) either when you plant or when the maggots are most likely to begin hatching. If the bulbs remain in the soil into the summer, a second

application may be necessary to combat later maggot generations.

Onion Thrips

A widespread pest that prefers onion crops, the onion thrips is also an occasional, but serious, pest of cabbage. It also feeds on bean, beet, carrot, cauliflower, celery, cucumber, melon, pea, squash, tomato, turnip, and many flowers.

White streaks or blotches appear on onion leaves, and the leaf tips may be misshapen. If the infestation is serious, the entire plant may appear white and dried out. An affected plant may wither, turn brown, fall over, and die.

The onion thrips is slender and only about 1/16 inch long at maturity; it may be white, yellow, or brown. It has four narrow wings that extend just past the end of its body. The larva is wingless as well as smaller, lighter in color, and slower moving than the adult. To see the insect, part the

onion's inner leaves and look under the leaf sheaths with a hand lens.

Both the adult and larva overwinter in alfalfa, clover, and wheat. In late spring and early summer, the insect lays eggs on the leaves of onion and other host vegetables. Most thrips are female; males are not necessary for reproduction. In mild-winter climates reproduction continues all year. Both adults and newly hatched larvae rasp holes in individual onion leaf cells and suck out the sap. The larvae form pupae in the soil at the base of onion plants. There is a new generation every 10 to 30 days.

Provide good growing conditions; healthy, well-watered onion crops are more likely to resist the onion thrips and to outgrow light infestations. Where outbreaks are common, early crops may escape infestation if you harvest before the thrips population builds up. Onion thrips are most damaging during hot, dry weather. Heavy rains can significantly reduce their numbers; if rainfall is scarce

Top: Botrytis can cause neck rot after onions are harvested.
Bottom: On growing plants botrytis causes a leaf blight.

Downy mildew–infected onion leaves are covered with gray or lavender spores, which often disappear in dry weather.

you may want to hose down plants as part of a control program. Do it early in the day so that you don't create a moist environment for diseases.

The onion thrips has many natural enemies, including several lady beetles, minute pirate bugs, syrphid fly larvae, lacewings, spiders, predacious wasps, and pseudoscorpions. Several types of wasps and mites parasitize the eggs and larvae. Also, various fungi infect thrips. A commercially available predatory mite, *Amblyseius cucumeris*, preys on onion thrips. Hosing off the plant may help by knocking off some thrips; also, the damp environment favors the predators. Insecticidal soap is more effective on the larvae, whereas sabadilla and ryania kill both larvae and adults.

ADDITIONAL INSECT AND ANIMAL PESTS

The black *blister beetle* (see BEET) may chew irregular holes in onion leaves. Onion is susceptible to several kinds of *nematodes* (see BEAN), including the cotton root-knot nematode, the northern root-knot nematode, and the southern root-knot nematode. Onion is often used in rotations to control the northern root-knot nematode, because the infested roots fall off before the pest matures. Thus, the population of the northern root-knot nematode declines following an onion crop. Although the onion bulbs are slightly smaller than usual, they still make an acceptable crop. Garlic has the same ability to reduce northern root-knot nematodes.

DISEASES

Botrytis Leaf Blight or Neck Rot

This widespread fungus disease strikes onion, garlic, and shallot. The leaves, especially older ones, are covered with sunken straw-colored lesions, often with vertical slits. The lesions are usually surrounded by a whitish halo. The leaves may die and the plant may be stunted. Harvested bulbs from both infected and healthy plants may decay from the neck, or stem end. Grayish mold develops between the scales, and hard black sporing bodies may form around the neck of the bulb.

The fungus spores overwinter in the soil, in plant debris, and in bulbs left in the garden during the winter. Two species of the fungus can infect bulbs after harvest; one of these also infects the leaves of growing plants.

Use certified sets where available, and rotate onion and its relatives with unrelated crops. Seek resistant varieties, such as 'Eskimo' and 'Norstar' onion. Pull up and destroy infected plants; do not compost them. Be sparing in your use of nitrogen fertilizer, especially late in the season. Discontinue irrigation as harvest approaches, and let the tops of the plants dry out. Avoid injuring bulbs when you harvest them, and store them in a dry, cool (35° to 40° F) place. Get rid of plant debris at harvest and don't leave any bulbs in the ground.

Onion Downy Mildew

Although this fungus disease can occur anywhere, it is particularly common in Gulf Coast and West Coast states. Onion, chive, garlic, leek, and shallot are susceptible to the disease.

Light green, yellowish, or brownish elongated spots appear on the leaves. During damp weather a downy lavender-gray substance covers these lesions. The down disappears during warm, sunny weather but returns and spreads on cool, moist days. Often the leaf tips die; although the plant usually survives, it may be smaller and the bulb may not store well.

The fungal spores overwinter in onion plant debris, perennial (bunching) onions, and the soil. The spores become infectious during moist conditions. New spores are produced every 11 to 15 days on infected plants.

Grow onion crops in well-drained soil and do not overwater them. Use certified sets where available. Use a two-year rotation if the disease has appeared in your garden; rotate onion and its relatives with unrelated crops.

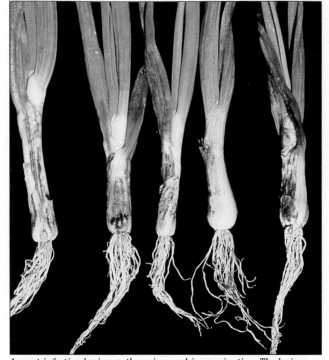

A smut infection begins as the onion seed is germinating. The lesions serve as entry points for decay organisms.

Plant only certified onion and garlic sets to avoid white rot, a disease that lives in the soil for several years.

Remove infected plants from the garden, clean up all plant debris after harvest, and do not grow perennial onions near bulb onions. Red onions, such as 'Calred', offer some resistance.

Smut of Onion

This fungus disease affects onion, chive, garlic, leek, and shallot grown in northern gardens. Black blisters or streaks appear on young plants. Seedlings may die soon after emerging, or they may not emerge at all. If the plant survives it is stunted and there are brown or black smut pustules on the bulb.

The fungal spores live in the soil for many years, but they can infect seedlings only until one true leaf has developed. Spores released from the leaf blisters of young plants either infect other plants right away or remain in the soil and infect plants later. Spores released from mature bulbs contaminate the soil.

Rotate onion and its relatives with unrelated crops to avoid a buildup of spores in the soil. Remove any infected

plants from the garden immediately. Use certified sets where available or start seeds in sterilized potting mix and transplant the seedlings into the garden. 'Evergreen', a bunching onion, is resistant.

White Rot

This fungus disease, which is becoming more widespread, damages onion, garlic, and shallot. Although leek may be affected, it is less vulnerable to infection. The injury to crops may be serious one year and nonexistent the next.

The infection most commonly occurs at the time of bulb formation, although it may happen earlier. The oldest leaves turn yellow, wilt, and die. A soft rot destroys the bulb and roots. Affected parts are covered with a thick white mat of fungal tissue bearing small black dots, which contain dormant fungus that can survive at least four to five years in the soil in the absence of a plant to infect. The

fungus begins to grow when the roots of onion and related plants are present, because it is stimulated by the chemicals that these roots normally release.

Obtain certified sets. Use a rotation of four to five years for onion and related crops. 'Festival' onion shows some resistance, but no variety is immune to the disease. Remove infected plants from the garden.

OTHER DISEASES

Onion may fall victim to *asparagus rust* (see ASPARAGUS); garlic and leek appear to be immune. Onion and its relatives are susceptible to *aster yellows* (see LETTUCE). The younger leaves turn yellow, beginning at the base and gradually moving upward. Affected leaves become flattened and develop green and yellow streaks. The disease is not as damaging on onion as it is on lettuce and carrot; however, it is serious if the onion crop is being raised for seeds, since the seeds of infected plants are usually sterile.

PARSNIP

INSECT AND OTHER ANIMAL PESTS

Insects that may feed on parsnip include the *carrot rust fly* (see CARROT), the *carrot weevil* (see CARROT), and the palestriped *flea beetle* (see EGGPLANT). Root-knot *nematodes* (see BEAN) and the *parsleyworm* (see CARROT) may also damage parsnip.

DISEASES

Leaf Blight or Canker of Parsnip

A problem in the Northeast, this fungus disease affects only parsnip. Small silvery leaf spots appear; they enlarge and turn brown with a darker border. Affected plants may lose their leaves. A dry chocolate brown rot, or canker, develops primarily on the shoulders of the roots. Cool, moist conditions encourage the disease. The fungus spends the winter in parsnips stored in the ground, and it may also survive in residue from diseased plants.

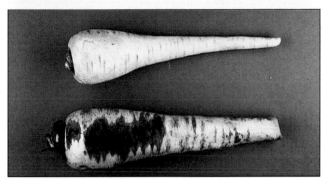

Top: Parsnips may lose all their leaves to blight.
Bottom: Top root is healthy; bottom root has canker.

Top: Pea aphids blend with the color of pea plants.
Bottom: A pea weevil larva has infested this pea.

Take preventive measures: Plant in well-drained soil and avoid planting parsnip in the same location two years in a row. Spray with a copper fungicide every 7 to 10 days to prevent spores from infecting leaves and exposed roots. Also, hill the plants gradually by adding a small amount of soil every 10 to 14 days until the roots are well covered. 'Model' is a resistant variety.

Other Diseases

Parsnip may fall victim to *aster yellows* (see LETTUCE), *potato scab* (see POTATO), and *watery soft rot* (see *lettuce drop*, under LETTUCE). The best control for potato scab is rotation away from susceptible crops. Reducing the soil pH to a level low enough to discourage the fungus is not a practical control, since a pH under 6.0 is considered too acidic for parsnip.

PEA

INSECT AND OTHER ANIMAL PESTS

Pea Aphid

A common pest throughout the United States, the pea aphid feeds on pea, alfalfa, clover, and sweet pea. Infested plants turn yellow and wilt and pods may fill out only partially. Pale green insects with black legs cluster on the plants. At ⅕ inch long, the pea aphid is larger than most other kinds of aphids.

The insect overwinters on alfalfa and clover, then migrates to pea and sweet pea. Usually, the migration takes place in April or May. In mild-winter areas, where the pea aphid breeds the year around, infestations may be worse in winter. There are 7 to 20 generations a year. As the pea aphid feeds, it spreads pea enation mosaic virus and bean yellow mosaic virus (see *pea enation mosaic*, page 113).

For general information about aphids and how to control them, see *aphids* under BEAN. Planting resistant varieties doesn't guarantee success, because there are several races of the aphids.

The *bean aphid* (see *aphids*, under BEAN) and the *potato aphid* (see POTATO) may also infest pea.

Pea Weevil

A widespread problem, the pea weevil attacks only pea. The adults are small (⅕ inch long) dark brown beetles that crawl around on blooming pea plants and feed on the blossoms. Later, partially eaten peas are found to contain ⅓-inch-long, fat white larvae with small brown heads.

The adult beetles overwinter in the garden, hiding in plant debris. In spring they seek pea plants; if they don't find any nearby, they will fly up to three miles to other gardens. (Although this is the most common pattern, pupae may remain in stored seeds for up to two years, emerging as adults when seeds are planted.) After the adults feed on the pea flower pollen and petals, they lay orange to white eggs on the pods. The larvae eat into the pods and then into the peas; they pupate inside. The entry holes in the peas are the size of small dots, but the exit holes left by the adult weevils are neat, circular holes ¹/₁₀ inch in diameter. There is only one generation a year.

Obtain seeds from a reputable source, or examine seeds carefully. If you suspect weevils are inside, kill them by heating the seeds: Wrap the seeds in cheesecloth, suspend the bundle in cold water, and heat the water rapidly; as soon as it reaches 140° F, remove the seeds and dry them.

Clean the garden in fall and till the soil to eliminate overwintering adults. Natural enemies of the pea weevil include many insects and birds. If you keep chickens try cooping them where you previously grew pea; they will eat the weevils. Check pea plants

A three- to four-year rotation is needed to clear the soil of ascochyta blight, a fungus disease of pea and sweet pea.

Pea plants with fusarium wilt are stunted and yellowish. The internal tissue of the stem near the ground is discolored.

often as they come into bloom; if you see any weevils, you can spray or dust with rotenone. Once the eggs have been laid, it is too late to prevent injury. Picking off infested pods isn't the answer, since the entry holes are difficult to discern. If the pea weevil is a problem in your garden, try growing snow pea varieties; there is a good chance that snow pea will reach the harvest stage without being infested.

ADDITIONAL INSECT AND ANIMAL PESTS

The *bean leaf beetle* (see BEAN), *blister beetles* (see BEET), the *cabbage looper* (see CABBAGE FAMILY), and the *corn earworm* (see CORN) may feed on pea. Three *cucumber beetles*—the spotted cucumber beetle, the striped cucumber beetle, and the western striped cucumber beetle (see CUCURBITS)—may feed on pea leaves. Another damaging pest is the palestriped *flea beetle* (see EGGPLANT). The *green stinkbug* (see BEAN) occasionally feeds on pea. Root-knot and other *nematodes* (see BEAN)

may harm the roots of pea plants. 'Burpeana Early' and 'Wando' are resistant to the southern root-knot nematode. *Thrips*—including the onion thrips (see ONION) and the bean thrips (see Additional Insect and Animal Pests, under BEAN) may also injure pea.

DISEASES

Ascochyta Blight
Also known as ascochyta pod spot, this fungus disease affects pea and sweet pea in the central, southern, and northeastern states. Small light brown to purple spots, which may enlarge into irregular blotches, appear on the pods. The stem at the soil line may darken and rot, and there may be elongated purplish black lesions on stems elsewhere on the plant. The stems may break and the leaves eventually shrivel and die. Any pods and peas that are only slightly blemished are still edible.

Because as many as three different fungi may be

involved in the disease, the symptoms are variable. The disease is transmitted by seed; an infected seed either fails to germinate or it produces a weak plant that soon dies. Also, fungal spores are carried in plant debris and are spread by splashing water and humid winds. Abundant rainfall and temperatures between 65° and 80° F favor development of the disease.

Obtain seeds from a reliable source; western-grown seeds are likely to be free of disease. Plant in well-drained soil. After harvest, dig under all pea plant debris or compost it. Pull up any infected plants and remove them from the garden. Use a three- to four-year rotation for pea. Copper oxychloride sprayed on the leaves is moderately effective.

Bacterial Blight of Pea
Common except in arid regions of the West, this bacterial disease damages the aboveground parts of pea plants. Large water-soaked spots appear on the pods, stems, and leaves. A slimy cream-colored ooze is prominent in the spots during wet weather. The spots turn

brown and papery during dry weather. If the bacteria reach the cells that circulate food and water, the foliage or the entire plant will wilt and die. The blight also causes a leaf spot in sweet pea.

The bacteria are carried in seeds; an infected seed will produce an infected plant that may not live to bear peas. The bacteria also survive in plant debris and in the soil. The disease can be spread by insects, splashing water, blowing soil, and gardeners working among the plants; the bacteria enter healthy plants through natural openings and wounds. High humidity promotes development of the disease.

Obtain seeds from a reputable source; western-grown seeds are likely to be disease free. Use a three-year rotation for pea. Sow seeds early in spring in well-drained, adequately fertilized soil. Remove diseased plants from the garden or compost them thoroughly in a hot compost pile, which should kill the bacteria.

Misshapen pods that often split open are evidence that a pea plant has become infected with pea enation virus.

Pea viruses often occur together so that clear symptoms are rarely visible. This plant has pea streak virus alone.

Fusarium Wilt of Pea

This widespread fungus disease causes stunting, yellowing, downward leaf curling, and wilting of pea plants; seriously affected plants may die. A reddish brown discoloration is noticeable on the lower stem and upper roots; when cut open, the stem tissue may be orange or brick red.

The fungus may be transmitted by seed, and it may also be spread when infected soil is windblown or flooded. It survives in the soil indefinitely, infecting plants through the roots. The disease spreads more quickly when the soil temperature is between 74° and 82° F.

Obtain seeds from a reliable source. Plant in well-drained soil and provide good growing conditions. Avoid overwatering or compacting the soil. Add compost or manure to the soil; both stimulate soil organisms that reduce this disease. Plan a three-year rotation for pea. Dig up infected plants, roots and all, and remove them from the garden. Clean tools thoroughly after using them in infected soil. No chemical controls are available.

Look for resistant varieties. Since there are two major races of the disease, make sure that you choose a variety that resists the race you have. 'Alaska', 'Daybreak', 'Little Marvel', and 'Perfection' resist race 1, the more serious wilt identified by yellow-orange internal stem tissue. 'New Era' and 'New Season' resist race 2, sometimes called near-wilt, which kills plants more slowly and can be identified by brick red internal stem tissue.

Pea Enation Mosaic

The most damaging virus of pea in the United States, this disease also strikes alfalfa, broad bean, and clover. There are yellowish areas on the leaves and blisterlike ridges, called enations, on the undersides of the leaves and on the pods. Also, the pods are misshapen and may split open. Flowering and pod set stop and the plant may die.

Grow resistant varieties. Good dwarf pea selections include 'Corvallis', 'Grenadier', 'Knight', 'Maestro', and 'Mayfair'. One of the most resistant snow pea varieties is 'Oregon Sugar Pod II', although 'Dwarf White Sugar' and 'Rembrandt' are often preferred by home gardeners. Grow pea as early in the season as possible, before the aphids that transmit the disease are active; if early planting is impractical, control the aphids. Pea enation mosaic virus is spread primarily by the pea aphid (see page 111); the green peach aphid (see SPINACH), and the bean aphid (see *aphids,* under BEAN) also transmit the virus. Control of aphids early in the season may allow you to escape this and other viruses of pea. Remove infected plants from the garden, since there is no cure for the disease.

Pea is susceptible to a number of mosaic viruses, which affect all or some of the same hosts as pea enation mosaic. *Bean yellow mosaic* (see *mosaic viruses,* under BEAN) is transmitted by bean and pea aphids. 'Perfection' and related varieties (used for freezing and canning) show resistance to this virus. 'Early Snap', 'Knight', 'Maestro', and 'Olympia' are also resistant.

If obvious purple-brown streaks appear on the stems and leafstalks, your peas have a pea streak disease. Other symptoms are curved, brittle growing points, flat dark purple-brown pods, and purple pitting on any peas that were formed before the infection. This disease may be caused by *alfalfa mosaic virus, cucumber mosaic virus, pea streak virus,* or a combination of *bean yellow mosaic* and *red clover vein mosaic virus.* Since all these viruses are spread by the pea aphid, controlling the insect will also control the diseases.

Powdery Mildew of Legumes

The same powdery mildew fungus (*Erysiphe polygoni*) that commonly infects bean also strikes pea. See *powdery mildew of legumes,* under BEAN, for more information.

Since the disease is transmitted by seed, obtain

Powdery mildew of legumes, which appears first at the bottom of plants, often affects pea as the weather warms.

The resting bodies of southern blight, which resemble mustard seeds, must be removed with infected plants.

seeds from a reliable source. If there is any doubt, treat the seeds for 30 minutes in 122° F water (see page 32). Resistant pea varieties include 'Bush Snapper', 'Knight', 'Maestro', 'Oregon Sugar Pod II', 'Snowflake', 'Sugar Bon', and 'Sugar Daddy'. Other controls include planting during cool weather, rotating pea with nonsusceptible crops, and removing infected plants right after harvest.

Although sulfur will not eradicate the fungus on plant parts that are already infected, it will keep the disease from spreading. You may be able to prolong the harvest by spraying at the first sign of the disease and repeating 10 and 20 days later. Light dustings of powdered sulfur are also effective.

PEANUT

INSECT AND OTHER ANIMAL PESTS

The fall *armyworm* (see CORN) and the palestriped *flea beetle* (see EGGPLANT) may damage peanut leaves. The potato *leafhopper* (see POTATO) injects a toxic saliva that causes a puckery condition, known as peanut pouts.

The northern root-knot *nematode* (see BEAN) is a particular pest of peanut. The plant is immune to the cotton root-knot nematode and southern root-knot nematode, but it is vulnerable to the Javanese root-knot nematode. In Florida it falls prey to the peanut root-knot nematode. In addition to root-knot nematodes, other kinds of nematodes identifiable only by laboratory analysis may injure peanut.

The *spotted cucumber beetle* (see CUCURBITS) may eat peanut leaves, and the *two-spotted mite* (see BEAN) may infest plants.

DISEASES

Southern Blight
Also known as stem rot, this fungus disease occurs mainly in the South. Nearly all vegetable crops except corn may be affected, but the disease is a particular problem on peanut. A wide variety of common flowers may also fall victim to southern blight.

Often, the first sign of the disease is a fan-shaped growth of white fungal strands at the base of the stem; the strands spread up and sometimes over the ground. This disease is also called the mustard-seed fungus, because it forms small resting bodies the size of mustard seeds. The resting bodies contain bits of fungus that may rest for years before they begin to grow again. White at first, they turn reddish tan or light brown.

Infected plants suddenly wilt, turn pale green, and die. They decay at the base where the fungus appears. Pegs (the stemlike connection between the flower and the developing nut) and pods are injured and break off during harvest. They may go unnoticed in the soil, thereby building up a reservoir of the fungus in the garden. The fungus survives for many years in infected debris and in the soil. Dry weather with temperatures between 85° and 95° F encourages infection.

As a precaution rotate peanut with corn every other year. If the disease appears plant corn for two or three years before trying another peanut crop in that location. At the first sign of the disease, dig up and remove the entire plant and surrounding soil for 6 inches in all directions; be sure to get rid of all the resting bodies. Adding organic matter to the soil will reduce southern blight, as will adding nitrogen fertilizer. Soil solarization (see page 30) has been used successfully to control the fungus.

OTHER DISEASES

Since *verticillium wilt* (see TOMATO) affects peanut, include peanut in a rotation with other susceptible crops and avoid planting in infected soil.

Top: Pepper weevil larvae feed in flower buds and fruit.
Bottom: Adult pepper weevils have antennae on their snouts.

Check pepper plants carefully for young corn earworms, since there is no remedy once they enter the peppers.

PEPPER (sweet and chile)

PHYSIOLOGICAL PROBLEMS

Pepper is subject to several of the same physiological problems as tomato. It can suffer from *blossom-end rot* for the same reasons that tomato is afflicted. *Poor fruit set* in pepper is caused primarily by extreme temperatures; 58° to 85° F is the optimum temperature range for fruit set of pepper. *Sunscald* may occur on pepper if the fruit is exposed to bright sunlight after the leaves have wilted or dropped due to drought, stress, or disease. See TOMATO for further information on these problems.

INSECT AND OTHER ANIMAL PESTS

Pepper Weevil

A problem from southern California to Florida, this insect feeds on sweet and chile peppers. Flower buds and fruit fall off; the remaining fruit is misshapen and discolored. The leaves are largely unaffected.

The legless white larva with a pale brown head grows up to ¼ inch long and feeds inside dropped or damaged flower buds and fruit. The small (⅛ inch long) brassy reddish brown to black adult beetle with a downturned snout half as long as its body can be seen crawling on the plant, feeding primarily on flower buds and fruit. The pepper weevil overwinters as an adult, hibernating in garden litter. There are five to eight generations a year.

Clean up garden debris to reduce winter hiding places. Remove infested pepper plants and plant debris. If the outbreak is serious, dust with rotenone.

ADDITIONAL INSECT AND ANIMAL PESTS

Pepper may be infested by many kinds of *aphids,* including the green peach aphid (see SPINACH), the melon aphid (see CUCURBITS), and the potato aphid (see POTATO). The *beet leafhopper* (see TOMATO) sucks plant sap, spreading beet curly

top virus as it feeds. The black *blister beetle* (see BEET) may chew irregular holes in the leaves. The *Colorado potato beetle* (see POTATO) occasionally feeds on pepper plants.

The *corn earworm* and the *European corn borer* (see CORN) feed on pepper, entering the fruit and spoiling it. The corn earworm eats leaves for a short while; when the caterpillars are about ½ inch long, they bore into the fruit. After feeding for two to four weeks, they fall to the ground to pupate in the top 6 inches of soil. There may be several generations a season. *Bt berliner-kurstake* sprayed every three to four days during egg laying and hatching will kill caterpillars before they enter the fruit; once inside, the pest is protected from the spray. The European corn borer is even harder to control, since it enters the fruit soon after hatching without stopping to nibble the leaves; repeated, thorough applications of Bt may help. Trichogramma wasps eat the eggs of both

these pests; large releases of the wasp during egg laying has proved effective in commercial fields. When using Bt or trichogramma wasps, careful observation is needed to determine the right time to apply the control. Remove and destroy infested fruit and clean up plant debris after harvest.

Other insects that may damage pepper include the potato *flea beetle* (see EGGPLANT), which feeds on leaves; *hornworms* (see TOMATO), which eat the foliage and fruit; and the serpentine *leafminer* (see BEET), which makes winding trails in the leaves. Since hornworms prefer pepper fruit to pepper leaves, it doesn't make sense to spray with Bt: The fruit would be seriously damaged, since the hornworms would have to ingest a fair amount of it in order to be killed.

Pepper is vulnerable to damage by various *nematodes* (see BEAN), including the cotton root-knot nematode, the

Top: Peppers with bacterial spot develop small corky areas.
Bottom: The disease causes spots on both sides of the leaves.

Top: Pepper anthracnose spots have concentric rings.
Bottom: Wet weather encourages pepper leaf spot.

northern root-knot nematode, the peanut root-knot nematode, and the southern root-knot nematode. 'All Big', 'Bontoc Sweet Long', and 'World Beater' are resistant to the southern root-knot nematode. Two types of mites—the *tomato russet mite* (see TOMATO) and the *two-spotted mite* (see BEAN)—may injure pepper plants.

DISEASES

Bacterial Spot
Common everywhere except arid regions, this bacterial disease damages pepper and tomato. One strain of the disease infects both pepper and tomato, and two other strains infect only pepper. Pepper race 1 is found throughout the range, whereas pepper race 2 is limited to Florida and the Caribbean.

Small (⅛ to ¼ inch) yellowish green spots appear on the new leaves; later, the spots develop dead, straw-colored centers and dark margins. The old leaves turn yellow and drop.

Small, corky, rough spots appear on the fruit, which is edible if the blemishes are removed. Other decay organisms may enter the fruit and rot it. The fruit is also susceptible to sunscald when the leaves drop. Blossoms on seriously infected plants may fall off, reducing the harvest.

The bacteria are carried on seeds, in the soil, and in infected plant debris. Splashing water and gardeners working among wet plants can spread the disease quickly through a planting.

Rotate pepper and tomato together on a three- to four-year basis. Obtain seeds, preferably western-grown seeds, from a reliable source. Avoid overhead watering and do not work among wet plants. If the disease strikes, clean up infected debris, fertilize to help plants replace lost leaves, and spray with basic copper sulfate every 10 to 14 days. If the disease is expected, begin spraying when the fruit forms. Although the spray does not eradicate the disease already in the plant, it will protect plants from further infection.

The success of a spray program depends on the amount of rainfall and dew; the chances for success are greater during dry weather.

Pepper Anthracnose
Pepper is the only vegetable host for this fungus disease, which is found in the central, southern, and Atlantic states. Marigold and tomato-family weeds are also hosts. Sunken dark spots with concentric rings appear on pepper fruit, and masses of pinkish spores develop on the spots during moist conditions. The disease is less obvious on the rest of the plant, although leaf and stem spots may be present.

The fungus is carried on and in seeds and in garden debris. Wet conditions and high temperatures, around 90° F, favor development of the disease. If pepper anthracnose is common in your area, take preventive measures. Obtain seeds from a reputable source, remove all pepper plant debris at the end of the season, and plan a three-year rotation.

Pepper is also susceptible to *tomato anthracnose* (see TOMATO).

Pepper Leaf Spot
Also known as stem-end rot and pepper cercospora leaf spot, this fungus disease strikes pepper most commonly in the southeastern and Gulf states. The leaves of affected plants develop water-soaked spots that turn white with dark brown margins. Soon, the leaves turn yellow and drop. The fungus may enter the fruit through the stem, causing a rot starting at the stem end of the pepper.

The fungus, which is carried on seeds, is more likely to be serious during very rainy summers. Obtain seeds—preferably western-grown seeds—from a reputable source. Leave two years between pepper crops in a given site. Avoid overhead watering and don't work among wet plants. If the disease strikes, clean up infected debris, fertilize the plants to help them replace lost leaves, and spray with basic copper sulfate every 10 to 14 days. If the disease is expected, begin spraying when

Developing tubers that are exposed to light form chlorophyll and become green. Cover exposed tubers with soil or compost.

When a potato tuber develops very rapidly, internal tearing may cause hollow heart, an irregular hole in the center.

the fruit forms. As with bacterial spot (see preceding page), spraying may not stop the disease in very wet weather.

OTHER DISEASES

The beet leafhopper may spread *beet curly top virus* (see TOMATO) to pepper. An affected plant is stunted and it may have a stiff, erect appearance. Early infection results in death early in the season. Plants infected later in the season have upward-curling, stiff, leathery leaves and little or no fruit; the roots gradually die. Plants surviving the virus can be identified by their stunted size and yellow leaves.

The green peach aphid may transmit *cucumber mosaic virus* (see CUCURBITS) to pepper. *Early blight of tomato and potato* (see TOMATO) occasionally infects pepper. Pepper plants are susceptible to *southern blight* (see PEANUT), which produces a stem rot.

Another *stem rot* may be caused by the fungi that

produce a host of diseases in many crops (see *lettuce drop*, under LETTUCE). A cottony white growth appears on the infected tissue of pepper; if the main stem is diseased, the plant gradually turns yellow and dies. Cutting open the stem where the white mold appears reveals pea-sized black fungal structures. Pepper is also susceptible to *tobacco mosaic virus* (see TOMATO), which is spread primarily by smokers; resistant pepper varieties include 'Bell Boy', 'Bell Captain', 'Bell Tower', 'Big Bertha', and 'Gypsy'.

POTATO

PHYSIOLOGICAL PROBLEMS

Green Tuber

The skin of a potato tuber turns green when the tuber is exposed to light. The green part contains naturally occurring toxins. Make sure that tubers are adequately covered by soil or a thick mulch, and always store potatoes in the dark. Don't eat a discolored potato until you peel off the green part.

Hollow Heart

A tuber has irregular cavities, sometimes with a brown discoloration on the surface. Generally, affected potatoes are very large. When a potato grows too fast, sometimes it develops internal rips that become cavities. Poor tuber set may be responsible for the plant directing its energy into a few large tubers instead of many moderate-sized ones. Another cause of hollow heart is too much space between plants. This allows a potato plant to develop a very large root system, which may fuel excessively rapid growth.

Use recommended spacing for the potato variety you are growing. Planting large seed pieces or whole seed potatoes may lessen the problem, since more tubers are likely to set. Keep potatoes from growing too fast by giving them only as much water and fertilizer as they need for healthy growth. Supply ample irrigation during tuber set (the two-week period after shoots appear above the

surface of the soil), but avoid very wet soil while the tubers are enlarging.

INSECT AND OTHER ANIMAL PESTS

Colorado Potato Beetle

Also called the potato bug, this pest is most destructive in the East, although it is found in all states except California and Nevada. It prefers potato but will eat eggplant, pepper, and tomato. Other hosts include tomato-family ornamentals and weeds.

The beetle appears as potato plants are emerging. It feeds on leaves and stems, often defoliating whole potato plantings. The pest is ¼ inch long and almost as wide, and is strongly convex. It has a yellow back, 10 black lines running lengthwise on its wing covers, and numerous black spots just behind its head. The brick red larvae, up to ⅜ inch long, are very humpbacked.

The adults overwinter in the soil in gardens and nearby weedy areas. They emerge in spring to feed as soon as potato plants are up, then they

Colorado potato beetle adults and larvae often feed at the same time, making short work of potato plants.

Watch for Colorado potato beetle eggs early in the season and crush them before they can hatch into destructive larvae.

mate and lay bright orange-yellow eggs on the undersides of the leaves. The larvae hatch in four to seven days and feed for two to three weeks, then pupate in the soil for one to two weeks. There are one to three generations a year.

Tilling the soil in fall will expose and kill some adults. It is possible to escape damage from larvae and later generations if you begin control very early in spring. Regularly handpick and crush adult beetles, larvae, and egg masses. Lacewings and lady beetles eat the eggs. *Bt san diego*, a new strain of the bacterial insecticide, is effective against the larvae. Rotenone or a mixture of rotenone and pyrethrins will kill adult beetles. You may want to try planting 'Sequoia' and 'Katahdin' potato varieties, which show resistance to the pest.

Leafhoppers
There are many kinds of leafhoppers, most of which feed on a limited range of host plants. The insects suck leaf sap, causing a light-colored stippling on the leaves. The saliva of some kinds of leafhoppers kills leaf tissue on certain types of plants. The resultant browning of the leaf edges and curling of the leaves is known as hopperburn. Leafhoppers spread several common virus diseases.

These insects are usually about ⅛ inch long and are wedge shaped; they hold their wings in a rooflike position when they are resting. Their large eyes are located on the sides of their blunt, rounded heads. Leafhoppers may be totally green or they may have red or white markings. The young leafhoppers, called nymphs, look like small wingless versions of the adults. Often, they scurry sideways when disturbed. Adults are able to fly quickly and far. Leafhoppers can generally be found on the undersides of leaves and in leaf folds.

In the South adults may hibernate in debris. In the North the insects overwinter as eggs attached to weeds and ornamental plants. Often, adults fly northward in spring. There may be several generations of leafhoppers a year, even in the North.

Depending on the crop and the leafhopper species, there may be resistant plant varieties available. Use small yellow sticky traps (see page 37) to monitor populations. When many leafhoppers are present, protect plants under a floating row cover, use large yellow sticky traps to reduce the number of adults, or apply insecticidal soap, pyrethrum, sabadilla, rotenone, ryania, or a blend of pyrethrum, rotenone, and ryania. Apply insecticides early in the day, when leafhoppers are less active. Be sure to coat the undersides of the leaves. Eradicate nearby weeds, particularly those harboring eggs of the leafhopper species you have. Lacewings may help control leafhoppers by eating the eggs.

Although widespread, the *potato leafhopper* is most common in the eastern half of the United States. A serious pest of potato, it also feeds on bean, celery, eggplant, peanut, and rhubarb. It prefers bean early in the season, when bean plants have a higher sugar content than potato plants. So likely is it to attack bean in the South that it is better known as the bean jassid in that region. Other hosts are alfalfa, apple, citrus, and ornamentals, including dahlia and rose.

The potato leafhopper causes stippling and hopperburn. On potato, hopperburn begins as a triangular brown spot at the tip of the leaf; then similar triangles appear at the tip of each leaflet. The brown areas spread until only the midrib is green. Leaves or entire plants, especially young ones, may die. Even if a plant survives, its yield will be seriously reduced.

The ⅛-inch-long adults are iridescent green, usually with six white spots just behind the head. Beginning in late May, they migrate northward on storm fronts. They may attack

Top: A toxin in potato leafhopper saliva causes hopperburn.
Bottom: Potato leafhoppers are blown north on storm fronts.

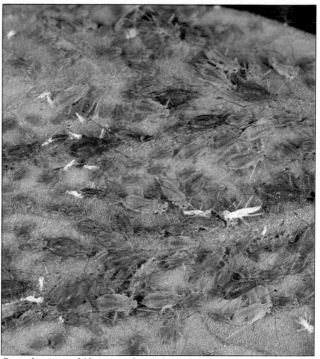

Control potato aphids on rose leaves in spring to prevent attacks on potatoes and other vegetables later in the season.

apple and alfalfa first, then swarm to potato and bean. The potato leafhopper completes its life cycle in about 20 days; there are one to six generations a year.

Among the resistant varieties, 'Delus' shows somewhat more resistance than 'Sebago', 'Pungo', and 'Plymouth'. Avoid planting alfalfa as a cover crop near susceptible crops in infested areas. Spray or dust apple leaves with an insecticide (see preceding page) when the insects first arrive. It is wise to protect young potato plants under a floating row cover, since large numbers of leafhoppers can appear suddenly. Although there are several natural enemies, they rarely provide adequate control. Commercial growers usually wait until there are 10 insects per 100 leaves before spraying vegetable crops with an insecticide.

A similar insect, the *western potato leafhopper,* infests potatoes in some areas of the Southwest. Other leafhoppers, including the *aster leafhopper* (see LETTUCE) and the *beet leafhopper* (see TOMATO), may also feed on potato.

Potato Aphid

This common insect feeds on potato and tomato. It may also attack eggplant, pepper, asparagus, bean, corn, lettuce, pea, pumpkin, squash, and sweet potato. Other summer hosts include many common flowers and weeds. Winter hosts are rose and occasionally apple and potentilla.

For general information about aphids and how to control them, see *aphids,* under BEAN. The potato aphid is $1/16$ inch long and is pink and green. Heavy feeding on the undersides of potato leaves causes the leaves to curl downward. An infested plant may turn brown and die. The potato aphid can spread virus diseases to potato and tomato.

Potato aphids overwinter as black eggs on one of the winter hosts. In spring they feed on young rose leaves and flower buds, then fly or crawl to summer hosts. After feeding and breeding all summer, the aphids mate and lay eggs on winter hosts. There are heavy outbreaks of the pest some years; it poses little trouble other years.

A dormant oil spray on the winter hosts or another control in spring should reduce the summer population of potato aphids. Don't plant roses near the vegetable garden. For other methods of control, see *aphids,* under BEAN.

The *green peach aphid* (see SPINACH) also feeds on potato.

Potato Tuberworm

Found in areas of the South and in California, this pest prefers potato but may also attack eggplant, pepper, tomato, tobacco, and tomato-family weeds. Shoots of affected plants wilt and die. The ¾-inch-long pinkish white worms with brown heads can be found tunneling in the stems and leaves. Harvested potatoes have holes at the eyes; the area around the holes is pinkish and soiled with insect webbing and frass.

The insect overwinters as a pupa in stored potatoes and in debris on the soil surface. The adult, a gray-brown mottled moth with a ½-inch wingspan, emerges in spring. Early-season moths lay eggs on the undersides of leaves; after hatching, the larvae bore into the tops of plants, then pupate in surface debris. Later generations of moths wriggle down through soil cracks to lay eggs on the eyes of tubers. The pest completes its life cycle in only a month, and there may be five or six generations a year. The pest is more active and numerous during hot, dry summers.

Rotate susceptible crops together. Remove infested plants and debris as soon as you notice them. Measures to reduce the formation of soil cracks will reduce egg laying. In some soils this can be accomplished by watering frequently. Cultivating the soil and mounding it so that tubers are at least

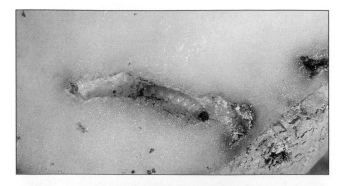

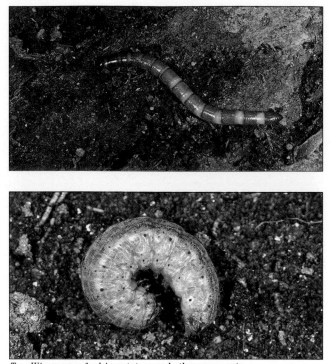

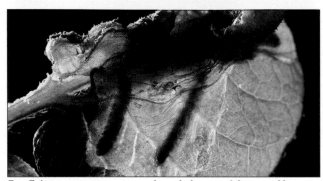

Top: Tuberworms enter potatoes through the eyes of the vegetable.
Bottom: Early in the season tuberworms mine in potato leaves.

Top: Wireworms feed in potatoes and other crop roots.
Bottom: Subterranean cutworms may damage potatoes.

2 inches below the surface is further insurance. Adding organic matter before planting reduces the tendency of the soil to crack, and a thick organic mulch makes access even more difficult for the pest. Cut infested potato vines at the ground and remove them from the garden before you begin to dig the crop. Examine potatoes before storing them, and do not leave them on the soil surface overnight after they have been harvested.

Wireworms

Common pests, particularly in irrigated areas of the West, wireworms feed on potato, bean, beet, carrot, celery, corn, lettuce, onion, sweet potato, and turnip. The insects are damaging in the larval stage: they ruin potato tubers by tunneling into them.

You are likely to see several stages of wireworms in infested soil. There are a number of wireworm species, each slightly different in appearance. Typically, the larvae are slender, tough-skinned white or yellow worms with a dark head and a dark tail section. They are ½ inch to 1½ inches long. The adults are called click beetles, named for the way they snap their bodies with a sharp click when they are trying to turn themselves upright. Slender and less than 1 inch long, click beetles are medium brown to black. You may also see the pupae, which are naked and resemble embryonic beetles.

The adult beetles spend the winter in pockets in the soil; in spring they travel a short distance to lay eggs in the soil. The larvae don't feed much the first year; they do more damage the second year and may feed for as many as six years before they pupate. They ravage root crops, large seeds, and seedlings. Often, wireworms are more serious pests in soil where a lawn was previously grown.

Do not plant susceptible crops where turf grew last year; if wireworms are a problem, wait three to four years before planting in that location. Rotate susceptible crops together. Till the garden several times before planting, and handpick the pests from the soil. You may lessen damage to potato by planting in late rather than early spring. Harvest the tubers promptly.

Try using a susceptible crop as bait. Gardeners report success with burying potato pieces or carrots 1 inch deep for one to three days, then removing the bait along with the worms. This will work only if the bait is appropriate for the species you have. Check with the cooperative extension office to find out which wireworm occurs locally and what might be an appropriate bait for it. Predatory nematodes (see page 42) will control wireworms.

ADDITIONAL INSECT AND ANIMAL PESTS

The *beet leafhopper* (see TOMATO) may feed on potato, spreading beet curly top virus in the process. The black *blister beetle* (see BEET), also known as the old-fashioned potato bug, may eat holes in potato leaves. Potato is also vulnerable to damage by other blister beetles. The *cabbage looper* (see CABBAGE FAMILY) may chew ragged holes in potato leaves. *Cutworms* (see SEEDLINGS) may feed on new growth and young tubers. Potato is susceptible to all generations of the *European corn borer* (see CORN), which bores into the aboveground stems of potato plants.

As adult potato *flea beetles* (see EGGPLANT) feed on young plants, they may spread potato virus diseases. The larvae may seriously damage roots and tubers, sometimes causing darkened, rough, or bumpy tubers. Other damaging insects include the *harlequin bug* (see CABBAGE FAMILY), which sucks sap; *hornworms* (see TOMATO), which devour leaves; and the serpentine *leafminer* (see BEET), which makes winding trails inside the leaves.

Blackleg, a bacterial disease, kills the lower stems of potato plants, causing them to collapse.

Potato leaves diseased by early blight show spots with concentric rings just as similarly infected tomato leaves do.

Potato is susceptible to damage by root-knot and other *nematodes* (see BEAN). It may be attacked by the cotton root-knot nematode, the peanut root-knot nematode, the northern root-knot nematode, and the Columbia root-knot nematode. When the nematode population is high, knobby swellings appear on the tubers of affected plants. Shallow cuts through the swellings reveal the white bodies of the female nematodes. The tissue around the nematodes is water soaked and may have brown flecks. When the nematode population is low, the tubers may not show any swellings; the only symptom may be small brown flecks under the surface of the tuber. Infected tubers serve as sources of infection.

The *seedcorn maggot* (see SEEDLINGS) may kill young potato shoots. Both the *spotted cucumber beetle* and the *western spotted cucumber beetle* (see CUCURBITS) eat holes in the foliage. The *tarnished plant bug* (see BEAN)

injects toxic saliva as it feeds on potato leaves. The *tomato russet mite* (see TOMATO) may infest potato; although an affected plant does not show much bronzing, the leaves may dry out so badly that the plant will die. The *vegetable weevil* (see CARROT) may defoliate potato plants.

DISEASES

Blackleg

A common bacterial disease of potato, blackleg causes yellowing of the lower leaves and upward curling of the top leaves. Black spots appear on the stem, and the stem base 3 to 4 inches from the soil is softened. A diseased plant wilts and often dies. Aerial tubers may form along the stems. The lower stem may be blackened and covered with smelly bacterial slime.

Blackleg is spread primarily by infected tubers. It may also be spread by the knife used to cut seed potatoes before planting. Infected seed

potatoes rot after they are planted, and the decay spreads to aboveground parts of the plant. The bacteria produce a toxin that causes the plant to wilt. Bacteria in the soil may infect healthy plants through the cut surface of the seed potato or through wounds. Healthy plants can usually resist infection but may succumb if the soil is overly wet or if the tubers are damaged by insects.

Obtain certified seed potatoes. Grow resistant varieties such as 'Atlantic', 'Katahdin', 'Kennebec', 'La Rouge', 'Red LaSoda', 'Red Norland', 'Red Pontiac', and 'Superior'. If you cut your own seed pieces, use 1 part household bleach to 9 parts water to disinfect the knife, then let the cut pieces heal overnight before planting them. As an alternative, plant whole seed potatoes; some sources sell small whole potatoes suitable for planting. Plant in well-drained soil, avoid overwatering, and be sparing with nitrogen fertilizer. As soon as you notice symptoms, remove

diseased plants and the soil from several inches around each plant. Avoid bruising the tubers when harvesting them. Don't wash the tubers before storing them. Keep them at 50° to 60° F for a week or two, then store them at 38° to 40° F. No chemical controls are available for blackleg.

Early Blight of Tomato and Potato

See TOMATO for general information about this fungus disease. On potato, symptoms usually appear after flowering. The leaf spots are very similar to those on tomato. Brown spots with a bull's-eye pattern and up to ½ inch in diameter appear first on the older leaves; the spots may enlarge and merge. When enough of the leaf surface is injured, the leaf dies and falls off. Dark, slightly sunken, roughly circular to irregular lesions may develop on tubers while they are in the ground or more likely in storage. The lesions

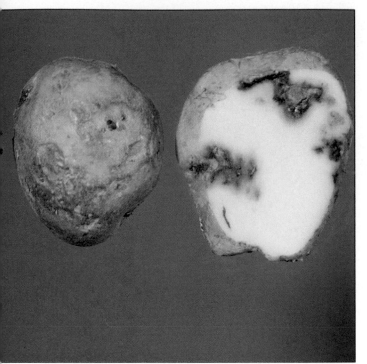

Early blight causes dark lesions, often with underlying areas of brown to black cork rot, on potato tubers.

During moist weather late blight lesions develop a white mildewlike growth mainly on the undersides of the leaves.

are up to ¾ inch in diameter with a gray to violet margin. There may be shallow areas of corky brown to black dry rot under the lesions, especially in stored potatoes.

The fungus overwinters on tomato-family plant debris, on infected tubers, and in tomato-family weeds. The fungus may be present on young potato plants, even though no symptoms appear until later. It is thought that the disease develops when the plant tissue is older and less vigorous. The fact that the disease is often more severe on potato plants stressed by drought, nutrient deficiencies, or insect damage tends to support this theory.

The fungal spores are spread primarily by wind. Alternating wet and dry weather encourages the disease. Tubers at or near the soil surface may be infected by spores dropping from the leaves. Tubers may also be infected during harvest, especially when they are injured. Once lesions develop on stored potatoes, other decay organisms may enter and rot the tubers.

Plant certified disease-free seed potatoes. Avoid very susceptible varieties, such as 'Norchip', 'Norland', 'Onaway', and 'Superior'. No varieties are immune but some are moderately resistant. If early blight is a continuing problem, consult the cooperative extension office for locally adapted varieties that show some resistance. Use a two- to three-year rotation that includes all tomato-family crops. Provide adequate fertilizer and water and avoid overhead irrigation. Catch an infection early by inspecting potato plants regularly after they are 1 foot high. Begin regular sprays of liquid copper fungicide just before bloom or at the first sign of infection, and repeat every 7 to 10 days. Mound soil over the tubers to reduce the chance of infection from leaves. Wait until the plants have died before you harvest the tubers; by this time the tuber skins will be tough enough

to resist the disease. Avoid bruising tubers during harvest and do not store any with signs of infection. Damaged potatoes may be eaten if the damage is superficial and the decayed part is cut off. Before storing potatoes, first hold them at 50° to 60° F for one to two weeks to allow any bruises to heal; then store them at 38° to 40° F.

Late Blight

This fungus disease, which caused the disastrous potato famine in Ireland in the 1840s, is most common on potato in the north central, northeastern, and Atlantic states. It is sometimes found in the Gulf states and in the West. Different strains of the fungus affect potato and tomato, but each is capable of infecting the other host (see also TOMATO). Eggplant is also vulnerable to infection.

Water-soaked areas appear on the leaves, stems, and leafstalks. These irregular patches become large and turn brown or black. They may be surrounded by a halo of light green, shading into the normal

green of the leaf. In moist conditions a downy white growth appears mainly on the undersides of the leaves. When severely infected the plants have a characteristic mildewlike odor similar to that of frost-killed potatoes. Infected tubers are covered with brown to purple patches, and just below the skin is a dry, corky dark reddish brown rot. Tubers that look healthy at harvest may develop symptoms in storage. Often, other decay organisms enter infected tubers and rot them.

The fungus overwinters only in living plant tissue. In mild-winter areas the fungus survives on tomato-family weeds and on volunteer tomato and potato plants. In cold-winter areas the fungus can survive on infected potato tubers that are left in the ground and don't freeze. The fungus may come into the garden on infected potato tubers and tomato seedlings that you

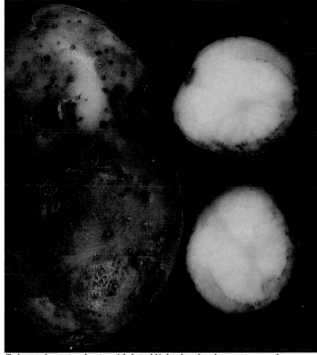

Tubers of potato plants with late blight develop brown to purple areas with reddish brown rot beneath them.

Leaf roll virus, which causes potato leaves to roll upward, may damage the tubers or leave them unblemished.

buy. High humidity and temperatures below 78° F foster the disease. Wind and splashing water spread the spores from plant to plant. The infection does not move downward through the plant to infect the tubers; rather, the tubers are infected by spores falling from the leaves and by airborne spores landing on them during harvest. There may be several generations of the fungus during a season.

Plant potato and tomato in different parts of the garden. Get rid of tomato-family weeds in and near the garden, and destroy any volunteer potato and tomato plants that come up from last season's crops. Obtain certified disease-free seed potatoes from a reliable source. When buying resistant potato varieties, it is important to obtain ones that are currently resistant, since the fungus has developed new strains. Avoid overhead watering of potato and tomato. Mound soil over potato tubers to lessen the chance of infection by spores falling from the leaves. Apply a fixed copper

fungicide on potato and tomato when symptoms first appear. The local cooperative extension office may be able to tell you if conditions are favorable for late blight in a given season. If the disease is expected, apply the fungicide beginning when plants are 6 inches high and repeat every 7 to 10 days until the plants die naturally or are cut back. Cut potato vines 1 inch below the soil surface 10 to 14 days before you harvest the tubers; remove the plant debris from the garden. Be sure that the tubers are dry before they are stored, and provide adequate ventilation to keep them dry during storage.

Leaf Roll Virus
A widespread problem, this virus infects potato as well as other vegetables and weeds in the tomato family. The whole plant may show symptoms or only a part of the plant may be affected. When an infected tuber is responsible for the

disease, damage usually appears throughout the plant. The lower leaves are severely rolled and leathery, the margins may be yellow or reddish, and the plant may appear stunted, yellowed, and unusually erect. When the harvested tubers are cut open, they may reveal brown spots in a ring around the edge and sometimes in the center. Since the disease isn't always apparent on tubers, a healthy-looking tuber can produce a diseased plant.

When the virus is spread by aphids, particularly the green peach aphid, the damage usually appears first on the top part of the plant, where the aphids were feeding. The upper leaves may be pale and rolled upward, and the undersides or margins may be reddish. The disease may spread to the whole plant.

Control leaf roll virus by planting certified disease-free seed potatoes, by suppressing the *green peach aphid* (see SPINACH), and by discarding infected plants and tubers.

Potato Scab
Also known as common scab, this widespread fungus disease is most damaging on potato. It occurs less frequently on beet, carrot, parsnip, radish, rutabaga, and turnip.

Roughly circular corky scabs, usually darker than the surrounding skin, appear on the mature tubers. The scabs may be scattered or they may merge to cover most of the tuber. The organism causing potato scab has some characteristics of a bacterium, but it is generally classified as a fungus. The soilborne spores are spread by wind, splashing water, and contaminated tools. The spores are also carried on infected tubers. The fungus can live on decaying organic matter in the soil in the absence of a suitable host. The disease develops readily when the soil pH is between 6.0 and 7.5 but is usually suppressed below pH 5.5. It is usually less serious in cool soil. The disease is more common in sandy

Planting certified disease-free potatoes and keeping the soil well watered will go a long way toward preventing scab.

Wilting leaves and discoloration on the lower stem (plant on right) are symptoms of verticillium wilt on potato.

or gravelly soil than heavier soil. It is also stimulated by dry soil, especially during the first two weeks after the plants are up, when the tubers are forming. Scab also tends to be more serious in soil containing large amounts of undecomposed organic matter.

Plant certified disease-free seed potatoes. Look for resistant varieties. Avoid very susceptible varieties, such as 'Denali', 'Katahdin', and 'Monona'. Russet potatoes are generally more resistant than smooth-skinned varieties. See page 146 for a list of resistant varieties. Use a three- to four-year rotation for susceptible crops. Acidify the soil where potato will be planted; test the pH and use the appropriate amount of aluminum sulfate to reach pH 5.2 to 5.5. If scab still develops, lower the pH to 4.8. (It may be impractical to acidify large areas of alkaline soil.) Don't amend the soil with lime, ashes, manure, or other materials that will raise the pH. Water adequately, especially during early tuber

formation, but take care not to overwater. If you add organic matter to a light soil to improve its water-holding capacity, choose compost or other well-rotted amendments. Although unsightly, scab blemishes are superficial. Remove them by peeling the affected tubers before you eat them.

Verticillium Wilt
See Tomato for general information about this widespread fungus disease. On potato, the disease appears late in the season. The older leaves at the bottom of the plant turn yellow, wilt, and drop. The plant dies prematurely, but the stems are upright and wilted leaves remain on the upper part of the plant. Cut open a stem and you will see a yellow or brown discoloration extending from the base well up into the plant. Verticillium wilt produces no symptoms on the exterior of infected tubers,

but a light brown discoloration may extend into the stem end of tubers. There may be cavities in the tuber as well. A pinkish discoloration around the tuber eyes, called pink eye, may develop, but it is due to a secondary bacterial infection.

Avoid cultivating the soil late in the growth of potatoes, because any damage to the roots will increase the risk of infection. Be particularly careful not to disturb the roots when mounding soil over the tubers. Resistant varieties include 'Green Mountain', 'Katahdin', 'Ona', 'Pontiac', and 'Shoshoni'. For other controls see Tomato.

Other Diseases
Sometimes, aster leafhoppers transmit *aster yellows* (see Lettuce), and beet leafhoppers transmit *beet curly top virus* (see Tomato), although neither disease is a major problem on potato. Take precautions to protect potato plants from *tobacco mosaic virus* (see Tomato).

RHUBARB

Insect and Other Animal Pests

Rhubarb Curculio
Common from New England to Idaho and south to Florida and Louisiana, this insect pest feeds on rhubarb and sunflower as well as curly dock and thistle weeds.

Dark gray adult snout beetles, which are covered with a yellow powder that rubs off, are seen resting on rhubarb stalks. The beetles are ½ inch to ¾ inch long. Small dots on the stems indicate where the beetles deposited their eggs; oblong and yellowish white, the eggs lay about ⅛ inch under the surface of the stalks.

The adult curculio overwinters in garden debris, emerging in late spring to feed and deposit eggs on host plants for four to six weeks; afterward, the adult dies. On all plants except rhubarb, the

Control nearby weeds with large stems, such as giant ragweed, to reduce populations of the rhubarb curculio.

Rhubarb anthracnose, which survives over winter, causes leaf spots as well as decay at the base of the plant.

eggs hatch into larvae; on rhubarb the eggs are crushed by the rapidly growing stems. Damage to rhubarb comes from the feeding and egg-laying punctures made by the adults. The stalks may ooze a shimmering sap from the puncture wounds, and partial decay may occur. The adults may also make notches in the stems and leaf margins as they feed.

On the plants on which they hatch, ¾-inch, legless white larvae with brown heads eat downward, reaching the soil level in eight to nine weeks; they pupate in the stem base just under the soil surface. The new generation of adult beetles emerges, feeds briefly, and seeks a place to hibernate. There is only one generation a year.

In early summer handpick any beetles that you see and destroy them. Further reduce next year's population by removing weedy hosts near rhubarb during July, when the larvae are still in them; shred the weeds and compost them. No insecticide is registered for use on this pest.

ADDITIONAL INSECT AND ANIMAL PESTS

Although rhubarb is susceptible to attack by a number of pests, the plant is not usually seriously affected. The *European corn borer* (see CORN) may enter rhubarb stalks. The plant may be visited by the potato *flea beetle* (see EGGPLANT), the *green peach aphid* (see SPINACH), and the *Japanese beetle* (see CORN). Rhubarb may also fall prey to the Javanese root-knot *nematode* (see BEAN), the *sugar beet cyst nematode* (see BEET), and other nematodes identifiable by laboratory analysis. The common *stalk borer* (see CORN) may infest rhubarb stalks.

DISEASES

Rhubarb Anthracnose

Also known as stalk rot, this fungus disease affects rhubarb in the central and eastern states. Oval, water-soaked spots appear at the base of the leafstalks; then entire stalks decay and the leaves wilt. The disease can spread rapidly through a rhubarb planting. The fungus can survive the winter in infected stems and attack again in spring.

Obtain rhubarb roots from a reputable source. As a preventive measure clean up rhubarb debris in fall. Remove affected plants and destroy them; purchase new rhubarb roots and plant them in a different location.

OTHER DISEASES

A variety of bacterial and fungal diseases can cause *crown and root rots* of rhubarb. Obtaining healthy roots and clearing debris in fall will help prevent these diseases, and replanting in a different location will give you a fresh start if a disease occurs. Since rhubarb is susceptible to *southern blight* (see PEANUT) and *verticillium wilt* (see TOMATO), don't plant in soil infected with either fungus.

SPINACH

INSECT PESTS

Green Peach Aphid

Also known as the spinach aphid, this widespread insect is particularly damaging to spinach and potato but also infests bean, beet, the cabbage family, celery, cucurbits, eggplant, lettuce, pepper, and tomato. It is a serious pest of peach and may damage apricot, cherry, citrus, and plum. The insect also infests many common flowers, including aster, calendula, carnation, crocus, chrysanthemum, dahlia, dianthus, forget-me-not, freesia, iris, lily, nasturtium, pansy, poppy, primrose, rose, snapdragon, sunflower, tulip, verbena, and violet.

A particular pest of spinach and potato, green peach aphids harm a wide variety of vegetable crops.

Although downy mildew of spinach can be destructive, it is readily limited by crop rotation and cultural practices.

For general information about aphids and ways to control them, see *aphids* under BEAN. The green peach aphid is a $\frac{1}{16}$-inch-long pale yellowish green insect with three dark lines lengthwise on its back. Shiny black eggs overwinter on the bark of fruit trees, especially peach, hatching approximately when the peach trees bloom. Two or three generations of the aphid live on the fruit trees, sucking sap from twigs. They migrate to vegetable and flower garden plants during the summer. There may be as many as 15 generations in a summer. In fall the insects mate and lay eggs on the fruit trees.

Grow flat-leaved rather than savoy-leaved varieties of spinach; the aphids are easier to wash off the smooth leaves. Reduce the number of green peach aphids in your vegetable garden by controlling them on nearby fruit trees; use either a dormant oil spray in winter or an insecticidal soap spray in spring. Avoid planting spinach and other host crops next to susceptible flowers.

The *bean aphid* (see *aphids,* under BEAN) and the *melon aphid* (see CUCURBITS) may also infest spinach.

ADDITIONAL INSECT PESTS

The *beet leafhopper* (see TOMATO) may spread beet curly top virus to spinach plants. The black *blister beetle* (see BEET) often chews irregular holes in the leaves. The *cabbage looper* (see CABBAGE FAMILY) may feed on the undersides of the leaves, and the *celery leaftier* (see CELERY) may roll the leaves as it feeds. Potato and other *flea beetles* (see EGGPLANT) may riddle spinach leaves, and serpentine and spinach *leafminers* (see BEET) may mine the leaves. Although several root-knot *nematodes* (see BEAN) may cause damage, the *sugar beet cyst nematode*

(see BEET) is the nematode most likely to attack spinach. The *vegetable weevil* (see CARROT) may defoliate entire spinach plants.

DISEASES

Downy Mildew of Spinach

Also called blue mold, this fungus disease affects spinach grown in southeastern and southern states. 'Bloomsdale' and related cultivars are especially susceptible. Large pale yellow spots on the upper surfaces of the leaves grow together to cover the leaves. On the lower surfaces a gray to violet mold forms. The bottom leaves are affected first, then the disease spreads throughout the plant. The entire plant may decay and dry up.

Fungal spores in the soil infect susceptible plants when the weather is very humid and temperatures are between 45° and 65° F for a week. New spores that form on the leaves spread the disease throughout the planting.

Since the fungus can survive only on spinach, limit spinach crops to once every three years in the same location. Plant resistant varieties, such as 'Aden', 'Badger Savoy', 'Early', 'Giant Nobel', 'Melody', and 'Skookum'. Plant in a well-drained, fertile soil; allow adequate spacing between plants; and avoid overhead watering. Chemical control is not very practical, because it is difficult to spray the undersides of leaves that are so close to the ground.

OTHER DISEASES

Beet curly top virus (see TOMATO), transmitted by the beet leafhopper, causes curled leaves and sometimes kills spinach plants. Spinach may get *cercospora leaf spot of beet* (see BEET), although spinach is somewhat less vulnerable than beet.

Cracking of sweet potato roots may be caused by root-knot nematodes or it may be an unrelated physiological problem.

Sweet potato weevils look like ants with snouts. Control these pests or they will devastate sweet potato crops.

Cucumber mosaic virus (see CUCURBITS) is transmitted by the green peach aphid. Spinach is infected often enough that the disease is also known by two other names when it strikes this crop: spinach yellows and spinach blight. The usual symptoms are stunting of the plant and curled yellowed leaves. Resistant varieties include 'Early', 'Melody', 'Old Dominion', and 'Virginia Savoy'.

In spinach plants *tobacco mosaic virus* (see TOMATO) produces general stunting, mottling of the leaves, and death of leaf tissue.

SWEET POTATO

PHYSIOLOGICAL PROBLEMS

Growth Cracks

The edible root is marred by lengthwise cracks; these may be present at harvest or they may develop in storage. Although unsightly, cracks do not affect the eating quality. Prolonged dry conditions followed by very wet conditions can lead to cracking, particularly in susceptible varieties. In storage, wide fluctuations in temperature and humidity encourage cracking. Control the problem by keeping sweet potato plants evenly moist during the growing season. 'Jewel' and 'Porto Rico 198' are resistant to cracking.

INSECT AND OTHER ANIMAL PESTS

Sweet Potato Flea Beetle

A pest of sweet potato and corn, the $\frac{1}{16}$-inch-long black adult beetle also feeds on boxelder, dichondra, grain crops, grasses, ornamental and weedy morning glory, raspberry, and sugar beet. It eats narrow grooves in the leaves along the veins, causing the leaves to wilt and the plant to turn brown. The larvae feed on the roots of bindweed and dichondra. Control bindweed in your garden and don't plant dichondra near sweet potato plantings. For additional controls see *flea beetles*, under EGGPLANT.

Sweet potato may also exhibit the more typical shothole damage of the potato *flea beetle* (see EGGPLANT), and flea beetle larvae may bore into the roots.

Sweet Potato Weevil

This insect wreaks havoc on sweet potato crops in areas of Texas, Louisiana, Mississippi, Alabama, Florida, Georgia, and South Carolina; it may also cause local infestations elsewhere. Harvested roots are honeycombed with ⅜-inch-long, legless, fat white larvae with a pale brown head. The damaged roots have a bitter taste. You may see the adult beetles, which look like large ants, feeding on aboveground parts of the plant. They may spread black rot of sweet potato (see page 128) to plants as they feed. The ¼-inch-long adult beetles are shiny and reddish with a bluish black head, bluish black wing covers, and a long, straight black snout.

The weevil spends most of its life inside sweet potato roots. The larvae feed inside the roots and then pupate there; the adults emerge, mate, and lay eggs under the surface of the roots. The insect can complete its life cycle in as little as three weeks during hot weather or as long as two to three months during colder weather. It can live only on sweet potatoes or on certain kinds of morning glory near the coast. With food adults can live for months; without food they can survive for only a few days during warm weather. The pest spreads through an area slowly, because it can fly only short distances.

Obtain certified weevil-free slips (cuttings) and seed potatoes. Avoid growing morning glories and get rid of wild members of that family. Also eradicate volunteer sweet potatoes. If you start your own slips, do it away from your vegetable garden; when you harvest the slips, cut them at

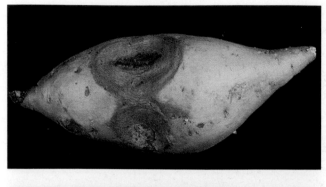

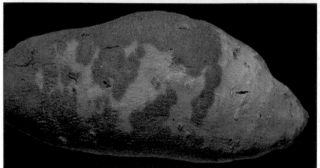

Top: Black rot causes rounded spots on sweet potato roots.
Bottom: Scurf blemishes are ugly but only skin-deep.

Don't risk introducing stem rot of sweet potato by using starts that are not certified to be disease free.

least 1 inch above the soil level to leave all or almost all insect eggs in the soil. Dig out and destroy the seed potatoes after you plant the harvested slips in your sweet potato patch. Mound the soil slightly around the stems of the growing crop plants to make it more difficult for the pest to reach the roots. After harvest, remove all plant debris, including leftover roots; the weevil's need to eat all winter is the weak point in its life cycle. Do not plant sweet potato in the same location each year; rotate it from site to site. If the pest strikes, remove and destroy any infested plants and roots.

Sometimes, when infestations are light, local nonplanting zones can be established to starve the weevil out of certain farm areas or communities. Contact the local cooperative extension office for information about your situation. Rotenone dust, which kills the adult weevils, can be used as part of a control program; dusting alone is insufficient.

ADDITIONAL INSECT AND ANIMAL PESTS

Sweet potato leaves may serve as food for *aphids,* particularly the green peach aphid (see SPINACH) and the potato aphid (see POTATO). The black *blister beetle* (see BEET) may chew irregular holes in sweet potato leaves.

Sweet potato is vulnerable to damage by two root-knot *nematodes* (see BEAN)—the cotton root-knot nematode and the southern root-knot nematode. Knots, or swellings, appear on the fine feeder roots; the nematodes also cause the feeder roots to rot. Damage to the edible roots includes scarring, pitting, and cracking. Scarring and pitting are more telling symptoms than cracking, which may not occur. Even when it does it may be due to a physiological problem unrelated to nematodes (see

Growth Cracks on page 127). The aboveground growth may not show symptoms if there is adequate rainfall and the soil infestation is light. When rain is scarce, severely infested plants—particularly those grown in light soils—may be stunted and yellowed. To check for nematodes cut the edible root into ⅛-inch slices and search for discolored brownish cavities with tiny pearly white nematodes inside. Next time try planting a resistant variety, such as 'Heart', 'Jasper', 'Jewel', 'Kandee', 'Nemagold', or 'Nugget'.

DISEASES

Black Rot of Sweet Potato

Common on sweet potato wherever it is grown, this fungus disease may ruin roots in the ground and in storage. An affected root has roundish, sunken black spots, which may spread to cover the root. The tissue just beneath the black areas has a bitter taste. Stems of slips or larger plants are black at their base and

just beneath the soil. Plants are stunted and the leaves turn yellow.

The fungus is carried in seed potatoes and in the soil. It is also spread by wind, water, and the sweet potato weevil (see page 127).

Obtain certified disease-free seed stock and look for a resistant variety, such as 'Allgold'. Before planting, wash seed stock in a 2½ percent solution of borax (1 pound borax to 5 to 6 gallons water). Grow slips in a location where sweet potatoes have not been grown for four years, or plant them in a sterile bedding mix; harvest the slips by cutting them 1 inch above the soil surface. Do not use fresh manure in sweet potato beds. Remove and destroy any plants that show symptoms of black rot. Rotate sweet potato with other crops on a three- to four-year basis.

Top: Blossom-end rot is among the most common tomato problems.
Bottom: Although unattractive, catfaced tomatoes taste fine.

Uneven watering and high temperatures combined to form radial and concentric cracks on these tomatoes.

Scurf of Sweet Potato

Found wherever sweet potato is grown, this fungus disease superficially mars the edible root but does not affect the eating quality. Skin-deep brownish to black discolorations develop on the surface of the roots during growth or storage. Also, the skin may crack and the roots may shrivel in storage.

The fungus is carried in seed potatoes and in the soil. Use the same controls as for black rot of sweet potato (see opposite page). The rotation can probably be reduced to two to three years if scurf is the only problem. 'Jasper' is a resistant variety.

Stem Rot of Sweet Potato

Also called wilt of sweet potato, this fungus disease is a form of fusarium wilt affecting only sweet potato. Plants have a yellowish tinge. Yellowing and leaf drop begin at the base of the plant and move upward. If you peel the stem, you will see a dark discoloration

that extends up the stem and down into the roots. The edible roots are small and decayed at the stem end; brown dots are visible in the cross section.

The fungus is carried in stored roots and can live in the soil for many years. Obtain certified disease-free seed potatoes or slips. Use resistant varieties, such as 'Allgold', 'Centennial', 'Jasper', 'Nemagold', 'Southern Queen', 'Triumph', and 'Yellow Strassburg'. Remove and destroy diseased plants. Rotate sweet potato with other crops; if the disease is in the soil, a 10-year rotation may be necessary.

TOMATO

PHYSIOLOGICAL PROBLEMS

Blossom-End Rot

This problem most commonly develops when the fruit is green and still enlarging. A water-soaked area appears on the blossom end (opposite the stem end). As the fruit develops, the discoloration spreads and turns dark brown and leathery. The blemish, which may be flat or concave,

extends slightly under the surface. It may remain dry and firm, or decay-causing bacteria or fungi may enter.

A deficiency of calcium in the plant causes the problem. Although calcium may be present in the soil, it is available to plants only when the soil is evenly moist. Other conditions that may lead to a calcium shortage in the plant are root damage, an imbalance of soil minerals, and heavy soil that does not permit development of a large root system.

Keep the soil evenly moist. Infrequent, deep waterings are better than frequent, light ones. A mulch on the soil surface will help conserve soil moisture. Do not plant tomatoes in heavy or poorly drained soil. Add plenty of organic matter to heavy clay soil before planting. Avoid damaging roots; do not cultivate more than 1 inch deep within 1 foot of the plant. Mulching not only conserves moisture but also eliminates the need

for cultivation. If these practices do not eliminate blossom-end rot, have your soil tested for a mineral imbalance.

Catfacing

The blossom end (opposite the stem end) of the tomato is deformed. There are rough brown blemishes and the surface may be puckered or have bulbous protrusions.

The problem seems to be caused by exposure to cold days and nights while the embryonic flower buds are forming. Waiting to plant until the weather warms up reduces the problem. 'Monte Carlo' and 'Walter Villemaire' are varieties that have shown resistance. Small-fruited varieties are also less likely to be affected by catfacing.

Growth Cracks

Radial or concentric cracks appear on the fruit, usually at the stem end. At first, the cracks are moist and open; later, the surface tissue may heal to a dry brown veneer. Early blight, anthracnose, and other decay organisms may enter through the cracks.

Poor light and inadequate soil fertility are among the factors that lead to spindly, late-blooming tomato plants.

Top: Exposed tomato fruit can be scalded by the sun.
Bottom: Beet leafhoppers spread curly top virus in the West.

Radial cracks form during periods of high temperatures and bright sunlight. Concentric cracks usually form when rain follows a dry spell. Both types of cracks are the result of sudden, rapid growth.

Keep the soil evenly moist. In hot, bright climates choose varieties that have good leaf cover, and schedule your planting to avoid ripening during temperatures higher than 90° F. To avoid concentric cracking, pick ripe fruit right after a rainfall. 'Burpee's VF', 'Floradel', 'Floralou', 'Homestead 24', 'Manalucie', 'Monte Carlo', and 'Pearson Improved' have shown some resistance to cracking. 'Roma', 'Square Paste', and other paste tomato varieties have shown marked resistance.

Poor Fruit Set

The plant bears little or no fruit, even though it appears otherwise healthy. There are many reasons for poor fruit set. Tomato flowers are usually self-pollinating; they rely on breezes to transfer the pollen from the male part of the flower to the female part. The optimum temperature, humidity, soil moisture, soil fertility, and sunlight are also needed for pollination to succeed. When nighttime temperatures fall below 55° F for more than four nights in a row, flowers fall off unfertilized. They also drop when the temperature rises above 90° F during the day or above 75° F during the night, when the relative humidity is above its ideal range of 40 to 70 percent, and when the soil is too dry or too wet. When tomato plants grow in soil that is too high in nitrogen, they produce leafy growth at the expense of blossoms. Conversely, if soil fertility is too low, the plant will be spindly and unable to support a crop. Plants growing in sites that receive less than six hours of sunlight a day form few blossoms; they may grow quite tall but without flowers or fruit.

Schedule tomato plantings to avoid unfavorable temperatures. Choose varieties that cope best with your growing conditions. If your nights are cool, plant in the warmest spot in the garden and use mechanical warming techniques, such as a 6-inch band of black roofing paper around the base of the tomato cage. Commercially available growth hormone sprays may help fruit set in cool weather. If the daytime temperature is between 90° and 100° F and the nighttime temperature below 75° F, improve fruit set by aiming a strong jet of water at the plants twice during the heat of the day. If the daytime temperature is above 100° F and the nighttime temperature above 75° F, this measure will not work. If the air is calm, flick each blossom to shake the pollen loose.

Pick a site where plants will get six or more hours of sunlight a day. Plant in well-drained, properly amended soil. Keep the plants evenly watered, and apply a mulch to conserve moisture. Several types of fertilizer formulations are suitable for tomatoes. Many have a higher amount of phosphorus than nitrogen or potassium—for example, 8-10-8 or 10-12-6. Others have similar amounts of phosphorus and potassium and a smaller amount of nitrogen—for example, 5-10-10. To check a plant's nitrogen needs, examine the stems 6 inches from the tips. If they are smaller than the diameter of your small finger, the plant needs nitrogen. If the growth is larger and rank, the plant has been receiving too much nitrogen. Correct a lack of nitrogen with a fertilizer containing mainly nitrogen; correct an excess of nitrogen with a fertilizer containing mainly phosphorus.

Sunscald

Both green and nearly ripe fruit may develop a blistered, shiny light area on the side facing the most intense sunlight. Later, this area becomes a flat, grayish white blemish. Sudden exposure of the fruit to the sun may initiate sunscald. Heavy pruning and diseases that cause wilting or leaf drop are common causes.

Tomato hornworms have a black horn, whereas tobacco hornworms have a red one. Both insects devour tomato plants.

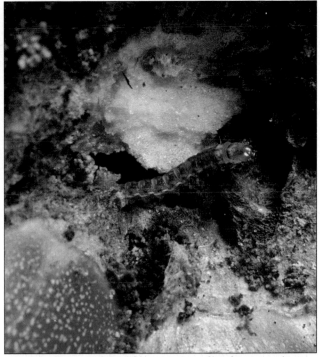

The stem was removed from this tomato, revealing the tomato pinworm and the damage it caused.

In areas where the summer sun is intense, choose tomato varieties with large, broad leaves. Avoid excessive pruning. Control wilt-producing diseases (see *fusarium wilt of tomato* on page 136, and *verticillium wilt* on page 139) and mites (see *tomato russet mite,* page 132). Erect a cloth shade structure a couple of feet above the plants: Drive four stakes into the ground and fasten the corners of a lightweight cloth or floating row cover to them. For tomatoes that sprawl on the ground, use a light covering of straw to protect exposed fruit.

Insect and Other Animal Pests

Beet Leafhopper
Primarily a problem in the West, except in the Pacific Coast fog belt, the beet leafhopper ranges as far east as Illinois and Missouri. The insect is a serious pest because it spreads beet curly top virus as it feeds on a wide range of vegetables, flowers, and weeds. (See *beet curly top virus,* page 135, for a list of hosts.)

The ⅛-inch-long beet leafhopper is usually pale greenish or yellowish but becomes darker in winter. It overwinters among weed hosts in the desert and foothills. In spring it lays eggs on weeds and it is here that the first generation matures. From early May to June, the first-generation adults fly in swarms to sugar beet fields. They feed on the sugar beets, spreading beet curly top virus. After the sugar beets are harvested, the leafhoppers fly to nearby gardens, where they spread the virus to vegetables and flowers. For more information about leafhoppers in general, see *leafhoppers,* under Potato.

For control measures see *beet curly top virus,* page 135.

Hornworms
The *tomato hornworm* and the *tobacco hornworm* infest tomato, eggplant, pepper, potato, and tomato-family weeds in localized areas throughout the United States. The hornworms are large (up to 4

inches long) bright green caterpillars with diagonal white stripes and a prominent horn at the rear. The two species have slightly different markings. The tomato hornworm has eight diagonal lines on each side, joined by a horizontal white stripe; its horn is green with black sides. The tobacco hornworm has seven diagonal white stripes on each side, and its horn is red.

The life cycles of the two species, as well as the damage they cause and control measures for them, are identical. Hornworms overwinter in the soil as hard-shelled brown pupae; the pupae can be identified by a narrow tongue that sticks out like the handle of a pitcher. Large moths, known as sphinx moths or hummingbird moths, emerge in May or June. They hover over petunia and other flowers at dusk, sipping nectar. The females lay greenish or yellow eggs singly on the undersides of leaves of host plants. The caterpillars hatch a week later and feed for three to four weeks on the foliage and fruit. There is one

generation a year in the North and two or more in the South.

Often, handpicking is enough to control these pests in a home garden. Leave any caterpillars with small white cocoons on their backs; they are being parasitized by a braconid wasp, which will soon produce more wasps to help with control.

Trichogramma wasps, lacewings, and lady beetles attack hornworm eggs. *Bt berliner-kurstake* is lethal to hornworms and is recommended in areas where handpicking is impractical. Tilling in fall will destroy pupae in the soil, although moths are likely to fly in from other gardens.

Tomato Pinworm
This insect attacks tomato in the South and in southern California. Serpentine or blotchy trails appear in the leaves, some leaves are folded and held together with light webs, and pinholes are bored into ripening fruit near the stem end. Feeding inside the fruit are up to ⅛-inch-long

It takes close attention to recognize the yellowing and bronzing caused by a tomato russet mite infestation.

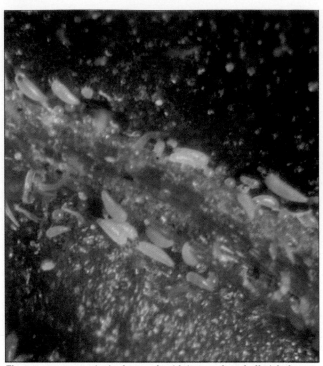

The tomato russet mite is elongated, with its mouth and all eight legs at the front end.

yellowish or gray caterpillars with purple spots.

The insect overwinters as a pupa in the soil, leaves, or fruit. The adult is a gray moth with a ¼-inch wingspan. Soon after emerging, the adults, which are active primarily at dusk, begin to lay eggs on the undersides of tomato leaves. The eggs hatch in a week and the caterpillars feed for several weeks.

Before planting, check transplants carefully for infestations. Till under all plants and unharvested fruit immediately after harvest; pupae buried more than 2 inches deep will not survive. Although some two dozen naturally occurring parasites attack this pest, they do not usually offer effective control. Releasing large numbers of trichogramma wasps at egg-laying time has provided some control.

Tomato Russet Mite

This spider relative is most common in California, although localized infestations have occurred in scattered locations. Attacks on tomato

usually kill the plant. The mite also infests eggplant, pepper, and potato, as well as tomato-family ornamentals including datura and petunia. Another host is wild morning glory (bindweed).

An infested plant takes on a dirty yellow-brown appearance usually described as bronze or russet, and the stems may develop lengthwise cracks. Damage begins at the bottom of the plant and moves upward. The leaves turn brown in another three to four weeks and the plant usually dies. Although the fruit is rarely attacked, it may be sunburned when the leaves curl.

The tomato russet mite is too small to see without a 30-power magnifying lens. The slow-moving orange-yellow pest is shaped like a dunce cap with eight legs at the wider end. It completes its life cycle in only eight days and reproduces continually during warm weather. A prolonged freeze kills the mite. It overwinters on any tomato-family

plants and on wild morning glory. Infested wild morning glory has leaves that appear dry, with a silver sheen on both surfaces. The mites may be spread by wind and by gardeners working among plants. The mites also move around by hitchhiking on insects.

Avoid growing tomato next to potato, petunia, or any other tomato-family plants. Eliminate any overwintering tomato-family crops and wild morning glory. Naturally occurring predatory mites help control low populations of the mite, but they cannot wipe out a heavy infestation. If the tomato russet mite has been a problem in the past, make one application of liquid sulfur or sulfur dust when the tomato plants are fairly large but before symptoms appear; this will probably reduce the tomato russet mite population to a level that the predators can handle. Repeat the application in three to four weeks if symptoms appear. Avoid applying sulfur when the temperature is over 94° F.

Also, apply only as much sulfur as recommended, since too much can injure tomato plants. Wash the sulfur-treated fruit before eating it and especially before canning; traces of sulfur will form sulfur dioxide, which may cause the containers to explode.

The *two-spotted mite* (see BEAN) may also attack tomato.

Whitefly

Plaguing gardeners throughout the United States, this insect attacks tomato, bean, cucumber, eggplant, lettuce, okra, potato, sweet potato, and many other vegetables as well as numerous ornamental plants and weeds.

When you brush against a plant, tiny white insects flutter around for a few seconds, then land on the plant again. Examination of the lower leaf surfaces reveals both the white winged adults and the even smaller (¹/₃₂ inch long), flat, oval, translucent pale green whitefly larvae, which

An adult whitefly, magnified greatly, rests on a tomato leaf. In a severe infestation all life stages will be present.

Potato aphids, which spread viruses to tomato and potato, can also cause blossom drop.

resemble scale insects. Often, an infestation begins at the bottom of a plant and moves upward. There may be a coating of honeydew, a sticky excretion of the insects, on the leaves. Sooty mold, a powdery black fungus, may grow on the honeydew deposits. An infested plant lacks vigor; the leaves may turn yellow and sometimes the plant wilts and dies.

Since the insect cannot overwinter in the North, outbreaks in cold-winter areas probably come from infested greenhouse plants. Such plants may also be a major source of problems in southern gardens, even though the insect can survive winters outdoors in warm climates. Adult whiteflies lay eggs on the undersides of leaves. These hatch into tiny mobile larvae called crawlers; after moving about for up to two days, they become immobile and remain in place sucking plant sap. At this stage they resemble scale insects. They stop feeding for a few days to pupate, and the

adults emerge. Soon, all stages of the insect are present on plant leaves. The life cycle takes approximately one month, and there can be many overlapping generations in a season.

If the infestation is confined to a few leaves, pick off the affected leaves. Often, the many natural enemies of whitefly are able to keep the insect under control. Among whitefly predators are lacewings, bigeyed bugs, and minute pirate bugs. There are also a number of naturally occurring parasites. *Encarsia formosa* is a tiny parasitic wasp sold for release in greenhouses; it is unsuitable for release in most gardens, except possibly those sheltered from the wind. Insecticidal soap, applied every 7 to 10 days, will kill whiteflies; be sure to spray the undersides of the leaves, including those near the ground. Pyrethrins and ryania also kill whiteflies, but try insecticidal soap first. A vacuum

cleaner will catch adults, although the larvae remain behind on the plant. Vacuum early in the morning, when it is still cool and the insects are sluggish. Place the vacuum bag filled with whiteflies in a plastic container and freeze it overnight to kill the insects. Repeat every few days to remove newly mature adults. Yellow sticky traps (see page 37) may be effective in reducing the number of adult whiteflies.

ADDITIONAL INSECT AND ANIMAL PESTS

Two types of *aphids*—the green peach aphid (see SPINACH) and the potato aphid (see POTATO)—commonly feed on tomato. The potato aphid may damage tomato blossoms so badly that they are unable to set fruit. The fall *armyworm* (see CORN) may also attack tomato plants. *Blister beetles* (see BEET), the *cabbage looper* (see CABBAGE FAMILY), and the *Colorado potato beetle* (see POTATO) may chew holes in tomato leaves.

When the *corn earworm* (see CORN) attacks tomato, it is known as the tomato fruitworm. It begins by feeding on foliage but soon works its way into the green fruit, usually entering at the stem end. It may destroy as much as one quarter of the tomato crop. The larvae move from fruit to fruit, as well as to nearby bean, broccoli, cabbage, lettuce, okra, and pepper plants. Bt may kill 40 to 60 percent of the caterpillars on tomato.

Cutworms (see SEEDLINGS) not only injure tomato seedlings, they may also gouge holes in the fruit. The *European corn borer* (see CORN) may damage tomato plants, especially if corn is planted nearby. Mostly young but also older tomato plants may show the shot-hole feeding pattern of palestriped and potato *flea beetles* (see EGGPLANT). The *green stinkbug* (see BEAN) occasionally feeds on tomato leaves. The *meadow mouse*

Although the Colorado potato beetle prefers potato, it will eat tomato plants. Here, a larva is eating into the fruit.

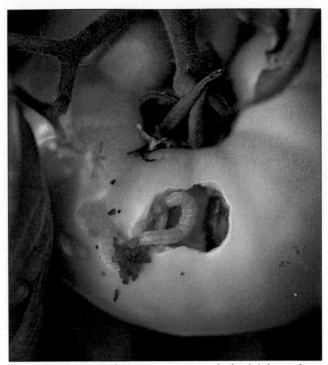

The corn earworm attacks tomatoes so commonly that it is known by a second name: the tomato fruitworm.

(see BEAN) may eat ripening fruit that is near the ground.

All the root-knot *nematodes* (see BEAN) affecting bean also affect tomato. Tomato is susceptible to a number of other nematode species as well. Nematode-resistant tomato varieties (identifiable by the letter *N* next to the variety name) are resistant to the cotton root-knot nematode, the Javanese root-knot nematode, and the southern root-knot nematode but not the northern root-knot nematode. Keep in mind that nematode resistance is not reliable in warm soil (above 81° F). See the charts on pages 144 to 145 for resistant varieties.

The *onion thrips* (see ONION) may attack tomato. Other thrips, including the flower thrips, sometimes feed on tomato and other vegetables. Both kinds of thrips transmit tomato spotted wilt virus. The *potato tuberworm* (see POTATO) may bore into tomato fruit; as a preventive measure avoid planting tomato where potato just grew. The *spotted*

cucumber beetle (see CUCURBITS) and the *vegetable weevil* (see CARROT) may damage tomato leaves. Tomato roots may be seriously injured by *symphylans* (see SEEDLINGS).

DISEASES

Bacterial Canker
Also known as bacterial blight, this widespread disease appears sporadically. However, it is so destructive that care should be taken to avoid it and to recognize it when it strikes. In addition to affecting tomato, it may be carried by ground cherry and tomato-family weeds, such as horsenettle, jimsonweed, and nightshade.

Variable symptoms make this bacterial disease tricky to identify. Seedlings grown from infected seeds may wilt and die quickly or they may show no symptoms until they have been transplanted into the garden. On older plants wilting of the lower leaves is the first symptom. The wilted leaves hang downward, but the

edges of the leaflets curl upward. Often, only half of the plant or half of the leaflets on a leaf will wilt. You may see light-colored streaks extending down the stem; these streaks break open into cankers. Squeezing the stem may cause a yellow slime to ooze from the cankers. If you cut open the stem, you will see a brown or yellow discoloration; there may also be hollow cavities. The most specific symptom of the disease is on the fruit—small light brown lesions surrounded by a white halo; however, this symptom does not always occur. Plants that survive the disease remain stunted and never produce a good harvest.

The bacterium causing the disease is carried on and inside seeds. It survives in infected plant debris, on plant stakes, and on tools, and it can live in the soil for up to two and one-half years. Gardeners handling infected seedlings and then healthy ones can spread the disease. Warm, wet weather encourages the disease.

Prevention is the best control, since there is no chemical cure and no known genetic resistance. Obtain seeds from a reputable source and buy certified disease-free seedlings if they are available. Control tomato-family weeds in and near the garden. If you grow your own transplants, use a sterile potting mix. Sanitize tools with a freshly made solution of 1 part household bleach to 9 parts water. Handle tomato plants as little as possible and try not to work among wet plants. A three-year rotation for tomato is a wise precaution, but it becomes essential if the disease actually appears. Remove and destroy infected plants and fruit as soon as you notice them. Place a bag over the plants and remove them without touching them. A copper fungicide spray may help protect healthy plants, but reports on its effectiveness are mixed.

White-ringed brown lesions on tomatoes, creating a bird's-eye effect, are the clearest symptom of bacterial canker.

Beet curly top virus symptoms are variable on tomato but are likely to include yellowed twisted leaves.

Beet Curly Top Virus

A problem west of the Continental Divide, especially in arid regions that are irrigated, this virus is among the factors limiting commercial tomato crops in some parts of the West. It also affects bean, beet, carrot, celery, cabbage-family crops, cucurbits, eggplant, New Zealand spinach, okra, pepper, potato, spinach, and Swiss chard. In addition, it attacks many flowers, including alyssum, blue flax, campanula, carnation, columbine, coreopsis, cosmos, delphinium, foxglove, geranium, larkspur, nasturtium, pansy, petunia, poppy, portulaca, pyrethrum, scabiosa, Shasta daisy, stock, strawflower, veronica, and zinnia. Weed hosts include curly dock, filaree, mustard, peppergrass, plantago, Russian thistle, and tumbleweed.

Tomato plants at any stage of development may be infected. Although symptoms vary, several are generally associated with the virus. The leaves of an infected seedling turn yellow, and often they are twisted and curled; usually the plant dies quickly. The leaves of older plants become leathery and stiff and there is a pronounced rolling, twisting, and puckering. When infected after mid- to late maturity, the plant turns greenish yellow, then yellow. The main stem and branches become abnormally erect, the leafstalks turn downward, and the leaflets twist and roll upward. The leaflet veins may turn purple. Severely infected plants are stunted and rarely produce fruit; if they do it ripens prematurely and has an off-flavor. In advanced stages of the disease, the roots may rot, causing the plant to collapse and die.

Beware of a hasty diagnosis. Some tomato varieties have leaflets that roll upward when the plant is growing well. Also, purplish veins and stunting may be symptoms of phosphorus deficiency.

The virus is transmitted by the beet leafhopper (see page 131). The insect feeds on wild vegetation between crop seasons, and at the height of the growing season it migrates into gardens and spreads the virus there. Often, the migration coincides with the drying up of wild vegetation. The disease is worst in areas with intense sunlight, prolonged summer heat, low humidity, and rapid evaporation. Usually, the period of greatest leafhopper activity is May and June.

Look for resistant varieties, although breeding resistant tomatoes is complicated by the fact that the virus has many strains. Recent research in Arizona found 'Payette' to be the most resistant variety tested. Other varieties showing resistance include 'Columbia', 'Owyhee', 'Rosa', and 'Saladmaster'. Controlling the beet leafhopper is of limited value, because the insect migrates long distances to feed on crops, and it may only be passing through your garden. Remove volunteer plants from a previous susceptible crop, because they may serve as a reservoir for the virus. Avoid planting tomato where it will be surrounded by other susceptible plants. In some areas it is possible to plant early enough so that the plants are past the seedling stage by the time the leafhopper migrates. In other areas the leafhopper may migrate at almost any time of the year. Check with the local cooperative extension office. Protect young plants with a floating row cover, and remove the cover when the plants are large enough to withstand attack. If the problem is serious, protect larger plants under 4- to 6-foot-high frames covered with fine-mesh cheesecloth or a floating row cover. The frame should be large enough so that the plant never touches the cloth. As an alternative, plant two or three

Look for a subtle bull's-eye pattern in the dark brown spots caused by early blight on tomato leaves.

The stem of this tomato plant infected with fusarium wilt has been cut lengthwise to show discoloration.

tomato plants in a single hill; if one or two are infected, you can remove them and still have a crop. If all the plants survive, the crowding may reduce the amount of fruit per plant but probably won't reduce total yield for the space.

Early Blight of Tomato and Potato

Also known as alternaria blight, this widespread fungus disease is less common in arid regions of the West, although overhead irrigation and frequent heavy dew promote the disease in these areas. The disease is frequently found on tomato and potato and occasionally strikes eggplant and pepper. It also infects tomato-family weeds.

Small, irregularly shaped dark brown spots, 1/32 inch to 1/2 inch in diameter, appear on the older leaves first and gradually move up the plant. They develop a bull's-eye pattern of concentric rings and often are surrounded by a narrow yellow halo. If there are many lesions, a leaf will turn yellow

and drop off. Elongated lesions on the stems also show concentric rings. When blossoms become infected they drop. On the fruit, early blight causes leathery, sunken dark brown lesions with the characteristic concentric circles. These form at the stem end and on growth cracks and other injuries. In humid weather the fruit lesions become covered with velvety black spores. Infected seedlings may have collar rot, a dark brown lesion circling the stem at the soil line.

The fungal spores overwinter in seeds and plant debris and are spread rapidly from plant to plant by wind and rain. To germinate, the spores require the moist environment of overhead irrigation, frequent rain, or heavy dew. Infection is most likely to occur during warm weather (75° to 85° F), although the symptoms develop

most rapidly when the temperature is less than 70° F.

Obtain seeds from a reputable source. If you doubt the quality, soak the seeds for 25 minutes in 122° F water (see page 32). The same treatment also controls septoria leaf spot (see opposite page) and tomato anthracnose (see page 139). Although some varieties are more tolerant of early blight than others, there are as yet no truly resistant varieties. Plant only healthy seedlings, allow for good air circulation, and provide adequate water and fertilizer. Avoid overhead watering. Remove infected plants from the garden and clean up plant debris after harvest. Schedule a two- to three-year rotation for tomato-family crops. Apply a liquid copper fungicide beginning shortly before or at blossom set, or at first symptoms, and repeat every 7 to 10 days. Be sure to coat the undersides of the leaves. (The same chemical will also control septoria leaf spot and tomato anthracnose; although there

are slight differences in the optimum spray schedule for each, a compromise schedule can be devised.)

Fusarium Wilt of Tomato

This is one of the most common and devastating diseases of tomato. There are several strains of the fungus: Race 1 is found everywhere; race 2 is scattered; and race 3 is a problem in Florida.

The lower leaves of seedlings turn downward, wilt, and die, and infected seedlings rarely survive long enough to flower or fruit. If the plants are infected when they are older, the lower leaves turn yellow, wilt, and die; often this occurs only on one side of the plant or one side of a shoot. The infected plant may be stunted and may produce either little or no normal fruit or a reduced crop of small, inferior fruit near the top of the plant. Part or all of the plant may die, with the brown leaves still attached to the stems. If you cut open an

On tomato, late blight lesions start out as large water-soaked green patches, which later turn brown.

Tomato fruit infected by late blight develops greenish brown greasy blotches, mainly at the stem end.

affected stem, you will see brown streaks under the surface.

The fungal spores live on decaying tomato material in the soil, and they continue to live in the soil after the debris has rotted away. In some soils they can live three to four years in the absence of a tomato crop. In other soils, especially light, dry, sandy soils, they can live indefinitely. Soil acidity (pH 5.0 to 5.6) seems to favor the disease; incidence of the disease decreases up to pH 7.2 but increases at higher pH levels. The disease is most active in warm soil (78° to 90° F). Although the fungus can be transmitted by seed, it usually isn't, because most infected fruit drops and is not saved for seed.

Obtain seeds and transplants from a reputable source. The chief method of control is resistant varieties. There are many resistant varieties for races 1 and 2 but none for race 3. Resistance is indicated by the letter *F* after

the variety name; varieties with *FF* are resistant to both races 1 and 2. Some resistant varieties are listed in the charts on pages 144 and 145. Maintain a soil pH around 6.0. Fertilize properly, since the disease is favored by too little potassium and too much nitrogen. Keep the soil evenly moist as the crop develops. Rotate tomato on a three- to four-year basis. Soil solarization (see page 30) has been shown to suppress the disease.

Late Blight
This fungus disease is a problem in humid areas, particularly east of the Mississippi River. Although different strains affect tomato and potato, each is capable of infecting the other host. Eggplant is also susceptible to infection.

On tomato the first symptom is a bending down of the leafstalks. Large, irregular, water-soaked greenish patches develop on the leaves and stems. These lesions enlarge and turn brown and papery. During wet weather the undersides of the lesions develop a downy white ring of

mold. Large, irregular, firm greenish brown blotches with a rough, greasy-looking surface appear on the fruit. They begin at the stem end and commonly occupy the upper half of the fruit. During wet weather all the leaves may become blighted and the mold may appear on the fruit as well. Infected plants have a foul odor.

For general information about the fungus and ways to control it, see *late blight* under POTATO. Purchase tomato seedlings from a reputable source or grow your own. Remove any diseased tomato plants, including fallen leaves and fruit, from the garden immediately.

Septoria Leaf Spot
Common in the north central, northeastern, and southeastern states, this destructive fungus disease affects primarily tomato. It may also strike eggplant, potato, and tomato-family weeds.

Many small water-soaked spots appear on the undersides

of leaves near the bottom of the plant. These become roughly circular, ¼-inch lesions visible on both sides of the leaves. Older spots are gray or tan with a darker margin and small dark brown dots in the middle. The infection moves up the plant, appearing on the leaves, stems, and blossoms but rarely on the fruit. Heavily infected leaves turn yellow and drop. The loss of leaf cover may expose the fruit to sunscald (see Physiological Problems, page 130). Septoria leaf spot can be distinguished from early blight of tomato and potato (see opposite page) by the larger number of spots and the presence of tiny dark brown dots inside older spots.

The fungus completes several generations in a season. The disease can overwinter in tomato debris and on tomato-family weeds, but it does not survive in the soil. The disease is also transmitted by seed; infected seeds produce diseased plants. Spores are spread by wind, splashing water, contaminated tools, and

Septoria leaf spot can be identified by the dark dots that form in the center of spots.

Narrow shoestring leaflets are a common symptom of tobacco mosaic virus on tomato, but symptoms are highly variable.

gardeners working among the plants. Warm, moist weather favors development of septoria leaf blight. Although the disease can strike at any time, it is most likely to occur after fruit set.

Obtain seeds from a reputable source. If there is any doubt, soak the seeds for 25 minutes in 122° F water (see page 32). The same treatment also controls early blight and tomato anthracnose. Get rid of susceptible weeds in and near the garden. Don't plant seedlings that show symptoms of the disease. Remove tomato debris after harvest. Rotate tomato, eggplant, and potato together on a four-year basis. Apply a liquid copper fungicide beginning when the first symptoms appear or shortly before or at blossom set; repeat every 7 to 10 days. (The same chemical will also control early blight and tomato anthracnose; although there are slight differences in the optimum spray schedule for each, a compromise schedule can be devised.)

Tobacco Mosaic Virus

Also known as tomato mosaic and pepper mosaic, this widespread virus affects tomato, eggplant, pepper, potato, tobacco, and nearly all other tomato-family plants, as well as spinach, and many weeds.

The symptoms are variable and may be almost invisible during hot weather. Also, there are many strains of the virus, each with slightly different symptoms. Light and darker green mottling on the leaves is a common symptom. Some strains cause a bright yellow mottling. Contrary to popular belief the leaves do not develop brown spots. During cool weather the leaves may show a shoestring effect—very narrow leaflets, similar to those caused by cucumber mosaic virus. A diseased plant usually produces fewer and smaller fruit than normal. Occasionally, the fruit has brown areas; this is most common on fully developed,

unripe fruit produced earliest on the plant.

Although the virus can be transmitted by seed, it is spread primarily by gardeners who smoke. It is estimated that 80 percent of all cigarettes contain the virus. A smoker who touches a susceptible plant runs the risk of introducing the virus. The virus can also be carried on tools that the smoker has handled. Infected plants can infect healthy plants by contact—by gardeners brushing up against plants and by infected plant debris in the soil touching the roots of healthy plants. Although the virus can survive for a century in dried plant debris, it disappears rapidly when the infected plant material decomposes. High soil moisture and shortages of nitrogen and boron in the soil are among the factors that make symptoms more severe.

Obtain seeds and seedlings from a reputable source. Choose resistant varieties; these are indicated by the letter *T* after the variety name.

Some resistant varieties are listed in the charts on pages 144 and 145. If you are a smoker, wash your hands thoroughly with soap and water before handling tomato plants. Ask the same of any family members and visitors to the garden. Milk helps to prevent the spread of tobacco mosaic virus. If the virus has been a problem in the past, spray seedlings with skim milk and dip your hands in milk frequently when transplanting. Do not actually dip the seedlings in milk, however. Clean your hands and tools often in a 3 percent solution of trisodium phosphate (TSP). Scrub under your nails and rinse your hands well under running water. Do not rinse the tools after washing them in TSP. Think of what you may have touched, including faucets and doorknobs, and wash them with TSP as well. Launder clothing that may have brushed against infected plants. Dig up any diseased

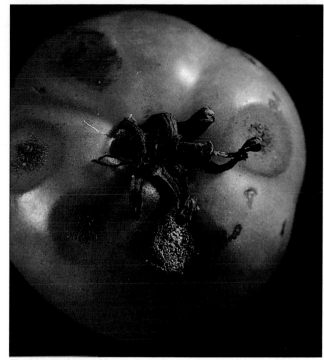

The fruit of plants with tomato anthracnose develops dark circular spots, followed by decay of the entire fruit.

Leaves with V-shaped lesions and tan discoloration of internal stem tissue are symptoms of verticillium wilt.

plants immediately and remove them from the garden. If the disease has occurred, plan a one- to three-year rotation for susceptible crops.

Tomato is vulnerable to other virus diseases, including *cucumber mosaic virus* (see CUCURBITS). The most typical symptom is a shoestring appearance of the leaves. The disease may also cause general stunting, unusual bushiness, and green mottling. The fruit is small and often misshapen. The disease is spread mainly by aphids, including the *green peach aphid* (see SPINACH) and the *potato aphid (see* POTATO), although it may be spread to some extent by gardeners working among the plants. Control aphids, eliminate host weeds, and remove diseased plants from the garden.

Tomato Anthracnose
Most common in the northeastern and north central states, this fungus disease infects the fruit of tomato and pepper. Other tomato-family crops may harbor the fungus.

Sunken, circular spots appear on the fruit of diseased plants; eventually, the whole fruit decays. The infection may begin when tomato fruit is still green, although the fruit looks normal until it ripens. On the ripe fruit the small spots enlarge until they are dime sized. They become dark in the center and are soon peppered with black dots arranged in concentric rings. During moist weather these dots develop the salmon pink spore masses typical of anthracnose (see *bean anthracnose,* under BEAN). Symptoms are not usually noticeable on leaves or stems.

The fungus lives in the soil. The fungal resting bodies tend to build up in the soil when tomato and potato are grown; they slowly decrease when less susceptible crops are grown. The fungus also lives in decaying plant material, and it may be carried in association with seeds. The disease is favored by wet

weather and poorly drained soil. Although the fungus can infect tomato at any temperature between 55° and 95° F, lesions grow most rapidly at 80° F. Fruit damaged by flea beetles, windblown sand, early blight, or growth cracks is more susceptible.

Obtain seeds from a reputable source. If there is any doubt, soak the seeds for 25 minutes in 122° F water (see page 32). The same treatment also controls early blight of tomato and potato (see page 136) and septoria leaf spot (see page 137). Plant in well-drained soil and avoid overhead watering. Mulch to prevent swirling of sandy soils and splashing of spores. Control insects and other diseases. Pick the fruit as soon as it is ripe; don't allow damaged fruit to decay on the ground. Remove diseased plants from the garden and clean up tomato debris after harvest. Rotate tomato-family crops together; if the disease appears use a three- to four-year rotation. Apply a liquid copper

fungicide, beginning no later than blossom set and continuing weekly until the end of the harvest. (The same chemical will also control early blight and septoria leaf spot; although there are slight differences in the optimum spray schedule for each, a compromise schedule can be devised.)

Verticillium Wilt
This damaging fungus disease occurs in the north central and northeastern states as well as in California, Washington, Colorado, Utah, and southern Florida. There are two races: Race 1 is widely distributed; race 2 occurs only in California and North Carolina. The tomato-family vegetables affected by verticillium wilt include tomato, eggplant, and potato; the disease is rare on pepper. It also commonly strikes beet, cabbage-family plants, cowpea, cucurbits, New Zealand spinach, okra, peanut, rhubarb, and spinach. Many common shade trees, fruit

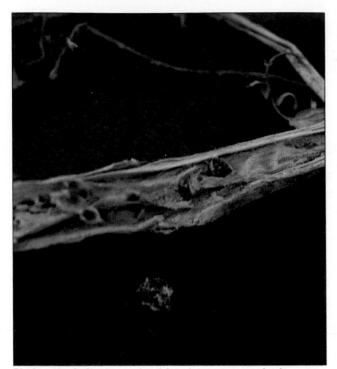

Black resting bodies (center front) form in tomato stems that have stem rot, also known as timber rot.

Raised rings ripen unevenly on fruit infected with tomato spotted wilt virus.

trees, berries, flowers, and weeds are vulnerable to the disease. Strawberry is very susceptible, although there are resistant varieties.

In tomato the symptoms begin on the lower leaves. They may turn yellow and wilt quickly or they may remain unwilted at first as the discoloration spreads. In the latter case, V-shaped yellow areas at the edge of the leaf develop, enlarge, and turn brown. The veins also become brown. Eventually, the lower leaves drop and the disease progresses up the plant until only the youngest leaves remain. Verticillium wilt produces symptoms uniformly across the plant, whereas fusarium wilt of tomato (see page 136) causes symptoms on one side of the plant or on one branch. A plant infected by verticillium wilt is stunted; the fruit is small and yellow around the stem end and it may sunburn because of the loss of leaves. If you cut across the main stem, you will see a light tan discoloration in the cross section.

The fungus lives in the soil for many years. Because it has many hosts, it can build up in the absence of susceptible vegetable crops. It may be transmitted by seed, although reports are conflicting. The disease develops most readily when the temperature is between 70° and 75° F. The wilt gradually plugs the vascular system, and the damaged plant has more trouble coping with the increased water loss on hot days. Plants are more vulnerable to infection when they have been overwatered and overfertilized with nitrogen. Plants that have been hardened off excessively are also more susceptible.

Resistant varieties are the best control measure. There are many resistant varieties for race 1 but none for race 2; the letter *V* after the variety name indicates resistance. Some resistant varieties are listed in the charts on pages 144 and 145. Obtain seeds and transplants from a reputable source. Rotate tomato-family crops together. If the disease

is present, a four- to six-year rotation may be helpful in controlling it. For the rotation to be effective, other susceptible plants must not be grown in the soil. See page 147 for lists of commonly grown resistant and immune plants. Soil solarization (see page 30) will reduce the disease. Water and fertilize plants adequately. Discard diseased plants and fruit as soon as you notice them, and remove tomato debris at the end of the season.

OTHER DISEASES

One strain of *bacterial spot* (see PEPPER) may also affect tomato. The leaf spots it causes on tomato are circular, water-soaked dark areas, usually less than ¼ inch in diameter. Later, the centers dry and fall out, leaving small holes. Fruit lesions on tomato are similar to those on pepper. There are no resistant tomato varieties, although varieties differ in susceptibility.

Southern blight (see PEANUT) causes wilting of tomato plants, followed by a coating of white fungal growth on the lower stem; embedded in

the fungal growth are the typical mustard seed–like reproductive bodies of the fungus. The wilt is unusual because the leaves do not change color before they wilt. If you fear that southern blight is present in the soil, you may escape damage by wrapping the stems of transplants in aluminum foil, 2 inches above and 2 inches below the soil surface, at planting time. Make sure that there is no soil contact above the wrap.

The fungi that cause *lettuce drop* (see LETTUCE) and a host of diseases in other crops produce a *stem rot* in tomato. The symptoms are similar to those of stem rot on cucurbits (see Other Diseases, under CUCURBITS). *Tomato spotted wilt virus*, which is transmitted by thrips, causes the following symptoms: general stunting, yellowing of the older leaves, circular spots and yellow speckles on the leaves, and unusual raised bull's-eye rings in green, yellow, and red on the fruit.

RESISTANT CORN VARIETIES

	Bacterial Wilt	Northern Leaf Blight	Southern Leaf Blight
Yellow Corn			
Apache	•	•	•
Aztec	•		•
Bellringer	•		
Bonanza	•		
Comanche	•	•	•
Early Sunglow	•		
Gold Cup	•		
Golden Beauty	•		
Golden Queen		•	
Gold Winner	•		
NK 199	•		
Seneca Chief	•		•
Summer Sweet #7210	•	•	
Summer Sweet #7410		•	
Summer Sweet #7620	•	•	
Summer Sweet #7630		•	
Summer Sweet #7710	•	•	
White Corn			
Alpine	•		
Country Gentleman	•		
Silver Chief	•	•	•
Silver Queen	•	•	•
Summer Pearl	•	•	
Summer Sweet #8601W	•		
Summer Sweet #8701W	•		
Summer Sweet #8801W	•	•	
Bicolor Corn			
Bi-Color	•		
Bi-Queen	•	•	•
Honeymoon	•		
Summer Sweet #7702BC		•	
Summer Sweet #7812BC	•	•	
Summer Sweet #8502BC	•	•	
Summer Sweet #8802BC	•	•	
Sweet Sue	•		
Extrasweet Corn (all colors)			
Bi-Honey Delight	•	•	•
Bunker Hill	•	•	
Crisp and Sweet 711	•	•	•
Miracle	•	•	
Pegasus		•	•
Sugar Loaf		•	

RESISTANT CUCUMBER VARIETIES

	Angular Leaf Spot	Cucumber Mosaic Virus	Downy Mildew	Powdery Mildew	Scab of Cucurbits
Slicing Cucumbers					
Amira		•	•	•	
Ashley			•	•	
Burpee Hybrid II		•	•		
Burpless Hybrid			•	•	
Centurion	•	•	•	•	•
Dasher II	•	•	•	•	•
Dynasty	•	•	•	•	•
Earliest of All		•			•
Early Surecrop		•	•		
Early Triumph	•	•	•	•	•
Elite		•			
Gemini 7	•	•	•	•	•
Jazzer		•	•	•	•
Marketmore			•		•
Marketmore 70		•			•
Marketmore 76		•	•	•	•
Marketmore 80		•			•
Marketsett	•	•	•	•	•
Palace King				•	
Pointsett	•		•	•	
Poinsett 76	•		•	•	•
Pot Luck		•			•
Salad Bush	•	•	•	•	•
Slicemaster	•	•	•	•	•
Slicemaster Select	•	•	•	•	
Slice Nice	•	•	•	•	•
Spacemaster		•			•
Streamliner		•			
Supersett	•	•	•		•
Sweet Salad		•	•	•	
Sweet Slice	•	•	•	•	•
Sweet Success		•	•	•	•
Victory		•	•	•	•
Greenhouse Cucumbers					
Carmen			•	•	
Gourmet #2					•
Superator			•	•	
Super Sandra				•	
Middle Eastern/Asian Cucumbers					
Hylares		•			
Saria			•	•	
Suyo Long				•	
Sweet Alphee			•	•	•

RESISTANT CUCUMBER VARIETIES

	Angular Leaf Spot	Cucumber Mosaic Virus	Downy Mildew	Powdery Mildew	Scab of Cucurbits
Pickling Cucmbers					
Armada	•	•	•	•	•
Burpee Pickler		•			
Calypso	•	•	•	•	•
Carolina	•	•	•	•	•
Conquest	•	•	•	•	•
County Fair		•	•	•	•
County Fair 87	•	•	•	•	
Hybrid Fortos		•	•	•	
Liberty	•	•	•		•
Lucky Strike	•				•
Patio Pik			•		
Pickalot				•	
Picklebush			•	•	
Pioneer	•	•	•	•	•
Salty		•	•	•	•
Salvo	•	•	•	•	•

RESISTANT MUSKMELON VARIETIES

	Downy Mildew	Powdery Mildew
Ambrosia	•	•
Aurora	•	•
Canada Gem		•
Can/Am Express	•	•
Charmel		•
Classic		•
Columbia		•
Dixie Jumbo	•	•
Early Dawn	•	•
Grande Gold	•	•
Hiline	•	•
Honey Brew		•
Honeymoon	•	•
Magnum .45		•
Market Star		•
Melon Gallicum		•
Pancha		•
Pulsar	•	•
Quick Sweet	•	
Road Runner		•
Saticoy		•
Summet	•	•
Supermarket	•	•
Texas Resistant No. 1	•	

RESISTANT TOMATO VARIETIES

	Fusarium Wilt	Nematodes*	Tobacco Mosaic Virus	Verticillium Wilt
Salad Tomatoes				
Basket Vee				•
Better Boy	•	•		•
Burpee's Big Girl	•			•
Big Seven	•	•		•
Bonita	+			•
Bonney Vee	•			
Burpee's VF	•			•
Campbell's #1327	•			•
Carmello	•	•		•
Cavallier	+	•	•	•
Celebrity	+	•	•	•
Duke	+			•
Earlirouge				•
Early Girl		•		•
Empire	+	•	•	•
First Lady	•	•		•
Floradade	+			•
Floradel	•			
Floralou	•			
Floramerica	+			•
Freedom	+			•
Hayslip	+			•
Heinz 1350	•			•
Heinz 1439	•			•
Heinz 1765	•			•
Homestead 24	•			
Hybrid Gurney Girl	+	•	•	•
Jackpot	+	•		•
Lady Luck	•	•	•	•
Lemon Boy	•	•		•
Liberty	+			•
Lorissa	•	•		•
Manalucie	•			
Monte Carlo	•	•		•
Mountain Delight	+			•
Mountain Pride	+			•
New Yorker				•
Olympic	+			•
Park's Whopper	•	•	•	•
Pearson Improved	•			•
Pink Girl	•		•	•
Pole King	+			•
Revolution	+			•
Rodade	+			•

RESISTANT TOMATO VARIETIES

	Fusarium Wilt	Nematodes*	Tobacco Mosaic Virus	Verticillium Wilt
Royal Flush	•	•		•
Rutgers	•			•
Summer Delight	•	•		•
Tropic	•		•	•
Ultra Boy	•	•		•
Ultra Girl	•	•		•
Walter Villemaire	+			
Beefsteak Tomatoes				
Beefeater	•	•		
Beefmaster	•	•		•
Burpee's Supersteak	•	•		•
Super Beefsteak	•	•		•
Cherry Tomatoes				
Cherry Express				•
Cherry Flavor	+	•	•	•
Cherry Grande	•			•
Small Fry	•	•		•
Super Sweet 100	•			•
Sweet Chelsea	+	•	•	•
Toy Boy	•			•
Paste Tomatoes				
Crimsonvee	•			•
Nova	•			
Roma	•			•
Royal Chico	•	•		•
Square Paste	•			•
Veepick	•			•
Veerona	•			•

* Nematode-resistant tomato varieties are resistant to the cotton root-knot nematode, the Javanese root-knot nematode, and the southern root-knot nematode but not the northern root-knot nematode.

+ These varieties are resistant to fusarium races 1 and 2; the other varieties listed are resistant to race 1 only.

Some Vegetable Varieties Resistant to Certain Pests

If any of the following pests are in your garden, or are likely to turn up in it, a good way to combat them is to plant resistant varieties. The southern root-knot nematode and the harlequin bug are prevalent in the southern half of the United States, cabbage yellows is most serious in the Midwest, and potato scab is widespread.

SOME VEGETABLE VARIETIES RESISTANT TO THE SOUTHERN ROOT-KNOT NEMATODE

Bean
Bountiful
Brittle Wax
Tender Pod
Wingard Wonder

Corn
Carmel Cross
Golden Beauty Hybrid
Golden Cross Bantam
Span Cross

Cowpea
California Blackeye No. 5
Colossus*
Erectset
Floricream
Magnolia Buckeye
Mississippi Purple*
Mississippi Shipper*
Mississippi Silver
Pinkeye Purplehull
Zipper Cream

Pea
Burpeana Early
Wando

Pepper
All Big
Bontoc Sweet Long
World Beater

Sweet Potato
Apache
Carver
Heartogold
Hopi
Jasper
Jewel
Nemagold
Nugget
Ruby
Sunnyside
White Bunch
Whitestar
White Triumph

SOME POTATO VARIETIES RESISTANT TO POTATO SCAB

Alama
Cascade
Cherokee
La Rouge
Lemhi
Nooksack
Norchip
Norgold Russet
Norland
Ona
Onaway
Ontario
Plymouth
Pungo
Russet Burbank
Shurchip
Sioux
Superior
Targhee

SOME CABBAGE VARIETIES RESISTANT TO CABBAGE YELLOWS

Blueboy
Blue Vantage
Charleston Wakefield
Charmant
Early Jersey Wakefield
Excel
Genesis
Globe
Golden Acre
Harvester Queen
Hercules
Jersey Queen
King Cole
Marion Market
Market Prize
Resistant Detroit
Rio Verde
Rocket Sanibel
Solid Blue Brand
Stonehead
Sun Up
Supermarket
Superpack F_1
Wisconsin All Season
Wisconsin Golden Acre
Wisconsin Hollander

SOME CABBAGE-FAMILY VARIETIES RESISTANT TO THE HARLEQUIN BUG

Broccoli
Atlantic
Coastal
Grande

Cabbage
Copenhagen
Early Jersey Wakefield
Headstart
Market 86
Savoy Perfection Drumhead
Stein's Flat Dutch

Cauliflower
Early Snowball A
Early Snowball X

Collards
Green Glaze
Morris Improved Heading
Vates

Kale
Vale

Radish
Champion
Cherry Belle
Globemaster
Red Devil
Red Prince
White Icicle

* These varieties of cowpea are also resistant to the Javanese root-knot nematode.

Plants Susceptible and Resistant to Verticillium Wilt

The following is a partial listing of many of the most commonly grown plants that are susceptible or resistant to verticillium wilt.* This widespread fungus disease causes wilting, stem and leaf discoloration, and the death of many plants. The fungus lives in the soil for years, even after the host plants have died.

SUSCEPTIBLE PLANTS

Vegetables
Artichoke
Beet
Brussels sprouts
Cabbage
Cowpea
Cucumber
Eggplant
Horseradish
Melons+
New Zealand spinach
Okra
Peanut
Pepper
Potato
Pumpkin
Radish
Rhubarb
Rutabaga
Spinach
Strawberry
Tomato

Trees
Almond, apricot, cherry,
  peach, plum, prune
Ash
Avocado
Black locust
Black tupelo
Camphor
Carob
Carrotwood
Catalpa
Elm
Goldenrain tree
Maple
Olive
Pecan
Persimmon
Redbud
Russian olive
Southern magnolia
Tree-of-heaven
Yellowwood

Shrubs, Ground Covers, and Vines
Barberry
Blackberry
Currant, gooseberry
Dewberry
Elderberry
Fuchsia
Heather
Ice plant
Indian-hawthorn
Lilac
Nandina
Privet
Raspberry
Sumac
Trumpetcreeper
Viburnum
Rhododendron

Flowers
Aster
Bellflower
Black-eyed-susan
California poppy
Cape marigold
China aster
Chrysanthemum
Clarkia
Cockscomb
Dahlia
Foxglove
Gayfeather
Geranium
Heliotrope
Lobelia
Marguerite
Painted-tongue
Peony
Petunia
Phlox
Rocket larkspur
Shasta daisy
Snapdragon
Stock
Strawflower
Sweet pea
Transvaal daisy

RESISTANT OR IMMUNE PLANTS

Vegetables
Asparagus
Bean
Carrot
Celery
Corn
Lettuce
Onion
Pea
Sweet potato

Plant Families
Cactus
Ferns
Grasses and cereal grains
Gymnosperms (cycads, ginkgo,
  and conifers, including
  cypress, fir, larch, juniper,
  pine, sequoia, spruce, and
  others)
Monocots (bamboo, banana,
  gladiolus, grasses, iris, lily,
  orchids, palms, and others)

Trees
Apple, flowering crab apple
Beech
Birch
California bay
Citrus
Dogwood
Eucalyptus
European mountain ash
Fig
Hawthorn
Honeylocust
Hornbeam
Katsura tree
Linden
Mulberry
Oak
Pear
Sweet gum
Sycamore, plane tree
Walnut
Willow

Shrubs
Boxwood
Ceanothus
Manzanita
Oleander
Pyracantha
Rockrose
White rockrose

Flowers
Alyssum
Anemone
Baby-blue-eyes
Baby's breath
Balloonflower
Beardtongue
Blanketflower
Candytuft
Carnation, pink
Cinquefoil
Columbine
Coralbells
English daisy
Evening primrose
Flossflower
Hollyhock
Lantana
Monkeyflower
Nasturtium
Pansy, viola
Persian buttercup
Pot marigold
Pouch nemesia
Primrose
Rose moss
Scabiosa
Spiderflower
Sunflower
Sunrose
Tuberous begonia
Verbena
Wallflower
Wax begonia
Zinnia

* Adapted from *Plants Resistant or Susceptible to Verticillium Wilt*, University of California Cooperative Extension leaflet 2703.

+ Watermelon, cantaloupe, and honeydew become infected but are tolerant. Persian, casaba, and crenshaw melons are very susceptible.

APPENDIX

NEMATODE PESTS

Although predatory nematodes help gardeners by eating the larvae of insect pests (see pages 19 and 42), other types of nematodes harm plants. These plant-parasitic nematodes, sometimes called roundworms or eelworms, are so tiny that in most cases you need a microscope to see them. Pest nematodes are widespread, although some of the worst infestations occur in the southern half of the United States.

These parasitic nematodes affect almost every crop. Some types injure a wide range of crops, whereas others attack only one or two crops. Most pest nematodes live on plant roots, although there are types that injure leaves.

A plant infested with root-parasitic nematodes exhibits symptoms similar to those shown by a plant grown with too little water or a combination of low fertility and not enough water. The plant is stunted and does not fruit well; it may show some yellowing and it may wilt at midday. Inspection of the roots usually reveals some kind of damage. Root-knot nematodes, among the most common kinds of parasitic nematodes, cause the roots to form enlarged knots, or galls, that are pea sized or larger. Cyst nematodes can be identified by cysts, which are actually female nematodes, attached to the roots. (See *nematodes*, under BEAN, and *sugar beet cyst nematode*, under BEET, for more information.)

Plant-parasitic nematodes use a spearlike stylet (right) to puncture plant cells and suck the cell juices.

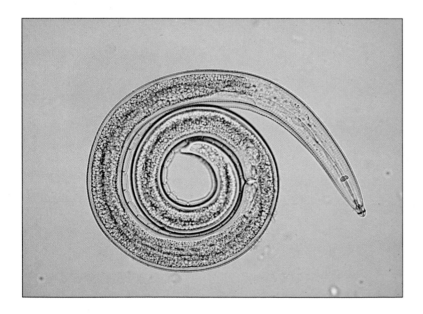

Many kinds of nematodes do not leave conclusive evidence of their presence. The roots may be unusually short, bushy, or decayed, or there may be no roots at all. The only way to know for sure which nematode you have—or even to confirm the presence of nematodes in general—is through laboratory analysis.

How Nematodes Damage Plant Roots

Most plant-parasitic nematodes feed by inserting a sharp stylet, or mouthpart, into the plant root and sucking sap. Some feed on the outside of roots; others enter the roots before they feed. Feeding not only steals strength from the roots, but it also allows entry of disease-causing organisms. In addition, galls and other deformities caused by the nematodes may block the passage of nutrients and water in the plant. Most nematodes complete their life cycle in about 30 days, so that many generations can occur in a single season. As long as susceptible plants are growing in the soil, nematodes will multiply. After the infected plants die, nematodes and nematode eggs can survive for a long time, either in dead roots or in the soil.

Typically, nematode infestations appear first in a small area of the garden, orchard, or lawn, then spread slowly from year to year. The infested area grows slowly because most nematodes travel only short distances—usually 3 to 6 feet a year—on their own. If they spread rapidly or appear suddenly in an area, they are being assisted. Nematodes can be carried from one area to another in contaminated soil, in running water, on plants, and on tools. They tend to be a worse problem in warm-winter climates; in these areas larger populations build up and more kinds of nematodes are able to survive. Some nematodes, including the root-knot types, are more common in sandy soils.

How to Control Nematodes

Methods of control depend on whether your garden is currently free of nematodes, whether you suspect that you have nematodes in a small area, or whether your whole garden is infested. In the first case, concentrate on preventive measures. If you suspect that you have a small infestation, identify the nematodes and keep them from spreading. If nematodes are causing widespread damage, identify the pests and then use several techniques to combat them.

After using tools in an infested garden area, clean them with a strong jet of water, making sure that the water does not run back into the garden. Dip tools in 1 part household bleach to 9 parts water, or douse them with boiling water.

Keep them out of the garden   Reduce the chance that nematodes will be introduced into your garden by being aware of possible methods of entry and avoiding them.

Purchased seedlings and rootstocks Always obtain plant material from a reliable source. If possible, buy stock that has been certified to be free of nematodes. Be particularly cautious of melon, pepper, tomato, and other crops that are highly susceptible to root-knot nematode damage. Examine plants and reject ones with suspicious knots on their roots. As an alternative, start your own seedlings in a sterile potting mix.

Gift plants from other gardens   Carefully inspect plants that may have been grown in infested soil. The only sure means of propagating plants that were grown in nematode-infested soil is to take stem or leaf cuttings and root them in clean soil.

Contaminated soil   Buy soil or planting mixes from a reputable dealer. Fill brought in from an empty lot or another questionable source may be infested.

Borrowed or rented tools   A rototiller, shredder, or other implement used previously in a nematode-infested garden will carry the pest into your soil.

Nematodes may be present in only certain areas of the garden, harming some plants and leaving others unaffected.

Prevent them from spreading   If you suspect that part of your garden is infested with nematodes, take preventive measures to confine the problem. Avoid moving plants or soil between the suspected infested area and clean areas. On any given day, work in the infested area last.

After using tools in an infested area, clean them thoroughly. Use a strong spray of water followed by 1 part household bleach to 9 parts water, or douse the tools with boiling water. Control weeds, particularly those related to susceptible crop plants. In the area of suspected infestation, don't leave crop plants in the ground after harvest. Dig them up, roots and all, and burn them or compost them thoroughly.

Confirm their presence and identify them
If you see root-knot or cyst nematodes on plant roots, you can be sure that you have nematodes, although you won't know which kind they are without analysis by a nematology laboratory. It is impossible to tell if other kinds of nematodes are causing problems in your garden without laboratory confirmation.

Unless the symptoms of nematode damage are definite, first try to eliminate other possible causes. To be sure that the problem is not poor care, give your crops the best possible growing conditions: ample organic matter in the soil, suitable soil pH, sufficient moisture, and adequate fertilizer. Examine your plants carefully for evidence of insect or disease problems. If you have no other explanation for the ill health of your plants, send samples of soil and plant roots to a laboratory. Take samples of live rootlets and some moist soil surrounding them. In an area where plants have been killed, take the samples from the edge of the planting, where the roots are still alive. Protect the samples from exposure to temperature extremes even for short periods.

The local cooperative extension office can provide you with exact sampling instructions; it will also let you know whether to send the samples to an extension laboratory or a private one. In most areas the cost ranges from $5 to $25. Once you know which nematode species you have—and you may have more than one type of nematode—you can schedule a rotation and plan other control methods.

Control them with a combination of tactics
If there are enough nematodes in your soil to cause damage, the best approach is to try to limit the damage by using a combination of methods over time. Start by providing good growing conditions, especially adequate moisture and fertilizer. Also, plant resistant varieties if they are available.

Crop rotation is very important, although it is more likely to succeed if you know which kinds of nematodes you have. That way, you will know which plants are immune. A green manure crop that is immune can help in a rotation, as long as susceptible weeds are not allowed to grow.

Dig in 3 to 4 inches of compost or composted manure each year, and use an organic mulch, such as straw, leaves, or pine needles. Organic matter helps by encouraging certain soil fungi and bacteria that help control nematodes. Some commercial products, such as those made from crab and shrimp shells, work by stimulating the same nematode enemies. These may help, but don't rely solely on them; a successful control program will combine several tactics. Take care in using these commercial products; they may contain nitrate levels high enough to harm a crop planted too soon after the product was used. Also, excess nitrate will leach into the water table in the same way that excess fertilizer does.

Sample Management Plans for Nematode-Infested Soil

	First Winter		First Summer	Second Winter	Second Summer	Third Winter		Third Summer
Plan A	Fallow		Fallow	Fallow	Summer Susceptible Crop	Winter/ Spring Crop	*	Summer Resistant Crop
Plan B	Winter/ Spring Crop		Summer Solarize	Fallow	Summer Susceptible Crop	Winter/ Spring Crop		Summer Solarize
Plan C	Winter/ Spring Crop	*	Amend Soil Summer Susceptible Crop	Fallow	Fallow	Fallow		Fallow or Summer Resistant Crop

* Early Harvest.   Adapted from *Pests of the Garden and Small Farm* by Mary Louise Flint.

In addition to improving growing conditions, using resistant varieties, rotating crops, and adding organic matter, you will probably need a fallow period if the infestation is serious. Use a complete fallow: bare soil only. Eliminate any weeds, since their roots may be nourishing the nematodes. Although moist soil encourages weed growth, it makes the fallow more effective because it causes more eggs to hatch. Since there is no food available, the young nematodes die from starvation. Tilling the fallow area several times reduces nematodes by exposing them to heat and drying. One year of complete fallow permits susceptible crops to be grown for one year; two years will lower the nematode population even more.

Solarizing your soil (see page 30) will also reduce the number of nematodes. The next year there will be fewer nematodes in the top foot of soil, allowing a crop of shallow-rooted plants to be grown. Replace a fallow period with solarization, or solarize the soil in summer and leave the soil fallow in winter.

Certain kinds of marigolds have long been known to decrease some kinds of root-knot nematodes. A notable exception is the northern root-knot nematode, which continues to reproduce in marigold plantings. To be effective in combating other root-knot nematodes, marigold must be the only crop in the infested area, and it must cover the area solidly. Use French marigold (*Tagetes patula*); common varieties include 'Nemagold', 'Petite Blanc', and 'Queen Sophia'. Be aware that marigold is probably the least reliable of the tactics discussed thus far.

Asparagus, garlic, and onion have also been reported to reduce nematodes, but fewer tests have been performed on them than marigold, and the reports are less consistent. A probable reason for the inconsistency is that the crops work against only certain nematodes. Asparagus roots produce a chemical that is toxic to the stubby-root nematode and lowers populations of root-lesion nematodes. Onion bulbs growing in soil infested with the northern root-knot nematode are somewhat smaller than

Laying down an organic mulch, such as straw, is a useful practice in a program of nematode control.

normal. Although the nematodes cause some damage, the onion plants shed their roots before the pests can complete a life cycle; consequently, the population of these nematodes declines in soil planted with onion. The same is true of garlic.

Although radish does not actually resist root-knot nematodes, it can lower the population, since it is harvested before the nematodes can complete a life cycle. For radishes to be effective, none can be left in the ground past maturity.

In addition to all these tactics, a few other techniques are useful. If you plant when the soil is cooler than optimum for the nematodes, damage will be minimal. In the South it is often possible to grow cool-season crops with little damage in early spring, whereas the warm summer temperatures will bring serious damage. Some nematode species cannot penetrate roots when the soil temperature is below 64° F; however, the northern root-knot nematode and certain other kinds of nematodes are able to infest plants at 50° F.

Dig up seriously affected plants, including as much root as possible, and destroy them. Even if plants are minimally damaged, do not leave them in the ground past the end of the harvest; it is a good idea to remove them a little earlier, because nematodes build up in the soil more rapidly toward the end of the season. Plants left in the ground an extra month or so may allow one or two more generations to occur. Since each succeeding generation is larger than the previous one, you will be paying a high price for the last few okra or cucumbers.

Researchers report that Vapam®, a soil fumigant and the only nematicide registered for use by home gardeners (and only in some states), gives results similar in variability to other control methods; perhaps this is due to improper preparation of the soil or to difficulties in applying the chemical correctly. Before resorting to a soil fumigant, try the other methods described above and the different management sequences described in the chart on page 150. If you do decide to use a fumigant, follow the instructions with great care.

'Queen Sophia' is among the varieties of French marigold that have been shown to decrease some root-knot nematode infestations—but only if marigolds are planted over the entire area for the entire season.

Seed Sources

If a local nursery doesn't carry the varieties you want, you may want to obtain them through a mail-order nursery. Most of these suppliers carry a wide variety of vegetable seeds; some specialize in seeds for one or two crops or for a particular growing region. Some of the sources charge a nominal fee for their catalogs.

W. Atlee Burpee Company
300 Park Avenue
Warminster, PA 18974

D.V. Burrell Seed Growers Company
Box 150
Rocky Ford, CO 81067
719-254-3318
Full line of vegetable and flower seeds.

Canadian Gardening Guide
Box 20
Bowden, Alberta
Canada T0M 0K0
403-224-3545
Short-season varieties and varieties for the West Coast.

The Cook's Garden
Box 53517
Londonderry, VT 05148
802-824-3400
FAX: 802-824-3027

Henry Field's Seed & Nursery Company
415 North Burnett Street
Box 700
Shenandoah, IA 51602
605-665-4491

Good Earth/Tsang and Ma
Box 5644
Redwood City, CA 94063
415-595-2270

Gurney Seed & Nursery Company
110 Capital Street
Yankton, SD 57079
605-665-1671

Harris Moran Seed Company
3670 Buffalo Road
Rochester, NY 14624
East: 716-594-9411
FAX: 716-594-9415
West: 209-544-0330
FAX: 209-544-0335

H.G. Hastings
Box 115535
Atlanta, GA 30310
In Georgia: 404-755-6580
Out of state: 800-334-1771
Seeds and plants for the South. Large selection of cowpeas, okra, and greens.

Ed Hume Seeds, Inc.
Box 1450
Kent, WA 98035
Seeds for short-season climates.

J.W. Jung Seed Company
335 South High Street
Randolph, WI 53957

Kilgore Seed Company
1400 West First Street
Sanford, FL 32771
Seeds for subtropical and tropical climates.

D. Landreth Seed Company
180–188 West Ostend Street
Baltimore, MD 21230
301-727-3922

Orol Ledden & Sons
Box 7
Sewell, NJ 08080
609-468-1000
Wide selection of untreated seeds.

Liberty Seed Company
128 First Drive SE
Box 806 B1
New Philadelphia, OH 44663
216-364-1611
Good selection of new varieties and old favorites.

Lockhart Seeds, Inc.
Box 1361
Stockton, CA 95201
209-466-4401

McFayden Seeds
Box 1030
Minot, ND 58702
204-727-0766
Seeds and plants for cold climates.

Earl May Seed & Nursery
208 North Elm Street
Shenandoah, IA 51603
800-831-4193

Mellinger's, Inc.
Dept. REF
West South Range Road
North Lima, OH 44452
216-549-9861

Meyer Seed Company
600 South Caroline Street
Baltimore, MD 21231

Nichols Garden Nursery
1190 North Pacific Highway
Albany, OR 97321
503-928-9280

Park Seed Company, Inc.
Cokesbury Road
Greenwood, SC 29647
803-223-7333

The Pepper Gal
10536 119th Avenue North
Largo, FL 34643
Over 200 varieties of pepper seeds.

Porter & Son, Seedsmen
Box 104
Stephenville, TX 76401

Redwood City Seed Company
Box 361
Redwood City, CA 94064
415-325-SEED
Old-fashioned, open-pollinated vegetable and herb seeds. Rare chile pepper varieties.

Seeds Blum
Idaho City Stage
Boise, ID 83706

Shepherd's Garden Seeds
6116 Highway 9
Felton, CA 95018
408-335-5311
Gourmet vegetable seeds and culinary herbs.

Southern Seeds
Box 2091
Melbourne, FL 32902
407-727-3662
Vegetable seeds for hot climates.

Stokes Seeds
Box 548
Buffalo, NY 14240
416-688-4300
Over 2,500 vegetable, herb, and flower seed varieties.

Territorial Seed Company
Box 157
20 Palmer Avenue
Cottage Grove, OR 97424
503-942-9547
FAX: 503-942-9881

Tomato Growers Supply Company
Box 2237
Fort Myers, FL 33902
813-768-1119
Tomato and pepper seeds.

Otis S. Twilley Seed Company, Inc.
Box 65, Dept. 636
Trevose, PA 19057
In Pennsylvania: 800-232-7333
Out of state: 800-622-7333

Vesey's Seeds, Ltd.
York, Prince Edward Island
Canada C0A 1P0
902-892-1048
FAX: 902-566-1620
Seeds for short seasons.

U.S. Measure and Metric Measure Conversion Chart

	Symbol	**Formulas for Exact Measures** When you know:	Multiply by:	To find:	**Rounded Measures for Quick Reference**		
Mass	oz	ounces	28.35	grams	1 oz		= 30 g
(Weight)	lb	pounds	0.45	kilograms	4 oz		= 115 g
	g	grams	0.035	ounces	8 oz		= 225 g
	kg	kilograms	2.2	pounds	16 oz	= 1 lb	= 450 g
					32 oz	= 2 lb	= 900 g
					36 oz	= 2¼ lb	= 1000g (1 kg)
Volume	pt	pints	0.47	liters	1 c	= 8 oz	= 250 ml
	qt	quarts	0.95	liters	2 c (1 pt)	= 16 oz	= 500 ml
	gal	gallons	3.785	liters	4 c (1 qt)	= 32 oz	= 1 liter
	ml	milliliters	0.034	fluid ounces	4 qt (1 gal)	= 128 oz	= 3¾ liter
Length	in.	inches	2.54	centimeters	⅜ in.	= 1 cm	
	ft	feet	30.48	centimeters	1 in.	= 2.5 cm	
	yd	yards	0.9144	meters	2 in.	= 5 cm	
	mi	miles	1.609	kilometers	2½ in.	= 6.5 cm	
	km	kilometers	0.621	miles	12 in. (1 ft)	= 30 cm	
	m	meters	1.094	yards	1 yd	= 90 cm	
	cm	centimeters	0.39	inches	100 ft	= 30 m	
					1 mi	= 1.6 km	
Temperature	°F	Fahrenheit	⅝ (after subtracting 32)	Celsius	32°F	= 0°C	
	°C	Celsius	⁹⁄₅ (then add 32)	Fahrenheit	212°F	= 100°C	
Area	in.²	square inches	6.452	square centimeters	1 in.²	= 6.5 cm²	
	ft²	square feet	929.0	square centimeters	1 ft²	= 930 cm²	
	yd²	square yards	8361.0	square centimeters	1 yd²	= 8360 cm²	
	a.	acres	0.4047	hectares	1 a.	= 4050 m²	